PRAISE FOR
SEPTEMBER UNIVERSITY

"*September University* is a nourishing feast of a book, replete with reasons to discover new meaning and purpose in the last chapters of your life, to welcome those years as life's most precious gift—an opportunity to cultivate wisdom and then put it to use in the world."

WALTER TRUETT ANDERSON
President Emeritus, World Academy of Art and Science

"*September University*, by leading scholar and visionary Charles Hayes, is a superb intellectual achievement by any standards. With sweeping scope and remarkable depth of knowledge across numerous disciplines, Hayes addresses the totality of the human experience—along with neglected questions surrounding life, death, freedom, authenticity, and truth—as he paves the way for a genuinely mature future in which citizens discover new degrees of potency and thoughtfulness. Rather than shying away from idealism, *September University* sets out a bold and timely blueprint for a post-consumer consciousness that is more culturally aware, media literate, and politically astute. Hayes delves with electrifying intelligence into the nature of meaning, identity, and community as he weaves together a comprehensive philosophy that enables people to transcend evolutionary baggage, social indoctrination, and illusions of limitation. *September University* is one of the finest books in print when it comes to the wisdom and existential bearings required to survive the current age of insanity."

JOHN F. SCHUMAKER, author,
*In Search of Happiness: Understanding an
Endangered State of Mind*, *Wings of Illusion*,
and *The Age of Insanity*

"This is an important work. Wisdom evolves from real life experience, and Charles Hayes has both. For those who aspire to a better world, this is a must read."

PETER C. WHYBROW, Director of the Semel Institute for Human Behavior at UCLA and author, *American Mania: When More Is Not Enough*

"*September University* is the first philosophy integrating the university without walls and transformative learning—essential reading for learning in the 21st century."

DANIEL S. JANIK, MD, PhD, author, *Unlock the Genius Within: Neurobiological Trauma, Teaching, and Transformative Learning*

"Engaging, convincing, and provocative. Given the collapse of the future most adults thought they had, and the involuntary mandate to shape a new one, *September University* calls those in the second half of life to step away from superficial things and commit to becoming wise guides for the generations that come after them."

DAVID L. SOLIE, MS, PA author, *How to Say It to Seniors*

"It's not too late to make your mark on the world and enjoy a new level of fulfillment in your life. Charles Hayes will inspire you to muster the courage to do it."

JEFF SCHMIDT author, *Disciplined Minds*

"*September University* is a wonderful book. It is wise and passionate and can teach us all about the rare art of growing old."

SAM KEEN, philosopher and author, *Faces of the Enemy*

SEPTEMBER UNIVERSITY

Donated to the

Dodgeville Public
Library

by

Michael Dearing

2010

ALSO BY CHARLES D. HAYES

*Existential Aspirations: Reflections
of a Self-Taught Philosopher*

*The Rapture of Maturity:
A Legacy of Lifelong Learning*

Portals in a Northern Sky, a novel

*Training Yourself:
The 21st Century Credential*

*Beyond the American Dream:
Lifelong Learning and the Search
for Meaning in a Postmodern World*

*Proving You're Qualified: Strategies for
Competent People without College Degrees*

*Self-University: The Price of Tuition is the
Desire to Learn. Your Degree is a Better Life*

SEPTEMBER UNIVERSITY

Summoning Passion

for an

Unfinished Life

CHARLES D. HAYES

Autodidactic Press

Printed in the United States of America

Mixed Sources
Product group from well-managed forests and other controlled sources
www.fsc.org   Cert no. SW-COC-002283
© 1996 Forest Stewardship Council
FSC

Printed on Recycled Paper

First Edition

0 9 8 7 6 5 4 3 2 1

Autodidactic Press
P. O. Box 872749
Wasilla, AK 99687

www.autodidactic.com

Index by Phyllis Linn
Book design by Shannon Bodie, Lightbourne, Inc.

Publisher's Cataloging-in-Publication
(Provided by Quality Books, Inc.)

Hayes, Charles D. (Charles Douglas)
September university : summoning passion for an unfinished life / by Charles D. Hayes. — 1st ed.
p. cm.
Includes bibliographical references and index.
LCCN 2009930291
ISBN-13: 978-0-9621979-7-0
ISBN-10: 0-9621979-7-1

1. Adult college students—United States. 2. College student orientation—United States.
3. Self-realization. 4. Adult learning—United States.
5. Middle-aged persons—Education—United States. 6. Older people—Education—United States. I. Title.

LB2343.32.H39 2010   378.1'98'0973
                                                QBI09-600091

*Dedicated to the memory of
my brother and sister,*

*Enoch Anthony Hayes and
Cheryl Elaine Wright.*

ACKNOWLEDGMENTS

This book has been taking shape for well over a decade, and the end result bears little resemblance to the original. I'm grateful to many people who offered feedback in varying stages of this work, and I want to attest that my including their names here does not necessarily mean that they agree with my assertions: Gertrude Batten, Gretchen Bersch, Mike Chmielewski, Christine Dittrich, Ralph Dumain, Kathleen Harrington, Lee Henrikson, Meg Hayes, Jessica Kiley, Connie McClellan, Chuck Oberst, John R. Roderick, Roy Shipman, and Karen Watterson. I'm also grateful to many of the authors referenced in the text, whose work has had a lasting effect on my thinking. Special thanks to John F. Schumaker, whose writing about contemporary culture is exceptionally insightful and whose encouragement is very much appreciated. Most of all, I'm grateful to my editor, LuAnne Dowling, whose editing talents bring my ideas to life.

CONTENTS

PREFACE

*Sapere aude! Have the courage
to use your own intelligence!*

IMMANUEL KANT

Perhaps you have sensed, as I have, a great spiritual hunger in the world. People want to believe that life is worth more than bottom-line entries on corporate spreadsheets, more than sporting event scores, and more than following the next fad. They seek something far more valuable: They are searching for meaning. I say, who better to figure out what that meaning is than those of us with enough life experience that we can't be fooled with platitudes, clichés, or doublespeak? For the generation now in the fall and winter of life, it's time to take Kant's advice and summon the courage to use our intelligence for the sake of posterity.

September University, in concept, is a metaphor for intellectual maturity and represents an ambitious quest on behalf of future generations. *September University*, the book, is a call to action, a social forecast, and above all a passionate argument that a bright future depends upon the experiential wisdom of aging citizens. The exploration you're about to begin has the potential to transform your worldview, heighten your aspirations, and elicit reflections about your personal legacy and the spiritual meaning to be derived from the last season of life.

Throughout most of human existence, older people have sustained civilization as repositories of knowledge. Historically, elders have been revered for passing information and culture from one generation to the next. But printing and advanced methods of storing information have eroded the perceived value of learned experience, resulting in an ever-persistent devaluation of aging citizens. There are, of course, exceptions. Some cultures still adhere to a tradition of revering their seniors, but lately there are signs that the time-honored esteem, so lavish in the past, is lessening. Nevertheless I'm hopeful.

If I've learned anything in my decades of self-education, it is that things are never as they appear. Although it may seem that knowledge gained through the experience of aging may be of decreasing value, precisely the opposite is true. Never before has perspective grounded in the wisdom of thoughtful experience been more important to the future.

In prehistoric times all humans lived in small groups, and survival depended entirely upon experientially based knowledge. Of particular concern was the immediate present—taking the wrong path or choosing the wrong thing to eat could result in death. Knowledge was critical, but wisdom from exceptionally alert and thoughtful individuals sometimes yielded breakthroughs that changed everything for the better. Reading the signs of the times was crucial to our ancient ancestors, and it is still so today. Through research in neuroscience and evolutionary psychology, and from computer modeling applied to social behavior, we now have compelling evidence that our culture is steeped in the practice of false attribution. We see connections where they don't exist and don't see them where they do. We are often irrational even as we perceive that we are reasoning. What we've always accepted as common sense is often little more than common deception. And what we think of as human nature is often egregiously out of sync with the realties of our social behavior.

In many ways the lives of our early ancestors required levels of alertness and attention to detail that were anything but primitive, and for us to judge them as simple beings is a big mistake. But environmentally we have very nearly come full circle. Today a person without a great deal of knowledge and experience is as far removed from the reality of what to do next as our ancient ancestors were from knowing which path to take. The dilemma of having so many choices presents a challenge that our brains were not designed to cope with. Now, like then, danger is everywhere. And while we no longer live in fear of being eaten alive if we make a false move, today the very complexity of our society is such that everywhere we look there is risk and confusion. Nature's savagery has been replaced by levels of complexity that we are ill equipped to cope with. According to the World Health Organization, psychological depression is escalating worldwide at alarming rates and is becoming a major cause of disability. Moreover, the sheer volume of advice available, some of it exceedingly wise, is far beyond an inexperienced individual's ability to sort through with confidence.

Never before has the quality of our lives been so dependent upon wise counsel. And yet, in spite of our best-intentioned educational theories, our long history of championing reason has created the false impression that we always reason first and then act, failing to appreciate the fact that what we actually do most of the time is the reverse. We depend upon an emotionally internalized moral guidance system to navigate our way through daily life. We act intuitively, relying on stored memory receptors in the emotional regions of the brain, and then we reason away the aftermath of our actions with explanations that sound profound but very often have little to do with the real motive.

We are surrounded by self-interested agents of every stripe, who tell us that they are looking out for us and that we have only to do this or that to succeed. More often than

not, however, it's not our interests but theirs that are best
served by doing what they ask. Thus, of necessity, one has
to be aware that sometimes the very suggestion of reward
may be reason to suspect deception. We are virtually
drowning in information; promises of access to vital knowledge are ubiquitous. Yet so much deceit and so many ideological black holes reside in our midst that matters of
trust have never been more central to the safety and security of daily existence. Whereas a misstep can still cost a
person their life, today it's more likely that a bad decision
can lead to an existence drained of vitality. Paying too
much attention to what others think one should do in personal or career matters can result in a long-term life trajectory from which one eventually awakens and realizes
that the major enterprise of their daily existence is bound
up in living out someone else's arbitrary ideology.

Many people experience lives today steeped in such
seething mediocrity that the beast-ridden savannah of our
ancient past seems inviting by comparison. Whereas life
may have once been "nasty, brutish, and short," these days
it can be confused, pointless, and headed toward a disaster that most people don't have time enough to recognize is
coming. Never before has reading the signs of the times
been more essential, and never has it been so imperative
that the concept of wisdom be a holistic notion favoring
humanity over the special interest of some excessively
needy individual, group, corporation, or nation-state.

When the hair on our heads turns gray, chances are
that the fruits of our brains are as ripe as they will ever get.
The saying "use it or lose it" becomes exceptionally pertinent now to addressing our serious problems. It's time to
turn up the heat on our politicians and our media who
choose the topics for public attention. For people who,
because of economic necessity during the "earning" years,
have lived on borrowed opinion, it's time to pay off the loan.
It's time for those of us who've always expressed strong
opinions about subjects that we've never really investigated

to actually do the research or keep quiet. Better yet, look it up, think it through, and speak out. If inspiration and some kind of mindful accomplishment for the sake of posterity do not precede our death, we must ask ourselves why, then, did we live?

The last few chapters of life are an appropriate time to apply the whole of our life experience and educational perspective to what it means to have been afforded the life of a human being. It's time to face life-stage theorist Erik Erikson's profound realization that our legacy is that which survives us and that our strength lies in a "detached yet active concern with life bounded by death, which we call wisdom." To confirm this sage advice we've only to recollect those who have passed on and then recall why we remember them.

Indeed, when we let go of our personal involvement with the present and contemplate a future that we will not live to see, the existential danger signs of today stand out as clearly as the fresh tracks of a saber-toothed cat stalking our ancestors in prehistory. I trust you will find in this book the kind of thinking that could cause our descendants to associate generativity with the tracks our generation leaves behind. The twenty-first century needs the wisdom of adults with a critical mass of life experience that's contrary to convention for convention's sake. We need people willing to confront the Stone Age mindsets and cultural contradictions that served us well in simpler times but today threaten our very existence. We need a fresh perspective about learning.

In spite of noble efforts on the part of our educational establishment, a liberal education has never been an adequate descriptor of what a person needs to know in order to sustain a level of authenticity far above a life of clichés, slogans, and platitudes. Deep down many of us with a half-century or more of life experience know this to be true. What a person needs, in my view, is an *existential education.* My hope is that you will find that this book provides a good start not only in helping you make insightful progress in existential matters, but also in helping you embody the kind of living example that inspires others do so as well. An existential education, in the sense that I have in mind, lessens one's fear of death, and ironically, even though it helps one to appreciate the practical limits of knowledge, it simultaneously increases one's curiosity and thirst for exploration. Perhaps most importantly an existential education has the power to dissipate our predisposition for bias against *otherness*.

Thomas Paine may be best remembered for his assertion, "These are the times that try men's souls." And thus, a hallmark of our culture has become that, regardless of the problems we face—flood, drought, earthquake, storm, war, disease, economic depression or recession—we expect it's fatefully ordained that we will prevail. In his pamphlet *Common Sense*, published in 1776, Paine declared that "we have it in our power to begin the world over again." At the time, the population of the thirteen colonies stood at about one-thirtieth of the size of today's baby-boom generation. Today each of us as an individual has the communication capabilities of a Thomas Paine pamphleteer writ large. If only a small percentage of us take up the mantle of Sept-U with the notion of shaping the future, we will represent a revolutionary force that has to be reckoned with.

Sept-U rests upon a simple equation: age + experience + curiosity x attitude = a greater quality of life and hope for humanity. If you haven't already done so, please enroll metaphorically in September University and encourage others to do so, too. The future depends on it.

ONE

DEMOGRAPHIC
TIDAL WAVES

*Change is not made without
inconvenience, even from worse to better.*

RICHARD HOOKER

mericans today are living longer, and the implications are profound. Little more than a hundred
years ago, the average life span in America did not
encompass what we now take for granted as the fall and
winter stages of life. If I'd lived a century earlier, I most likely
would have not reached my current age, nor would most of
the people reading this book. Not because we didn't have the
necessary genes for a longer life, but because of the absence
of recent lifesavers like antibiotics and other medical
advances that now keep us going without a second thought.
Longevity for growing numbers of people means that we are
on the verge of a new frontier, where a majority of adults can
expect with some confidence to live into old age. The baby-
boom generation drives the lead wagons in this trek.

Most demographers define baby boomers as those born
from 1946-1964, but for the purpose of this book I'll begin
with the year when I was born, 1943. This is the group
I envision as participating in September University—an
abstract arena, with no central administration and no

1

walls, devoted to self-directed learning and the search for better ideas.

Predictions abound about the baby-boom generation's effect on the future in the twenty-first century. In his book *The Greater Generation*, Leonard Steinhorn claims that it is this generation, and not Tom Brokaw's *Greatest Generation*, that deserves credit for coming to grips with the grievances, inequities, injustices, and hypocrisies of American life. You may or may not agree.

The baby-boom generation has been called everything imaginable: selfish and selfless, stingy and generous, self-centered and caring, the "me," "us," and "we" generation, and the New People. They can't be all of those things, but then again why not? The older I get and the more I learn, the less I am sure about the chance of reaching universal truths about anything to do with the behavior of human beings. Similar categories, yes; universals, not so fast. Abraham Maslow, Erik Erikson, Jean Piaget, Sigmund Freud, and the like all have been helpful with their models of human behavior, but their theories are only approximations.

Having been born in 1943, I've always lived under the illusion that I'm a little ahead of boomers in perspective because of my slight edge in experience. But I was clearly out of step with the boomers in the 1960s. While I have always felt that I shared many of their views, I missed out on their antiwar activism during the Vietnam War. I was at the time an ex-Marine who came very close to reenlisting, and I was an avid supporter of the war. It has only been from the perspective of hindsight and vigorous self-study that I now view things differently. In the 1960s any suggestion that the generation of my peers, who were protesting a war that I thought was legitimate, might have resulted in something resembling Leonard Steinhorn's future claim would have made my blood boil. But the pace of change in American life continually ratchets up, and sometimes it takes a long look into the past to appreciate how dramatically our views shift over time.

America is headed for a reckoning. If you are middle-aged or older, you are directly involved. Regardless of your age, if you are fortunate enough to live far into this century, you will be a witness. A high-tide demographic, a huge force of seniors, is set to come ashore—in successive waves—bringing with them a special brand of wisdom available only through the process of aging. This population of wise citizens no longer believes in the metaphor that time is money or that money is more valuable than life,[1] and they're on a collision course with free-market global capitalism.

Any way we consider the matter, it will amount to a profound shift in values. Those dedicated to leaving something of lasting value for the generations that follow may soon outnumber those focused on looking out only for themselves and their own. One need point no further for a demonstration of this ethos in actual practice than to the work underway by the Bill and Melinda Gates Foundation. Gates, a titan of business who became one of the richest men in the world, is devoting the majority of his retirement to philanthropic activities for the benefit of worthy causes. Financier Warren Buffet has joined forces with the Gates Foundation. Former Microsoft executive John Wood left the company to help bring literacy to the world's children, a truly inspiring story told in his book *Leaving Microsoft to Change the World*.[2] Wood's Room to Read foundation continues to grow with the goal of educating thousands of children each year who otherwise would have had no chance for an education. To date, Wood's foundation has established over 7,000 libraries, 765 schools, 6,800 scholarships for girls, and has published 327 local language children's book titles in eight countries in the developing world.

A natural disaster, a terrorist attack, or a war may render moot the clash I'm anticipating. But, calamity aside, we are in for a neck-snapping correction in what we care most about as a culture. My hope is that one day history will refer to it as a moral reckoning of global proportion.[3] If you are one of the many millions of citizens who lost a significant portion of your retirement funds in the roller-coaster stock market of recent years, you may have to work longer and you may have less time for participatory democracy. This situation alone is all the more reason to get involved to whatever degree you can.

ILLUSIONS OF TIME

Life is too short by half. Far too many of us spend three-quarters of our time on earth just getting to a stage where life starts to make sense. Sometimes, the only sense we gain is that life doesn't make sense and that there is no meaning unless we supply it. Then, when the reality that time is short overrides everything else, the whole world begins to look different. There is something about consciousness that gives us the feeling throughout our lives that we have always existed and always will. Although we know this isn't true, we have difficulty getting our minds around the notion of nonexistence because imagination cannot imagine itself out of existence. Unfortunately it is this aspect of perception that can prevent us from appreciating the wonder of being alive in the first place. It's as if the routine of everyday life lulls us into a stupor, and life streams by without our taking notice of what a fantastic opportunity is slipping out of reach.

As we age through the fog of midlife, superficial issues begin to diminish, and what is truly important becomes clearer. Trivial matters actually seem trivial. When the time we have left is significantly shorter than the time we have lived, then what we do with our time matters as never before. In a flash we are better prepared than anyone else on the planet to make objective decisions concerning posterity. This realization and how to make the most of it are what this book is about.

STONE AGE MINDS

We are equipped with bodies and brains designed for survival in the Stone Age. As scientist Robert Winston puts it, "We are forced, as a species, to walk through life laden down with the genetic baggage of five million years of savannah psychology and the inherited traits that preceded the hominids."[4] Cultures in the Western world are so technologically contrived that the word *nature* has nearly lost its meaning. Artificiality looms so large that we can't tell where reality begins or ends. The result is that daily life plays havoc with tribal tendencies that most of us don't even acknowledge we possess. "For good, or for ill," writes David Berreby in *Us and Them,* "Homo sapiens is inescapably a tribal animal."[5]

When time is short value stands tall, especially when, because of our progeny, our stake in the future is so high. If what we do is going to affect our offspring in a positive way, we need to outwit our tribal programming.[6] The late philosopher John Rawls fashioned an argument about fairness and justice using the example of a pie as a representation of our economic largesse. In it the participants charged with slicing the pie would not know which piece they themselves would eventually receive. In light of our history on the subject of justice, it was a stunning application of reasoned thought. Similar reasoning would say that the wisest course for the future might best be determined by those who won't live to see it but who fervently hope that their children and grandchildren will thrive there. Just as one is more mindful cutting the pie to keep from cheating oneself by carelessness, it is easier to see the real barriers to quality of life when one no longer has to focus on getting one's share of the pie.

PARADOXES OF AGING

We have yet to experience a demographic the size of the baby-boom generation growing old in such great numbers. It's therefore reasonable to expect that current attitudes toward older people will shift as those numbers increase. Even though we already acknowledge that we do indeed learn a great deal from our elders, there is still something in the way our culture views aging that discounts those over an arbitrary age as folks who no longer matter. To the contrary, I believe time and the demographics of aging will soon render this attitude absurd.

In his book *What Are Old People For? How Elders Will Save the World*, William H. Thomas, a medical doctor, asks and then partially answers his own question with his sub-title. Thomas is a geriatrician who presides over two non-profit organizations devoted to positive aging. He tells us that "the people who will grow old in this century will be better educated, more widely traveled, better read, and thus more aware than any generation in history."[7] Further, he points out that "elders have long been granted social shelter in the last decades of life, not as an act of charity but because old people possess notable talents that make them useful to their families and communities. Elderhood came to life when elders became the bearer of human culture. When it comes to retaining, refining, and transmitting culture, elders outperform adults."[8]

Thomas describes the full circle that elderhood completes: We are born as human beings, change to human doings, and then back again to human beings. One of his most interesting observations is a bit like reverse engineering in answering the question about the value of grandparents. For example, in viewing the history of Homo sapiens, he calls our attention to what anthropologists call the "grandmother effect." Thomas writes, "One million years ago on the plains of Africa, a hominid child cries out for hunger.

Her mother has recently given birth and is distracted by the needs of her helpless infant. The delivery was long and difficult and much blood was lost. The mother barely has the strength to nurse the infant. She can neither feed nor care for her older child. On this day, in this place, a miracle occurs. An older female, the mother of the new mother, the grandmother of the crying child, is moved to act. For the first time in the history of life on Earth, a grandmother intentionally shares food with her grandchild."[9]

This, as Thomas points out, may well have been the first step in the development of modern human beings by putting a virtuous cycle of caring into motion. So, perhaps the question about what old people are for would best be replaced with a celebration of the fact that we may owe our very existence to grandparents.

Come forward a million years and consider this observation by historians Will and Ariel Durant: "For civilization is not something inborn or imperishable; it must be acquired anew by every generation, and any serious interruption in its financing or its transmission may bring it to an end. Man differs from the beast only by education, which may be defined as the technique of transmitting civilization. . . . Let us begin before we die, gather up our heritage, and offer it to our children."[10] Indeed, as I established in an earlier book, the process by which we learn and then transmit our heritage to the next generation comes with sufficient reward to be characterized as the rapture of maturity.

Now, when we ask what old people are for and we consider our history in both an anthropological and a modern intellectual sense, it would seem that those of us who are considered old may hold the very key to the future. We are the bearers of some of the most important aspects of our culture, and at the same time we are in the best position to transmit to the next generation the most valuable lessons we've learned. By extension, then, we could ask, what are young people for, if not in turn to become valuable enough to add to the grandparent effect?

A shortcut to the kind of wisdom that enables us to learn life's most valuable lessons, as the ancient philosophers suggested, is found in the same level of thinking that ponders the wonder of existence. In my view, it's at the very dividing lines that separate us into camps of opposing worldviews where the discoveries and the inspiration from the wonder of existence need to be acknowledged, explored, and put to use. I believe there are three major obstacles that represent serious challenges to discovering the genuine wonder of existence. We must address each of them if we are going to complete the virtuous cycle of caring.

The first impediment is existential anxiety: the fear of death and nonexistence, which American culture is so ill prepared to deal with. Apprehension about death is so great that we go to extreme lengths to divert ourselves from thinking about it. Where death and nonexistence are concerned, we live in fear of fear.

The second obstacle to recognizing the wonder of existence resides in cultural conflict: in the ethnocentric contempt for others that we internalize from our own culture as all other peoples do from theirs. Such contempt is a major distraction and an impediment to problem solving. Class derision is ubiquitous, and the disdain for "the other" is coded into every part of our society. It may best be illustrated as a clash of worldviews: one religion versus another or religion versus the secular. This psychological and ideological divide is the fallout from our historical affiliation with small groups. It is so severe and threatening for some that new knowledge is shunned lest something be learned that threatens one's worldview or one's association with the "right" group. Thus, even though it is popular to claim we are a classless society, issues of class pervade every avenue of life from our taste in art and entertainment to the very clothes we wear.

The third obstruction is that, for far too many people, an uninspiring experience with traditional education stifles the desire to learn (even for many of the people we assume to be well educated), resulting in intellectual disaster. Literacy should be a foregone conclusion in America, but it's by no means something that can be taken for granted. Every year more books are published than one person can possibly read, while more of the people who do read books are reading less. Further, the need for media literacy is ever more critical for navigating daily life, but too many of our number are accustomed to being spoon-fed information rather than thinking for themselves.

Ralph Waldo Emerson recognized the debilitating effects of these existential anxieties more than a century ago. He said, "We are afraid of truth, afraid of fortune, afraid of death, and afraid of each other."[11] It's ironic that the very mention of Emerson's name brings the notion of self-reliance to mind, although his work is rich with insights suggesting that we can understand ourselves only by understanding ourselves in relation to others. In the chapters that follow, I intend to show that an existential understanding of ourselves in relation to others is critical to a sustainable culture. Not only are the three obstacles outlined above pervasive in diminishing the quality of our lives and our respective societies, they also stand in the way of the natural neurological rewards that come with learning. Simply put, these three impediments represent formidable barriers to furthering civilization. Of course, these are not the only obstacles to replenishing a lost sense of curiosity, but in my estimation they loom so large as to diminish any others. The fear of death, cultural conflict, and a lack of curiosity have the characteristics of an insidious virus that keeps morphing into new disguises to prevent us from recognizing them for what they are and thus ridding ourselves of the problem. I have been studying, reflecting, and brooding over the confusion brought about by these maladies for years, and I never cease to be amazed at how much effort is required to see through the latest camouflage. So don't be surprised that this subject crops up in unexpected places throughout this book.

The late Neil Postman argued that an education is, in effect, a defense against one's culture. I mention this at every opportunity because I believe it's nearly impossible to overstate the case. Finding ways to transcend our culture while facing the tumultuous times in which we live is the purpose of this book. I'm convinced that, provided one has good health, the fall and winter of life are the most meaningful ages of our existence. If you are past middle age, then you and I are in the same boat. Whether we have made a serious effort in the past to make sense of our lives is now beside the point. We are going to die soon, and if we don't put things into perspective now we may not get another chance. Having the courage to use our own intelligence sounds easy, but in actual practice it is an extraordinary achievement. Our culture focuses far too much on the material aspects of life. Even the so-called "golden years" have incurred so much commercial emphasis that little else that's positive about aging receives public attention. It is more appropriate to think of golden years as a metaphor for perspective, nothing more and nothing less. Perspective is why the final chapters of life are important.

Our lives seem to matter more with age because of the context that our evolving perception brings to bear on our past experience and on our hope for the future. The more we learn and expand our knowledge of the world, the more meaningful our understanding becomes. Wisdom is an ally of age and a friend to experience, but it's more like a lover to a reasoned effort to better understand the world and our place in it. Circumspective reflection is a characteristic of maturity, and once this effort achieves critical mass, it becomes an unrelenting thirst for insight. Many people despair about failing to experience the joy that the media lead us to expect during the golden years because aging alone is insufficient to produce such experience. Connecting with others, feeling a sense of purpose, and sustaining the effort to understand the mysteries of life are the added ingredients necessary to yield such rewards.

This is why so many others, even in ill health, seem to defy hopelessness with enthusiasm to their very last breath.

In any number of ways, the ethos of self-education has never been stronger, and yet there are instances, as we shall observe, where too many of our citizens are not measuring up to the intellectual standards of earlier generations. Golden years in the present have to live up to the golden achievements in the past in order for us to respond maturely and accept responsibility for our legacy. This is a call to rise to the occasion that our era demands.

TWO

RISING TO THE OCCASION

There will never be any substitute for twenty years of life and experience.

ALBERT CAMUS

SELF-EDUCATION IN PERSPECTIVE

Through the simple prospect of good fortune, I have been able to devote an extraordinary amount of time to my own learning. I've developed an insatiable appetite for discovering as much as I can about the world before I am no longer in it. The process has left me with clear insights about the power of self-directed inquiry and a profound appreciation for Ralph Waldo Emerson's notion of self-reliance. What I intend to show with *September University* is that self-education has the potential to radically change our worldviews for the better, that it's never too late to begin, and that in fact the future depends on it.

Self-education is usually thought of in terms of an alternative to traditional education. But self-education is a process in which we are all participants. It more accurately describes the method we used when we learned to speak and understand spoken language. In similar fashion, we

13

self-educate ourselves throughout our lives, often learning life's most valuable lessons in a manner peculiar to our own aptitude. Regardless of what level of formal education we've achieved, self-education becomes our post-graduate means of navigating our way through life. By comparison, even for those with advanced degrees, classroom experience is short-lived. Self-education is something we do without realizing that that is indeed what we are doing. It's like breathing: we don't need to think about it in order to do it.

In a word, what I advocate is a broadening of perspective—to examine your past experience and to deliberately seek new learning, with the goal of creating thoughtful, reasoned ways to address current problems and influence the future. Some of us feel that we are pulled through life; others feel pushed. Some of us are under the illusion that we are in control of what happens to us, and for the most part we try to pass this notion on to the generations that will follow us. Some of us choose to believe that what happens to us is preordained, and some of us do not. Some of us believe in life after death, and some of us do not. But none of us has a lock on reality, and therefore none of us has the moral authority to demand that everyone else should believe and act as we do without providing a knockdown argument to support our claim.

Rolling these subjects over and over in our minds may indeed bring us no comfort, but it can help immensely toward improving our understanding of those who have taken very different paths and those whose beliefs about the world differ greatly from our own. That others did not choose as we did does not make their decisions necessarily better or worse than ours. Too much deliberation, though, about the paths others have taken, often leads to envy. The result is a fearful attitude toward curiosity and an artificial barrier to experiencing a meaningful existence.

I didn't begin my effort to become self-educated until my mid-thirties. So I still remember what it was like to be viscerally anti-intellectual and to bristle and scoff at the very idea that literature and the arts might have something to offer that could add significant meaning to life. I recall being intolerant of minorities and being convinced that the way that I grew up viewing the world was the right perspective and that there were no close second opinions worthy of consideration. The most troubling aspect of these memories is that the time when I was most adamant about my worldview was the time when I had very little knowledge to support it, but I was willing, as most people are in similar circumstances, to use force to see that my view prevailed. In other words, in the preparation for conflict or for all out war, nothing is as useful as ignorance.

Ignorance lives off its own surplus of misspent emotion. Unfortunately, the emotion manifests itself in a positive light as the flip side of hatred when those who believe they belong to the right group come together in opposition to those regarded as other. Negative emotion bonds members in common cause simply by association. The result is that no matter what the collective group does as a result of its aggregate ignorance, loyalty to one another will always and forever outweigh any evil actions that may have been undertaken because of a lack of knowledge. Simply put, truth by association trumps morality. Every nation forgives its own excesses in war, but not those of its enemies. In tribalistic matters Stone Age minds still default to the perception of being right, even when there is overwhelming evidence against the position. The easiest of all cases to be made in such minds are those that rely on ethnocentric self-justification.

Now, with every passing year, I am more and more appreciative of the fact that I have been fortunate enough to vigorously pursue my own self-education. The result has been a profound change in my worldview and a dramatic dissipation of the hostility I grew up directing toward anyone I perceived as different. I believe the influence of education, and of self-education in particular, has the power to remake the world because of the awareness it generates for the need to change our conduct toward the peoples of other cultures. For each of us as individuals, I believe, there is a tipping-point when the defensive nature of our Stone Age minds will give way to a dramatic shift in perspective under the exponential weight of information that renders our rigid worldviews absurd. When you embrace a multitude of ideas about the world, narrow viewpoints begin to appear imma- ture. Achieving this threshold of knowledge on a very large scale seems to me the only way possible that we might be able to manage a truly sustainable environment, because to do that will require cooperation on a global scale. Assuming this kind of responsibility, though, requires a rethinking of and a rededication to the ethos of self-education.

While I was working on my first book in the 1980s, I ran across an article by a popular scientist that was so com- pelling I wrote to him and asked for permission to use the piece in my book. At the time I didn't know the protocols for requesting permission or that I would need to show how I would use the material and in what context, etc. So, a few months passed and one day I received a note from Carl Sagan's agent saying that Sagan respectfully declined my request to use his material because he was not familiar with my work, but that Dr. Sagan was intrigued by the idea of Self-University, which was the title of the book I was writing. It was as if the concept of conducting one's own university education was a novel suggestion.[12]

Contrast Sagan's response with this brief quotation from Joseph F. Kett's history of adult education titled *The Pursuit of Knowledge Under Difficulties*: "In the eighteenth century the idea of liberal education was bound intimately to that of self-education, both in the general sense that a liberal education included the acquisition of the qualities of character, for example, the habit of placing civic duty above self-interest, and also in the sense that a liberally educated person possessed a knowledge of many subjects—history, the law of nations, modern polemics, and modern poetry—that rarely formed part of the collegiate curriculum."[13]

How did we get so far off track with our expectations about self-education that one of America's leading twentieth-century scientists would find intriguing what in an earlier century simply would have been taken for granted? In the eighteenth century it was still possible to be offered a professorship at a college without ever having attended one. Knowledge and experience were taken at face value.[14] One either had the knowledge or did not. How one obtained the expertise did not matter. Today a lack of formal education too often takes on the guise of a particular kind of learned helplessness. Many people are boisterous about their political views, but down deep most of them are afraid to take seriously their own views about any number of subjects simply because they have not been officially recognized as being knowledgeable. On the other hand, at the highest graduate level, Ph.D.'s often can't reach agreement about any matter above a kindergarten level of sophistication.

Throughout history the price of citizenship has escalated correspondingly with the continuous rise of technology. The more we are able to do as individuals, the greater our impact on the environment. This fact is very seldom publicly acknowledged, however, because of an overemphasis on freedom instead of responsibility. Not surprisingly, the expectations for adult education are now unacceptably low. Why does the term adult education conjure images of remedial education? Perhaps, at least in part, it's because for millions of people, years of stop-start, by-the-clock school subjects, endured in arbitrary sequence, and taught by teachers who themselves were just going through the motions and were disrespectful of the students' enthusiasm or lack of it has had such an erosive effect on their curiosity that they have lost the desire to get beyond a superficial understanding of anything that can be avoided. For many of us, I suspect it's even worse. Years of having no control over our very state of attentive consciousness and being expected to answer questions that we did not ask is a profoundly traumatic experience.[15]

So much so that it seems to result in the death of curiosity. Add the ubiquitous growth of credentialing, and it's not surprising that for many people it seems futile to claim to know anything worthwhile without having an advanced degree in whatever subject is under discussion. Regardless of the reasons for this kind of thinking, none are good enough to justify a breach between one's experience and education that allows us to discount the former because of a perceived lack of the latter. Our personal knowledge about the world we live in gives us the democratic authority to influence decisions that affect both our foreign and domestic policy.

Did the baby-boom generation oppose the Vietnam War because they valued their civic duty above and beyond their own self-interest, or was it because it was simply in their self-interest not to go to war? My experience prompts me to believe that the reasons for the antiwar protests during the 1960s are as varied as the people who participated in them. The more I study history and human behavior, the less I am inclined to use generalizations. But I'm also very much aware that the character of self-education has eroded since the eighteenth century. Over time, self-education has come to be regarded as self-help, and the latter has to do much more with technique than with developing indisputable expertise or building character. Self-help has evolved in large part as a shadow of the American business management ethos. It's become a genre for developing what business wants, and it has little to do with whether what is wanted is actually desirable from an ethical point of view. Long, long ago in the American workplace *why* gave way to *how* and *when*. Since then, bucking the system has taken an extraordinary amount of effort. Worse, the self-education that equated to a liberal education and was so esteemed in the eighteenth century, after gaining prominence in colleges and universities for a time, has now lost respect and appears to be growing less important with each passing year.

I'm not suggesting that we should long to go back to the eighteenth century. Far from it. We are better off in countless ways. We are aware that students learn in differing modes and that one style of teaching does not fit all. We have classroom computers, broadband Internet connections, more libraries than ever before, more books, more museums, more research papers, and more dynamic web pages than we can ever visit. We need to ask, though, whether these are technological tools for people or whether people are becoming tools for the machines. We have to question why our expectations for liberal arts learning are so low. What would prompt college president Leon Botstein to say, "No generation of young people has been subjected to as much adult discouragement as today's schoolchildren and college students"?[16] You have to wonder why there was so much hope when America had so little and now so little hope when we have so much.

Although it's true that there has been an astonishing amount of progress in countless social arenas during the past three centuries, I believe it is also true that we are living in the shadow of some of the most formidable problems that our civilization has ever faced. Ideological wars are still pitting nation against nation, religion against religion, worldview against worldview. We are living through the greatest *preventable* environmental destruction in the history of the planet. In America and throughout the world, the gap between rich and poor is extreme, and during economic downturns, those with very little are subject to losing everything. If self-education were still largely experienced as it was in the eighteenth century, I suspect many more people would be reacting to these developments by putting their own self-interests aside and engaging in matters of civic duty.

No question, a lot of people are working for the public good already, just not nearly enough of them. In a culture that values self-education, people see themselves as being capable of improving not just their own lives but the conditions that make our lives possible. In a self-help culture, however, when stress and daily problems become too much to bear, the response for many is not to act thoughtfully, but to self-medicate in ordinary circumstances and extraordinary circumstances alike. Feeling bad and being depressed about the state of things used to be a basis for action; today's self-help remedy is not to fix the system but to drug oneself into fitting in. Neil Postman thought there is something deeply amiss about contemporary society— something that we've lost from the eighteenth century— something so important that he wrote a book about building an educational bridge to a time when people accepted more responsibility for their circumstances and worked very hard for the sake of posterity.[17] I suspect that those who founded this nation would have seen very little virtue in so many people desperately trying to fit into a system that makes them ill enough to require prescription medication for coping with daily life.

The seventeenth- and eighteenth-century Enlightenment thinkers still represent the most inspirational and courageous ideas in our history. In their day, the wonder of existence was for many citizens a self-evident reality. How can we get back to that?

ENTER SEPTEMBER UNIVERSITY

In the mid-1990s science writer John Brockman published a book titled *The Third Culture: Beyond the Scientific Revolution.* The book suggested that an evolving third culture—a science-based culture—was about to override philosophy and literature in defining what is important in life. I now propose the idea of a fourth culture made up of seniors with enough life experience to have something worthwhile to say and enough time on their hands to examine new theories and add wisdom to the discussion. A fourth culture may not be necessary in the sense of a different way of thinking or reasoning than Brockman's third, but the concept of it is needed to set the expectation that in the fall

and winter of life one should join the fourth culture, recognizing it as the last opportunity to speak up or forever
remain silent. This is a time to put Edward O. Wilson's
notion of *Consilience* to work, bringing all disciplines
together in an attempt to squeeze the last drop of value
from every avenue of our learning and experience.[18]

Getting to this point requires rediscovering the wonder
of existence by a thorough examination of our culture and
its history and by sorting through the foundational issues
which have made our lives possible. Textbook history is
often boring, but what really happened in the past is fascinating. We owe it to succeeding generations to think with
the same affinity for posterity that gave this country a start.
You may slip under the metaphorical fence or climb over the
top, but you must get a view of culture from all sides to gain
any sense of what might be considered objectivity. Those of
us with many years of life experience have already seen
enough of culture to get down to the important details, if
we're willing to spend time reflecting on what we've learned.

Valid warnings throughout our literature and philosophy caution against taking ourselves too seriously. Do not
confuse this with taking too seriously the times and the
culture in which we live, because doing so is the only way
we have to determine our complicity in good or ill. Let's
start with some of the dissonance we've kicked up in our
decades of life on this planet. It's long past time to question
the sanity of a world hell-bent on environmental destruction in the name of progress—a world that requires willful
ignorance on our part to disregard the problems we've created. It's time to admit that in some very real sense many
of us have been living a lie; millions of us have spent years
working at jobs that robbed us of the ability to speak our
minds about the issues that were most important to us.
Karl Marx was wrong about many things, but he was on to
something in acknowledging the ubiquity of worker alienation. Too many of us have endured mind-numbing jobs
that stifled our sense of worth and dulled our natural

curiosity and creativity. We spent years thinking things would get better. We went along to get along and, unless we are willfully blind, we are watching now as the same thing happens to our children and grandchildren. When do we decide to expose absurdity as absurdity? Do we dare raise controversial subjects? Or do we simply acquiesce and hope that others will speak for us?

For centuries people have pointed out those among them who they thought deserved less than a fair shake. Instead of demanding equal opportunity for everyone, they've allowed these various groups scapegoat status so as not to broach the subject of fairness to those with the power to effect it. The fall and winter of life is the time to awaken from this culturally induced trance and speak our minds. Reflective thinking can bring insightful solutions to bear on our problems when those doing the thinking have many years of life experience to sift through.

September University is a state of mind: it has no physical address, no faculty, and no staff. Instead, September University is a concept for a new way of aging, with the aim of erasing the notion of retirement from our vocabulary. It's a vision of retreat that replaces a time devoted to doing very little with a time for rigorous thought. It's here that people who've entered the September of life have the opportunity to make their greatest contribution to the generations to follow. September University is another kind of social security: it's a way to cash in one's life experience and exchange it for making payments on the tax of our existence. We don't have to be geniuses, advanced scholars, or ivory-tower residents to participate. But we do have to think at the best of our ability to whatever level of intellectual capacity that we possess. There is nothing much at stake except the fate of civilization. The level of mental effort required to fix the world's hardest problems is the same threshold that gives rise to the greatest quality of life for sentient beings. We discover the wonder of existence even as we wonder how long we will exist if we don't start thinking.

September University does not suffer the psychological poverty associated with most groups because there is no surrendering to authority here. We are all professors of lived experience and students in search of the better argument, seeking the wisdom of hard-won morality.

A September University frame of mind means anticipating having the time to examine our life experience, to discern those things that are truly important and those that aren't, and to discover ways to pass along that good judgment. Sept-U has to do in part with purposeful reflection about all of the many paths we've noticed in life but did not take. All of the things we could have done but didn't. All of the jobs we could have sought but did not. All of the places we wanted to go but have not yet seen. The many individuals we might have married but did not. And all of the subjects that held our interest for a time that we did not and have not yet pursued.

We look back on our youth and wish we had known then what we know now. But when we reflect deeply on the matter, some of us will realize that if we had had such knowledge back then it would have smothered the spirit and naïveté that gave our youthfulness its vitality. The lesson is not that we should have taken the paths not chosen, married someone else, or pursued another line of work, although in some cases the alternatives might have been the wiser choice. What matters most in hindsight is that reflecting on these themes will bring the present and possibilities for the future into sharper focus. We realize that the choices we make determine what we get from life. If we fail to expect the most, we are very likely to succeed in settling for less.

LEGACY MATTERS

The September of life offers one last opportunity for living a life that really matters, one last chance to feel the intellectual exhilaration that we very clearly have the capacity to experience, one last chance to get up to our elbows in the wonder of existence. Regardless of how or where we find ourselves on the road to maturity or wisdom, there is still time enough time to forge ahead if our health permits. The only thing we need is willingness and determination to advance. To proceed, however, we must ask ourselves what comes naturally to people in the fall and winter of life. In his book *How to Say It to Seniors,* David Solie explains the drive to discover our legacy. He writes, "When we start to realize that we're not going to be here forever, we become aware that it's not clear what it meant to be here at all."[19] Indeed, I've long suspected that for many people a midlife crisis occurs precisely because at a subconscious level they are beginning to realize that their current life trajectory is void of meaningful accomplishment.

Solie speaks of a legacy as the need to be remembered. For most people, he suggests, this plays out as an unconscious but unrelenting drive that cannot be satisfied without some feeling of attainment. I'm reminded of the movie *Patton,* when George C. Scott, portraying the general, arrives unannounced to inspect an army base. After questioning a number of soldiers who fail to give satisfactory answers about what they are up to, he comes across a soldier lying on the floor. Upon hearing the general's question about what he's doing down there, the soldier jumps to his feet and says, "Sleeping, sir," to which Patton replies, in effect, "Get back down there, son, you're the only SOB in this outfit who knows what he's trying to do."

I sympathize with the general; I don't want to be moved toward a feeling that I need to address something without knowing what's happening to me. If I'm going to be moved toward figuring out what my legacy amounts to, then I want to be able to recognize it when it happens. Nor do I want to see other people muddling through this rite of passage. Solie explains that a "well-facilitated life-review process" affects "how peacefully we face death."[20] Legacy issues are not optional, he says, but are in fact a developmental mandate for those privileged enough to survive to old age. Again, all the more reason to know up front what it is that beckons us in the fall and winter of life. Nothing is better than knowing what it is that you are up to at the *start* to get something accomplished. Hitting a target in any enterprise is easier if you take aim first.

Now, before I go any further with this line of reasoning, let me clarify that I do not believe there is a universal need throughout human culture driving people near the end of life to engage in a review process to tie up loose ends. Nevertheless, many of us are so inclined, and I would submit that American culture promotes this tendency in a feverish way. For example, we learn to expect a satisfactory ending to movies, books, plays, television dramas, and real-life experiences that we celebrate with congratulatory ceremonies. We long to interpret dreams with some kind of contextual significance. In nostalgic reminiscences we try to put our memories into meaningful perspective. Even television commercials and magazine ads sometimes tell a story. Someone's death in a spaghetti western has to have context for a life to end properly. In more movies than I can recall, especially westerns, the shootouts are incomplete until such time as the dying gunfighter knows who has shot him and why. With such knowledge he can die in peace, even the bad guy.

In a nutshell, we are conditioned to discern a plotlike framework all of our lives. It's something we've learned to accept and to expect. Conceiving of our lives as driven by narrative can feed the idea of creating a legacy for ourselves. If you have a plan for the future, then you are already on your way. If not, ask yourself if indeed it might be useful to put your life in contextual order, whether you feel the need to do so or not. Maybe now it's time to look death in the eye without blinking.

THREE

CONQUERING
FEARS

Anxiety is not fear, being afraid of this or that definite object, but the uncanny feeling of being afraid of nothing at all. It is precisely Nothingness that makes itself present and felt as the object of our dread.

WILLIAM BARRETT

One bright sunny afternoon in Oklahoma, when I was about ten years old, I saw something that few people ever live to see. Indeed, it was so rare that I expect a person has a better chance of winning the lottery than witnessing a similar event. Looking skyward, I was watching a sparrow fly in a straight line across the horizon when the bird suddenly died in flight. For reasons unknown, maybe a stroke, heart attack, seizure, or any number of physical calamities, it was in precision aerodynamic glide one moment and dead the next. In the blink of an eye, the sparrow became a lifeless weight, crumpled up like a discarded sheet of paper dropped into a wastebasket. It was a visual metaphor—an existential short story, with no drama, save the end, when life and death are separated by nothing but a moment in time. I have replayed this indelible memory many times during the past fifty-plus years, and it never ceases to portend a

simple lesson of mortality: We are here one minute and
gone the next.

THE EXISTENTIAL ABYSS

Many years later, when I was a police officer in Dallas,
Texas, I witnessed events that left me with a permanent
inclination for skepticism and an existentialist philosophy
of life.[21] The best description I've encountered of this perspective was written in 1956 by Walter Kaufmann: "The
refusal to belong to any school of thought, the repudiation
of the adequacy of any body of beliefs whatever, and especially of systems, and a marked dissatisfaction with traditional philosophy as superficial, academic, and remote
from life—that is the heart of existentialism."[22]

In existential philosophy the metaphor of the abyss
stands for uncertainty, death, annihilation, and thus
nonexistence. In other words, the abyss stands for all
of the fears that come naturally to human beings.
Furthermore, it is accepted generally by most existential-
ists, myself included, that these fears are best dealt with by
facing them directly. If we fail to do so, these uncertainties
will manifest themselves in subtle disguises that will haunt
us with innumerable false anxieties that can never be sati-
ated because they are not really what is bothering us.
Unfortunately, existential anxieties have a way of creeping
into social relations such that we readily blame others for
the things we're truly afraid of but are loath to confront.
The three psychic maladies mentioned earlier, the fear of
death, cultural identity conflict, and indifference or a lack
of curiosity have a way of overlapping so that we can't tell
one from another. We don't know whether our fears are real
or whether they are simply distractions that appear more
fruitful than getting to the bottom of what's really eating at
us. Moreover, our lack of inquisitiveness gets in the way
even as it ups the ante of our anxiety. We can't tell who or
what is the matter except that scapegoats and bigoted

assumptions override serious deliberations nine times out of ten.

The fear of nonexistence has a way of resurfacing as a resistance to change and fear of the other or of the unknown. Uncertainty and nothingness become interchangeable expressions. Existential angst even works its way into our appreciation of art and our acquisition of knowledge because of our predisposition to use these aspects of culture to forbid association with new ideas and to adhere to our tribalistic needs for small group affiliation.

Perhaps the idea of the abyss will become even clearer if we construct a mental image. Imagine the shape of a triangle: the left side represents the fear of death, the right side represents the conflict of cultural identity, and the base is indifference, ignorance, and an anti-intellectual stance toward life. This triangle represents the existential abyss at the heart of human anxiety: a metaphorical and cerebral traffic sign warning of fear ahead. Philosopher Søren Kierkegaard captures the essence of it as "despair unaware that it is despair."[23] Now you can see how individuals who harbor this internal motivational force are so easily distracted from their real fears, how and why their fear of death manifests itself as a resistance to change and intolerance for uncertainty, and how their need to cling to unexamined cultural truths leads to cultural conflict: contempt, bigotry, hatred, and obsessive patriotism in the extreme can lead all the way to genocide. Fear of knowledge that threatens someone's worldview leads that person to being uncomfortable with the unfamiliar; it manifests as anti-intellectualism on one side and snobbery on the other. This three-sided triangle is a contrivance used by people at all social and educational levels in society. Even intellectuals can be anti-intellectual at times. We all use existential angst in varying degrees when it suits us. It's always in the background like a black hole in space, ever ready to drain us of whatever goodwill we possess that we do not consciously and carefully safeguard against our worst instincts.

This predisposition is a barrier to experiencing the wonder of existence and an impediment to civilized behavior. Our social and existential angst comes to us so frequently and with such vehemence that it can easily distract us, while those with a hidden agenda manipulate these archaic tendencies for misrelating to achieve their own ends. Waving a symbol that the populace identifies with is often all it takes to raise the ire of those who are unreflective and unthinking to such a level of outrage that they abandon their ability to reason. All of us are vulnerable to becoming prisoners to our fears and useful pawns to bigots and tyrants of every political stripe.

Our preoccupation with and psychic apprehension about our own mortality are so powerful that simply being reminded about our inevitable death is enough to elicit hostile feelings toward those who take issue with our worldview.[24] And what actually happens when our worldview is threatened? It's simple: we feel less secure. Our ethnocentric inclinations escalate; our existential angst skyrockets. We are reminded that life can end in a flash, and thus our fear of death resurfaces, even though we may not make the conscious connection and deal with it directly. If our take on reality is suspect, then our anxiety must of necessity intensify.

The first order of business for participants of September University is to put our contempt for others and our fear of the unknown into perspective. Nietzsche warns us that "whoever struggles with monsters might watch that he does not thereby become a monster."[25] Life's major distractions must be recognized for what they are before we can begin to apprehend the wonder of existence.

For centuries a heated philosophical conversation has been underway about the meaning of human life. It ranges from affirming that life is a miraculous gift to denigrating life as both absurd and meaningless. I've learned to accept that life may very well be absurd if you deem it so and that it is very likely not if you don't. But the biggest lesson of all comes from realizing how prone we are to turning into monsters to deal with those we regard as others.

We are partially shielded from the pathetic shortness of human life by a neurological split-brain architecture that enables us to facilitate self-deception on demand. Through a mental device characterized as faith, we can seemingly partition conflicting ideas and squelch dissonance. That dissonance, however, often resurfaces as contempt for those whose worldview would challenge our faith. To my mind, the suggestion that if there is no God then everything is permissible is similar to the juvenile notion that if I don't like the rules I will "take my marbles and go home." Life is meaningful precisely because it is short and because it cannot and will not be repeated.

Old age and failing health bear a close association to the abyss, and sometimes nothing can be done to diminish the effects. In Gore Vidal's memoir, *Point to Point Navigation,* it's clear that the existential specter of death was never far from his awareness when he wrote the book. Philip Roth offers us an existential left hook to the solar plexus in his novel *Everyman,* showing us that the physical effects of aging are for many of us debilitating and unavoidable. And yet, I suspect that the actual fear of death may depend more on our temperament than on our beliefs. For some, religion may ease the fear of death, but for others it seems to up the ante. My own personal experience has been that some of the people who appeared to fear death the most were deeply religious, or so it seemed. Moreover, I infer that religion sought specifically to lessen one's fear of death may in fact magnify it, at least for some people.

My solution to the problem of the abyss is to face the reality of death without reserve, to smother it with thoughtfulness and with attention to matters that add value to life.

FACING DEATH WITHOUT FEAR

Philosopher Arthur Schopenhauer offered the sobering observation that we should view our life as a loan from death and that sleep is the daily interest we pay on the loan.[26] The temptation to study death is often irresistible, but the trouble is that the only thing any of us know about is living. Shortly before he died, Carl Sagan, in his book *Billions and Billions: Thoughts on Life and Death at the Brink of the Millennium*, wrote, "The world is so exquisite, with so much love and moral depth, that there is no reason to deceive ourselves with pretty stories for which there's little good evidence. Far better, it seems to me, in our vulnerability, is to look Death in the eye and to be grateful every day for the brief but magnificent opportunity that life provides."[27]

An ancient shard of Socratic wisdom is that the study of philosophy is preparation for death. Yes, it is that and more. Philosophy, as we shall see in a later chapter, is a sure-fire way to get caught up in the wonder of existence through an exploration of wide-ranging views about what is and isn't important. One of the fundamental tenets of existential philosophy says that if you can look into the face of death and fully accept its inevitability without compunction then the remainder of your life will come into sharper focus and the really important things will tower over the trivia. Even so, it is a primary characteristic of Western culture that we do everything possible to avoid the subject of death. We cover the dead immediately, not to protect ourselves from their gaze but to protect ourselves from looking at the dead. We often refrain from speaking of the deceased, and most taboo of all is to speak to the dying about death, although the hospice movement has begun to turn the tide.

In his book *Unweaving the Rainbow*, Richard Dawkins writes, "The feeling of awed wonder that science can give us is one of the highest experiences of which the human psyche is capable. It is a deep aesthetic passion to rank with the finest that music and poetry can deliver. It is truly one of the things that makes life worth living and it does so, if anything, more effectively if it convinces us the time we have for living is finite."[28] Indeed it has not escaped existential philosophy that social conformity is in part desirable because culture itself is associated with permanence whereas we as individuals are not.

I've learned to trust that our lives are meaningful in direct proportion to the psychic investment that we undertake to make them so. The subjective nature of human existence would suggest that life is not meaningless at all. Since the very characterization of meaning is a subjective experience, then meaning is to be found everywhere we look, that is, if we truly expect to find it. But, and this is a very important but, what we ultimately discover as meaning may be, in and of itself, profoundly unsatisfying. Questions often give rise to answers not of our liking.

Analogies are often very useful in providing perspective. Ever since the English publication of Albert Camus' *Myth of Sisyphus* in 1955, existentialism has been written off by a lot of people after only a cursory look. They equate the futility of pushing a boulder uphill, only to have it roll down again, with the absurdity of existence. Were it not for the fact that most people in the Western world have lived for centuries in cultures friendly to the notion of eternal life, I doubt that Sisyphus' predicament would have been afforded much credence as an analogy to human life in the first place, nor would existential philosophers have felt a need to write about it. The absurdity at hand is not whether life is or is not absurd, but that people who think themselves educated can deem it so based upon another's authority, thereby negating the intrinsic value of their own personal experience. The greater the effort we make to add something of lasting value to life, the more complexity is involved in the process and we are able to appreciate the quality and context all the more. We thus derive meaning. We have to ask ourselves whether the thrust of our lives can be compared to pushing a rock uphill, only to have it fall again.

Most any first-year philosophy student can make a case for the absurdity of human life. Yes, life is absurd if left to smolder in the cold ash of passionless mediocrity. But does it make sense to suggest that it's futile to learn anything because you can't know everything? Is there no awe or wonder, no enthralling enthusiasm to be discovered in the art of living? The existential hurdle is to embrace the absurdity and turn one's anxiety into a passion for living. Laugh when your boulder rolls downhill; smile as you begin to push it up, not because it's expected, but because you *will* it so. Learn to do this because you are engaged in a passionate pursuit of life, and relish the moments when you experience, as I do, the sheer joy of having the opportunity to live the life of a human being, knowing that the chance of its happening is one in many trillions.

Indeed, Camus imagines that Sisyphus does not find his existence absurd—quite the contrary. Camus writes, "One does not discover the absurd without being tempted to write a manual of happiness."[29] And if we do not find happiness then whose fault would that be? These are advanced-level questions within September University, for as Camus reminds us, "We get into the habit of living before acquiring the habit of thinking."[30] For millions of people the metaphor of the abyss suggests that life is empty of meaning. But that's only if there is no pushing back. Human consciousness is a receptacle of, by, and for meaning. The really big question asked of each and every one of us is the continuous and unrelenting question of life itself. Our moment-to-moment lives, our very breath, is a part of our response to the question: life is the query, and what we do with our lives is the answer. The far bigger question about meaning is not whether it exists but how much and to whom do our accomplishments matter? If our lives truly matter to us, and we've done all we can toward that goal, then we have to prove it no further. The cessation of the movie projector does not mean that there was never a film or that it had no meaning just because the theater collapsed. If it is true that there was once meaning, it will remain so, even if we no longer experience it as such.

Of one thing I'm quite certain: in order to live in the shadow of the abyss, only a stance of healthy skepticism contains enough integrity to keep a person from the crippling effects of self-deception and an irrational fear of the unknown. I have faith that the sun will shine tomorrow; I have faith in gravity, but I've learned that it can be disastrous to believe anything simply because others claim it is so. Am I hostile to the notion of faith? No. It takes a lot of trust to get through daily life. But I cannot favor belief over disbelief simply because it is a belief.

Skepticism is abhorred by millions of people for no other reason than it is intolerant of accepting baseless assertions as the foundation for dogmatic assumptions. I'm for believing things for very good reasons, and I do take some things on faith. I respect everyone's right to believe, but if you tell me that you can appeal to supernatural forces and suspend the rules of gravity, you do not have my support. Talk to me, though, about compassion, justice, and treating all of the human beings on this planet as if they really matter, and you will gain my attention and respect.

I agree with Daniel Dennett's assertion, in *Breaking the Spell*, that "religion *seems* to many people to be the source of many wonderful things, but others doubt this, for compelling reasons, and we shouldn't just concede the point out of a misplaced respect for tradition."[31] From an evolutionary perspective, religion is a method that enables people to come together and experience intense feelings of belonging—of belonging to something larger than oneself—simply by the societal nature of the group, regardless of their belief system. What you discover in a September University state of mind is that, simply by trying harder to better understand the world and our place in it, you can have this same spiritual experience without the inevitable ethnocentric side effects.

Arthur Schopenhauer gained prominence as the philosopher of pessimism, but he was much more than that.[32] He gave us "the will" as life's driving force. He stares down the abyss and cuts to the quick of our illusions about the morality of Nature. He writes, "The pleasure in this world, it has been said, outweighs the pain; or, at any rate, there is an even balance between the two. If the reader wishes to see shortly whether this statement is true, let him compare the respective feelings of two animals, one of which is engaged in eating the other."[33] A harsh assessment, no doubt, but who can deny its reality? Here is Robert Wright, author of *The Moral Animal,* on Darwinian selection: "The insidious lethality of a parasitic wasp, the cruelty of a cat playing with a mouse—these are, after all, just the tip of the iceberg. To ponder natural selection is to be staggered by the amount of suffering and death that can be the prize for a single, slight advance in organic design. And it is to realize, moreover, that the purpose of this 'advance'—longer, sharper canine teeth in male chimpanzees, say—is often to make other animals suffer or die more surely. Organic design thrives on pain, and pain thrives on organic design."[34] It's little wonder that so many people feel the need to embrace illusions in coping with the realities of life and death.

In some ways Schopenhauer's work is the mirror opposite of my thinking. Where he thought the complete denial of the will to be the pinnacle of existence, I believe the summit is experienced through thoughtfulness and striving for comprehension.[35] Though he clearly focused obsessively on the misery and suffering in the world, I find Schopenhauer's philosophy extraordinarily meaningful for the winter of one's life. At times I'm not certain why, but I suspect it has something to do with the fact that he seemed so eager to confront the harshness of reality. Not only did Schopenhauer not believe in a kind and loving God, he also imagined a manifest and seething malevolence at the very core of existence. More often than not, I think his boldness for staring down the abyss yielded him a surplus of courage, which makes sense when his cynicism is measured against his scholarship. He was indeed a pessimist, but his pessimism wasn't a working part of his philosophy.

Schopenhauer subtly suggested that we calculate our efforts so as to add something of value to society and that, in doing so, we then take a careful aim at posterity. He himself demonstrated that it is possible to acknowledge the harshness of life at its worst without giving in to it. Schopenhauer disparaged the worth of living, but he didn't commit suicide. His social life was one of continuous disappointment and despair, but he lived an extraordinarily rich life of the mind and made a serious contribution to philosophy. He looked through a glass darkly, but he understood the importance of compassion in the human predicament. In effect, he did what he argued could not be done: he conquered the abyss with thoughtfulness and in so doing made a compelling case that compassion constitutes the interior of morality. A somber advocate for compassion, Schopenhauer put forth his ideas more than a century before the Buddhist notion of compassion became popular in the West.

Schopenhauer was his own existential contradiction; he declared that the supreme goal of one's life should be an end of passionate involvement in life, even as he was speaking as passionately as he could about the life of the mind. He was one of the most articulate philosophers of the past three centuries, writing lucid prose that could be readily understood by the general public. And yet, I would argue that he was seduced by Eastern philosophy in the way that so many of us are—overwhelmed by the powerful satisfaction of seeming to conquer our desires and forgetting that if all human yearning is extinguished, the result is nihilistic oblivion. I'm reminded of the late existential psychologist Rollo May who said that "despair is a desperate refusal to be oneself."[36]

To compensate for the disturbing fact that pleasure must always give way to pain and that happiness is fleetingly disappointing, Schopenhauer constructed a complex illusion to override simpler ones. The effect is like using one magic trick to hide another. We are so awed by the first deception that we do not see the one put in its place. Accepting a preposterous belief is one way to escape reality; so is pretending one is free of desire or that nothing in our lives really matters simply because life is too absurd to care. And here is an existential question of my own that I trust deflates Schopenhauer's pessimistic view of the value of existence: If life is so meaningless and absurd, then why is the fear of death universal and so palpable that we associate it with terror? If Schopenhauer were right, then death would be something most of us should look forward to.

Moreover, if there is nothing to be passionate about, then what's the point and purpose of anything? We humans get our meaning from our commitment to care about things to the degree that the passion we derive from the experience makes dying regrettable. In my view, it would seem the Buddha cheated himself out of some of the best experiences life has to offer, if not for the fact that he himself was participating in a passionate pursuit of ultimate knowledge. So, for you and me, having anything short of the Buddha's enthusiasm to follow our own inclinations as he did his would seem to be a diversion and an exercise of bad faith. Are our selfish desires as individuals all that truly matter? Are we not asked to overlook the fact that the Buddha abandoned his family for reasons that today verge on extreme self-indulgence? How does the Buddhist notion of compassion fit in with family desertion?

The flashes of insight and euphoric shifts in perspective that often result from efforts to gain comprehension might be compared to the Buddhist concept of nirvana. A practice of continual learning seems much more productive and socially useful, in my view, than simply emptying one's mind because a semblance of nonexistence is thought superior and preferable to anything desirable. Of course, an ultimate goal of Buddhism is to gain a sense of unfettered compassion, and I am sympathetic with this aspiration. Still, even as the Buddha himself admitted, the odds of becoming like the Buddha are so formidable that few ever attain such a state. Absent a fundamental understanding of human relations, arresting the will, as Schopenhauer advocated, or overcoming one's yearning in Buddhist fashion, cannot be a surefire means of achieving a compassionate or Buddha-like temperament. Expecting everyone to come to the same conclusion once their desires are in check seems to me overly idealistic. It's much more realistic that we learn to engage both our emotions and our intellect in order to act when we have good reasons for doing so.

There is much to be lauded in acquiring a sense of self-control that stills desire, and Eastern notions of achieving enlightenment are praiseworthy, but to will nothing, is to do nothing, to be nothing, to achieve nothing and to leave nothing of value for posterity, save a mind purposely emptied to avoid the existential pain of disenchantment. Why should we have a brain at all if the most we aspire to do is to defuse its power with emptiness?

Pardon me, but there is much more to life than trying to escape from it, which is why my idea of an existential education is to face reality head on. I don't know about you, but my memories of pleasurable human experience, even in the presence of pain, make my brief existence on this planet seem worthwhile. That said, if you think I'm being too hard on the Buddha, then you should also know that if I had to choose among the many beliefs systems in the world, I would indeed be a Buddhist.

My scholarship suggests that deep within the existential human condition is a gulf between skeptics, who view worship as a squandering of human affection on needless illusion, and the believers, who view those who deny the meaningfulness of life as purveyors of a thinly veiled contempt that shields their own personal disillusionment. I am a skeptic and a nonbeliever, but I find myself somewhere in between these extremes. My life will be blotted out soon enough, so I'm for being passionate about living while time permits. Anything less seems to me a crass expression of ingratitude for having had the opportunity to experience life as a human being.

COLLIDING WORLDVIEWS

Time is too short for mincing words. Far too many of us are timid about discussing our deepest anxieties about mortality for fear offending people who, beloved as they may be, accept the bliss of illusion over reason. Billions of words have been written about the notion of life after death. Millions of people attest to its certainty. But the wishful thinking, the prayers, the yearning, all of it, every last thread, in my opinion, flies in the face of physics. Thinking does not occur without brains; there is no seeing without eyes, no hearing without ears, and no awareness without a conscious mind to provide the context for thought. How can anyone agree with the premise that the human brain is one of the most marvelous creations in the known universe and then accept that we still have use of it when it has decayed?

It is no wonder that people who cling to the possibility of life after death don't want the subject examined in depth; any elementary investigation reveals the idea can't possibly be true. Every kind of argument imaginable has been used to perpetuate the illusion of life after death, but none is as effective as indoctrinating children with sufficient force and support so that they will go through their whole lives fending off evidence to the contrary.

There is nothing to fear from death, however, because, as the stoic philosopher Epictetus observed, we will not experience what cannot be experienced. When our bodily functions are dead, so are we—not for a moment but forever. Give it some thought, and you will realize that since death is nonexistence, we have all been dead before. Therefore those who yearn for immortality have it precisely backwards: There is no life after death, but there is death before and after life.

People who can't face the objective certainty of death take the pursuit of illusion as their primary orientation in life, and the contempt they have toward people who question their sanity is often equal to or greater than any wickedness ever attributed to Satan. This attitude helps to explain the evangelical fervor for "saving the damned," which, when examined closely at the subconscious level, is less a concern for others than a feeling that the more people there are who will embrace an illusion, the greater the chance that it could be true.

Nietzsche captured the essence of the anxiety wrapped up in the thirst for immortality when he declared that investing the center of one's gravity in the notion of the afterlife is to lose one's center. He put it this way, "To live so, that there is no longer any *sense* in living, *that* now becomes the 'sense' of life."[37] And thus, all meaning to be derived from real life experience is egregiously undermined. It's sad that the distraction of a promised afterlife robs so much richness from living and that for millions of people an imaginary existence becomes more important than a real one. How ironic that for many people a deception under the guise of brotherly love hides a real agenda for eternal revenge against those unwilling to adopt the illusion. Organized religion's concern for humanity as a whole masks a virtual cauldron of contempt for otherness spewing with the venom of anti-ness: anti-gay, anti-intellectual, anti-feminist and most of all toward nonbelievers and all of those who question the piety of the in-group.

Sadder still is the reality that getting rid of the illusion of life after death may be the only chance we have for genuine social progress. This makes it highly unlikely that we will ever achieve a state of sustainable civilization. We will likely destroy ourselves over matters of perception. Let me demonstrate: If, on the one hand, you feel that what you are reading in this chapter is an attack on religion or, on the other, you are cheering because your own views seem somehow vindicated, I would argue that this is only a small taste of the intense emotional range that contributes so readily to the explosive possibilities when differences in worldview are present. It is long past time to grow up and put away childish notions about eternal life. That *faith* is a euphemism for *illusion* is one of the easiest of all assumptions to prove. It takes but a few simple questions to discern that faith, in each and every case, is nothing more than a shelter from uncertainty.

It may come as a surprise to people of a religious orientation that many nonbelievers view the believers' piety as selfish and immoral—selfish because their pretentious devotion expects to be rewarded, immoral because injustices that could be remedied by responsible citizens in this world are instead left to God in the imaginary next one. Many believers cannot face the fact that an entity that is not powerful enough to stop the needless suffering in the world cannot be good, and one without the power cannot be God.[38] Moreover, how is it possible for anyone but insufferable narcissists to believe God intervenes to help their favorite sporting teams win a game, but then turns a blind eye of indifference to events like the Holocaust? The very idea of God drains us of personal responsibility. We foul the water and poison the air. We kill each other without compunction and generally live without regard for the long-term consequences of our acts, even though our lives are pathetically short in comparison to the lasting residue of our deeds. True morality as Walter Truett Anderson said, is the "product of hard-won wisdom" and the "never ending result of understanding and reunderstanding life, constructing and reconstructing the rules of relationship between self and others."[39]

Rabbi Michael Lerner is a tireless advocate for bringing the world together through mutual respect and through recognition that at a deep level all of us value the same things in life. In his book *The Left Hand of God,* he says that the human race "longs to be part of a world in which kindness, generosity, nonviolence, humility, inner and outer peace, love and wonder at the grandeur of creation stand at the center of our political and economic systems and become the major realities of our daily life experience."[40] I can aspire to this kind of a world, and I call on those readers who are religious to apply the virtue of forgiveness to those of us who do not share your views on religion and let those who believe as I do return the goodwill.

I respectfully disagree, however, with Lerner's overreaching definition of scientism. He seems to believe that religion is so powerful that in its absence something must be substituted to take its place, at least to the degree that it can be called an ism.[41] But, in my view, it is entirely possible to go through life insisting on believing things for good reasons without being guilty of scientism. If you follow the logic of those who disparage science because of its affinity for skepticism, then simply by using our brains we are guilty of brainism. Carl Sagan and Ann Druyan said it best in *Shadows of Forgotten Ancestors*, "If the universe were really made for us, if there really is a benevolent, omnipotent, and omniscient God, then science has done something cruel and heartless, whose chief virtue would perhaps be a testing of our ancient faiths. But if the universe is heedless of our aspirations and our destiny, science provides the greatest possible service by awakening us to our true circumstances. In accord with our own unforgiving principle of natural selection, we are charged with our own preservation—under penalty of extinction."[42]

My experience suggests that to reach this kind of attentiveness requires a deep and invigorating exploration of our culture and its literature and art. Failing to appreciate the joy of such discovery is an impediment to embracing the humanities and reviving our enthusiasm for learning on a far grander scale than we ever thought practical. Once, during his presentation of the Gifford Lectures, Carl Sagan characterized science as something like "informed worship."[43]

Engaging in exploration with this degree of passion can help neutralize the threat of the abyss by rendering it secondary to meaningful experience. Such work is especially valuable to those of us in the fall and winter of life because we have our own life experiences to evaluate in contrast to conventional wisdom. The first step is to determine whether traditional education has dampened our drive to learn and if so, why. If the flame of our curiosity has been reduced to a flicker, why and how did it happen and what do we need to do to rekindle the flame?

FOUR

RELIGHTING THE FLAME OF CURIOSITY

The man who does not read good books has no advantage over the man who can't read them.

MARK TWAIN

I n my experience, learning becomes its own reward when a person's collective knowledge achieves a critical mass of satisfaction—a tipping point where learning becomes something one does for its own sake. A close examination of our culture suggests that millions of people never make this connection. They never learn that a serious effort to learn more and more about the world is a shortcut to a higher quality of life experience, even as it lays the groundwork for transforming society qualitatively.

For many people, getting past the drudgery of traditional education is the hard part. The mandatory acquisition of knowledge tends to dampen recognition of the intrinsic value of learning rather than inspire it. It's common today for writers to appeal to the notion of "knowledge for its own sake" as something of a virtue. I've frequently done so myself. Nietzsche ridiculed the very idea of knowledge for its own sake as an illusion of failed morality.[44]

Although I think he was mistaken, knowledge for its own sake seems to me to be a misnomer. The sake at stake is the sake of our selves, not of the knowledge per se.

Daniel S. Janik, a researcher in the field of neurobiological trauma and transformational learning, defines trauma as "any unwanted violation of one's body, mind, and/or spirit."[45] This supports my personal experience and my long-held suspicion that traditional education can often be a very traumatic experience.[46] One of the prominent features of trauma is a loss of memory, and that may help explain why I have no memories at all from many years of schooling. And it may reveal a grain of truth in the old saying that children begin school as question marks but end as periods. If you have didactic issues of your own that you feel a need to resolve, you can find both solace and validation in Kirsten Olson's *Wounded by School*.

Having very little control over one's front page of consciousness in a classroom environment for so many years can be destructive to one's sense of curiosity. It's little wonder so many people never fully recover from this orientation toward teacher-student instruction. I'm not suggesting that traditional education needs to be entertaining or even exciting, although I do favor the latter approach when possible. What I'm advocating is that all real education, in a meaningful sense, is self-education. Until our own volition comes into play, we are simply observers. We must become deeply involved in our own learning and turn the rental of our conscious awareness into a purchased transaction followed by acknowledged ownership of the learning experience. Only then does something lasting take place.

DISCOVERY

I've always felt a little sympathy for saddle horses, who spend most of their lives traveling about without the slightest clue of where they are going or why. A saddle horse has no control over its direction from one moment to the next, and this makes it an apt metaphor for discussing education. I don't think it's too much of a stretch to suggest that domesticated horses miss a great deal of what it truly means to be a horse for a horse's sake. Likewise for humans, traditional education weakens the part of the brain that houses curiosity. As with the saddle horse, perpetually deprived of the ability to go where it wants to go, too much direction in formal education can deprive us of meaningful experience for such long periods that it extinguishes our internal sense of wonder.

This diminishment is not because of the student-teacher relationship per se. Rather, the culprit is something we do that seems natural but is actually contrived: We arrange our students in groups of the same age and then expect them to proceed intellectually in lockstep. It is intellectually debilitating to be in the second grade and able to do fifth- and sixth-grade work, only to be held back because you are not yet the right age. Worse still is being expected to learn what you're not yet ready to learn, possibly because it is presented in the wrong way. For some people this leads to a crippling lack of self-worth that can last a lifetime. The one-room schoolhouse in the nineteenth century, where students of all ages worked together helping each other, was much more in keeping with the way people have learned through the ages. Peer pressure is an incredibly powerful force, and it's not given nearly as much credence in child development as it's due. Socializing children in like groups seems like a natural thing to do, and yet it makes children hyperaware of their differences at a time when they are trying desperately not to stand out. These practices severely tighten the reins on a child's intellect with long-term consequences.[47] One such aftereffect is that millions of people live the remainder of their lives in a stultifying intellectual maze, a state characterized by James Côté as arrested adulthood.[48]

One of the major reasons cited for students dropping out of high school is boredom. In my view, saddle-horse boredom is the vacuous residue of a loss of curiosity about where one might go next and why. Adapting to mediocrity is in part what boredom is about and thus is the antithesis of wonder.

Have you ever felt surrounded by people who are supposed to be well educated but who seem to have an interest in nothing beyond a little undemanding entertainment? I have, and it never ceases to amaze me, even though I think I understand why they are so intellectually jaded. I myself didn't begin to "thaw out," as Janik puts it, until my early thirties. Up until that time my curiosity was muted from having mistaken schooling and behaving for learning. Then I started to read material of interest to me and began posing questions of my own. Before long, I had learned to enjoy the process for its own reward. Based on that experience, I can say, don't worry too much about what to study on your own; just go with what interests you and take it far enough that it becomes its own compensation.

I've found that the brain rewards volitional learning with an endorphin rush so powerful that it could be sold as an illegal substance, if someone had the means to bottle it. Were the truth about its rewards fully recognized, learning would be considered seductive. I can think of no better way to inspire combustion of the learning process than through a voracious barrage of questions. Let a saddle horse run wild for a year or two, and it will relearn how to decide when and where it wants to go. After that, it will have built up enough resolve to require serious convincing before accepting a saddle again. Ask enough questions and you will begin to wonder why you haven't been doing it all along. Let me emphasize again that it doesn't matter what path you take to reinvigorate your curiosity. Even faking an interest in a subject will eventually result in a real interest, if the fakery is of your own volition and you follow through.

The late and great teacher Neil Postman said that for thirty-five years he had tried to figure out "why question-asking is not considered a core subject in school."[49] When I try to break through to new levels of understanding in a subject that I want to learn about, I spend whatever time is necessary reading everything I can get my hands on about that area of interest. When the time feels right, I begin to pose questions to myself about the nature of what I'm after—vague questions at first that in time become clearer and more precise. I ask these questions of myself over and over in differing ways, and I do it for days, weeks, and even months if necessary. I focus on these queries before, during, and after sleep, and in time a strange and mysterious feeling comes over me. I've learned to recognize this feeling as the preliminary signal that I'm about to receive answers to my questions. The feeling becomes more and more pronounced until at some totally unexpected moment, in the shower, on the telephone, on a walk, sitting at a red light, or paying a bill in a restaurant, I'm hit with a sudden cerebral downdraft of ideas. Answers to my questions burst forth with the force of a spring thunderstorm, and as soon as it happens I see everything I've been working on in a new light. It's a feeling of intense exhilaration, and for several days afterward I'm left with an enhanced sense of well-being. On reflection I've come to the conclusion that the eerie feeling in this process likely stems from the seldom acknowledged fact that thoughts do not come to us in words, but have to be put in words.[50]

Perhaps someday there may be something identifiable at a neurobiological level that can be shown to drive curiosity, some physical presence that makes a new book title so enticing that you can't wait to get your hands on it. Maybe there's a place in the brain that can be shown to light up when we are curious and that goes dark and fades when we lose the spark that makes a horse a real horse or awakens a human as a deeply intellectual being. At present, though, it seems to take an extraordinary amount of stimulation to jump-start the brain sufficiently to keep it from sliding into neutral when idle.

In the meantime, I suspect that the act of writing is itself a form of defiance against having had one's mind co-opted for long periods of time. Writing is a process of discovery. Sitting down to write is like priming a pump. It may be very hard at first, but it gets easier with time. Before long it becomes more like throwing a switch or turning on a light instead of pumping a handle. Read, read, read about what interests you most; then write about it. The pressure of your experience and prior learning will generate the cerebral quakes that we commonly call insight and creativity. Then comes the realization that "creating is living doubly," as Camus reminds us.[51]

READING

Book critic Maureen Corrigan has likened reading to a search for authenticity. I think it's that and more. An intense desire to read represents compelling evidence, albeit likely beneath consciousness, of a need to express the feeling that the chance to live one life is clearly not enough. One teacher, Mark Edmundson, put it this way, "Those aghast at having only one life on earth are drawn inexorably to books, and in them find the deep and true illusion of living not just their own too short life but of inhabiting many existences, many modes of being, and so of cheating fate a little."[52]

Life is a maze that offers an infinite number of paths from which to choose. Books provide little more of practical value than familiarity along the trail, and yet the advice we glean can sometimes make all of the difference in the world. Books make us aware that life is much more than we imagined. Serious reading enables us to free ourselves forever of the need to speak and write using clichés and platitudes. Clichés betray a lack of interest in life and a kind of awareness that is born of mediocrity. To demonstrate an element of maturity all adults are called upon to enter the great conversation of humankind, and we cannot do this effectively if we don't have some sense of what's been said.

So what do we choose to read in the fall and winter of life? How about material that will awaken us to some of the denial we have experienced over the years? Read something that raises your ire and makes your blood boil. Then reflect on why you react the way you do. Start asking questions. We've only got a short time to live, so let's make it count. Reading amplifies the richness of life experience, and it offers a surefire method for getting beyond mediocrity.

Reading is a process with the ever-increasing capacity to amplify the wonder of existence. In his book *How To Read and Why*, Harold Bloom writes, "The ultimate answer to the question 'Why read?' is that only deep, constant reading fully establishes and augments an autonomous self."[53] Reaching new levels of understanding is something akin to imagining our intellectual apparatus as a very large kaleidoscope: much effort and strain in the form of independent scholarship are required to turn the cylinder to observe from a fresh perspective, but, once this is accomplished, we are enthralled with the new image. We appreciate it, that is, until time renders it quaint or circumstances render it obsolete. To transcend, to become larger than oneself, to move beyond, is an apt metaphorical description of the very process of reading and learning in general. Reading enables us to utilize to our own ends the experience of others; reading sensitizes us to elements in the shadows of our experience that lie in our subconscious, waiting for acknowledgment and clarification.

Reading increases our ability to discern value from living and to learn how to gravitate toward that which is truly valuable, not because of the claims of others but because we learn to depend upon our own thought processes. As a means of breaking through barriers to new levels of knowledge, reading is a quest for authenticity, a path toward maturity and responsible citizenship. Reading in a September University frame of mind presents us a challenge to climb Lawrence Kohlberg's ladder of moral development[54]

and to learn to see ourselves as Socrates suggested we
should: as citizens of the world.[55]

One of the very last things most of us who love books
like to do is to doubt our own objectivity. If we don't pay
careful attention, however, and fail to read skeptically, we
are all the more susceptible to illusion, delusion, and self-
deception. If the postmodernists have taught us anything
it's that all text is biased, not in some diabolical conspiracy
but as a direct representation of the author's worldview at
the time of authorship. That these points of view are discernable is critical to understanding context. The fact that
people do not intuitively seek to know these things, but vigorously resist, seems to me at times incomprehensible.

Books used wisely are aids for expanding our awareness and deepening our understanding. They represent a
rhythm of intellectual awareness that, by design, is higher
than ordinary thought and thus is likely to be more intoxicating than everyday conversation. This is easy to understand, since good books are the result of a sustained effort
to get it right, involving countless rewrites and revisions.
Good writing is a product of composed and focused
thought. Once we become accustomed to thinking at this
level, nothing fills the void but still more rigorous thought.

Reading as a means to gain a sharper sense of reality
and to reach for ever higher levels of knowledge is a quest
for intellectual maturity and an attempt to transcend the
world by better understanding it. Reading, in and of itself,
is a life-affirming activity. Imagine a fifty-year reading life
as an adult devoted to reading one book per week. That's
roughly 2,600 books in a lifetime, which amounts to less
than half of one percent of the books published in the
United States in a single year. If a person reads only one
book per month, then the lifetime total is 600 books. When
the rate is only one book per year, the sum is fifty during a
person's adult life. From this you can see that the choice
about what to read can be very important, and it reveals
the potential loss in giving secondary books priority over

the classic originals that prompted them. Reading original works reinforces the notion that it's more important to think for ourselves than have others do it for us.[56] What makes classics worth reading is that so often they dramatically enlarge our perceptual awareness and forever sensitize us to nuances of life that can seldom be discovered in any other way.

Regardless of how and where we received our formal education, continuous reading informs the quality of our worldview and our very take on reality throughout our lives. From the time we first learn how, reading provides a key method of navigation in both new and familiar circumstances. And the value of reading becomes even more apparent as we grow older. Later adulthood is a prime time for examining our experience and for deepening our understanding about what really matters in life.

Of course, lived experience brings forth its own perspective, whether one reads or not, but reading aimed at better understanding the world ratchets up the whole process. Purposeful learning is to perspective as oxygen is to life. Humanity cannot survive—has no hope of long-term survival—without an exponential increase in perspective by an ever-growing percentage of its population.

REREADING

Purposely learning more about the world is a meaningful way of coping with the anxiety inherent in the human condition. The process pushes the world back for a more comprehensive view, and it holds at bay the forces we don't understand while we try to figure them out. In short, reading and aging go hand-in-hand.

Perhaps it's a holdover from traditional education that we seldom think it necessary to go back and read a book again, even when we recall our first reading as an exceptionally rewarding experience. The vaccination theory of education says that if we take a course or read a book, we are thus inoculated and will remain forever free of the need to revisit the material. Sometimes I think this is why we have so much difficulty in knowing our own minds and being truly aware of our own sense of what we do and do not understand about the world. Only by going back, and often, can we truly understand a subject thoroughly. As our own perspective changes with time, our understanding grows, and this is why reading and rereading are so important in the fall and winter of life.

At times when I reread a book, the experience feels completely different than the first time. My sense of reality has changed so much, it's as if, not I, but someone else read the book earlier. It's startling to reread a book you thought was difficult a few years ago only to read it now and perceive it to be easy. Moreover, the experience is far more satisfying than receiving a good grade for your effort. Any of us can use this technique to gain a deeper sense of understanding about our own intellectual progress.

Reread in the September of life a book that inspired you in your youth, and you'll have a gauge with which to compare those things you once thought were most important in life against the way you understand their relevance today. Rereading books that we thought were important to us when we were young exposes many of the false or mistaken assumptions so often missed by a youthful perspective. In many cases it lays bare our failure to notice the injustices that we grew up with, having taken them for granted as just the way things are.

Sometimes I think that much of what passes as psychotherapy for millions of people in America could be replaced if only the participants could become truly interested in something other than themselves. Think of how fulfilling it would be if more people learned to think deeply about life instead of skimming over it like stones across a pond. How much richer their experience would be if they simply spent the time they normally do dwelling on themselves and their perceived problems in a serious effort to read and better understand the world around them. Reading and then rereading is one of life's greatest pleasures and perhaps one of the most underrated.

No matter how fast you read, or for how long, or how hard you try to read everything you can get your hands on, you will realize eventually there will always be wide, deep holes in your reading experience. This can be discouraging, but it's no reason to give up the effort. It merely highlights that if the kind of reading material you seek does not in some way challenge your sense of reality, then nothing much of value may come of it.

My advice is to read critically. Read for insight, not for answers. Imagine the authors' thoughts as starter-stone strikes—theirs against the flint of your own intellect. Use your life experience as fuel, and light a fire in your mind. With practice you'll likely get into the daily habit of applying this kind of critical awareness to other forms of knowledge acquisition—the media surrounding us all.

FIVE

SOCIAL LITERACY

*The medium is the message. This is merely to say
that the personal and social consequences of any
medium—that is, of any extension of ourselves—result
from the new scale that is introduced into our affairs by
each extension of ourselves, or by any new technology.*

MARSHALL MCLUHAN

Technology is wonderful in myriad ways, but it has also put Americans and much of the developed world in a deplorable predicament. Ours is the first culture in the history of civilization whose members are exposed daily to hundreds of messages expertly designed to cause them to act—or to feel the worse for not doing so. Little wonder that we refer to ourselves less often as citizens and more often as consumers—consumers of products, images, symbols, icons, and manufactured reality.

It's an open secret that the advertisers who try their absolute best to influence us are attempting to contrive reality itself. It's also openly acknowledged that merely being aware we are targets of such an enterprise is not an adequate defense against it. An equal defense requires diligence, conviction, and effort—a staggering proposition in light of our willingness to substitute reality television for entertainment.

If you recall Rowan and Martin's *Laugh-In* from the late 1960s, you might also remember the frequent question from out of the blue, "What are you doin' Marshall McLuhan?" Marshall McLuhan was a college professor who was born in Canada but taught in the U.S. An extraordinary cultural explorer, he read media images in the same manner that frontier scouts used to read animal tracks. He pointed out things that should be obvious to us, if it weren't for the socially myopic way we live. Spinning off from McLuhan's work, Theodore Roszak has suggested that "context is more important that content" and that commercialism is "media's greatest offense to maturity."[57]

While I don't think technology is a panacea for human social problems, I am very much aware that technology is the best hope for getting ourselves out of the mess of having too many of our numbers populating a planet too small to bear the burden without severe degradation. As Peter Whybrow points out, however, the down-side of technology is that it "magnifies our instinctual craving."[58] Let us hope this subject will occupy Sept-U members well into the second half of this century.

MEDIA LITERACY

Those of us in the fall and winter of life have memories of a media reality that is stunningly different from that experienced by today's youth. We remember when the special effects of cinema were not up to the task of convincing us that what we were watching was real. Something about Buster Crabbe's spacesuit just didn't do it for us. Werewolves were scary, but it was the idea of them that made them so, not their screen image. Being afraid of the Blob and Frankenstein took some added imagination. The soundstage had its limits. But, over the years, things improved. *The War of the Worlds* in 1953 demonstrated that the special effects folks were working hard, just not there yet.

By comparison, today's special effects are out of this world: Compare the old *War of the Worlds* to Steven

Spielberg's 2005 version. Special effects today are more *real* than real. If you can imagine it, it can be simulated. Puzzling as it may seem to younger people, many of us past fifty find this to be both disturbing and disappointing. Don't get me wrong. I like great movies and I like to be fooled by the magic of film, but I still remember what it was like being in charge, so to speak, of my own assessment of reality. When we're being fooled by magic, we know we're being fooled, even though we can't tell how it's done. Not so with current film technology. These days, it's nearly impossible to distinguish between actual and simulated reality.

For decades social critics have been commenting on the way rapid developments in technology are changing our society and our sense of reality. The effects of these advances, along with the perception that public education has been corrupted by glitz, have given us new terms to describe the chaos of everyday existence. Some refer to this apparent unhinging of life as we have known it as "postmodernism." New York University anthropologist Thomas de Zengotita has coined what I think is a better word for our perpetual state of confusion: *mediated.*

At the fundamental level, de Zengotita says, "*mediation* means dealing with reality through *something* else." He writes, "Our minds are, as a matter of sheer quantitative fact, stocked with mediated entities. Ask yourself: is there anything you do that remains essentially unmediated, anything you don't experience reflexively through some commodified representation of it? Birth? Marriage? Illness? Think of all the movies and memoirs, philosophies and techniques, self-help books, counselors, programs, presentations, workshops. Think of the fashionable vocabularies generated by those venues, and think how all of this conditions your experience. Ask yourself: if I were to strip away all of those influences, could I conceive of my life?"[59]

When I was growing up in the 1940s and 1950s, media were mostly absent from daily life. I remember watching June bugs on the front porch for hours on end. At most, I would lie on the floor and deliberately listen to the radio each evening. Contrast that with today when we can rarely escape the effects of an unrelenting media assault on our senses. It is worth noting that the first year of the baby boom marked the beginning of commercial television, and things have never been the same. In the spirit of Marshall McLuhan's "global village," some cultural critics would have us believe that we are about to come full circle and experience a kind of retribalization as a direct result of the capabilities of instant mass communication. The jury is still out, though, and it may be a while before such effects make themselves known.[60]

That we are confused is obvious. Neil Postman likened postmodern deconstruction of literary texts to a form of mental madness, but in my view, the penchant for unbounded analysis has never been more appropriate. It is only by using every means we have available and by scrutinizing the ways that media are mediating our daily lives that we are going to discover anything meaningful about the positive or negative effects of technology. We must do as McLuhan advocated and pay very close attention to the things that we take for granted.

De Zengotita says, "We have been consigned to a new plane of being engendered by mediating representations of fabulous quality and inescapable ubiquity, a place where everything is addressed to us, everything is for us, and nothing is beyond us anymore."[61] In a mediated culture everything is taken seriously except that which should be. And to be a mediated person is to have been commercially compromised. The only way to get beyond this level of immersion is to leap outside ourselves and learn enough about the world we live in to sort the simulated from the realties of what's possible and what isn't.

Apparently those in charge of our educational establishments are willfully ignorant of the need for media literacy as a core subject. Otherwise, why is media literacy not a major topic at all levels in public education? If we were to plan to spend a year in the Amazon jungle, would we not study the terrain and the wildlife in preparation? Would we not consider it a dangerous place to be uninformed? Today's children grow up in a state of media saturation. The media have become the elephant in the room, whose effects are ignored even as its presence overshadows everything we do, see, and experience. We are in constant danger of being overwritten by the sheer volume of media we're exposed to. Nevertheless, some features of media culture can be profoundly empowering.

Media literacy depends in large part on literacy itself, although one could make a case for having an ability to read cinema and television without being able to read text. Today, for those who cannot read media, both young and old alike, there's a danger of becoming engulfed by a language they can indeed feel but cannot speak. All text, all film, all communication is value-laden. If we cannot tell where the values are in the text and where they appear on the screen, if we cannot tell how these values are contrived and why they may have been presented as they are, then there can be no defense against those who would seek to push our motivational buttons. To go through life enveloped in media most of your waking hours without understanding the ways and means of media manipulation is to live as if your imagination has been smothered or as if you're wearing a saddle but are unaware of its presence. You become not a human being or a human doing but a human seeing, a human stimulated, a human reacting, who is not really autonomous.

To be free, to experience freedom, requires the ability to read the text of life with enough insightfulness to be able to tell when anyone or everyone would have us do something other than what we would do ourselves, complete with the ability to figure out our reasons for our actions. Stop the film, mark the page, freeze the frame, make a note in the margin, and figure out what they are up to and why. Until most people can do this, we are not free in our most sincere definition of the term and we are but tools for those who would have us act for their purposes.

My experience suggests that when you raise the topic of media literacy with high school students by showing examples of their favorite programming, they are fascinated, spellbound that something they have long been suspicious of is real and can be figured out. This exercise is every bit as meaningful for those of us with many years of lived experience. Break the code, and the plot thickens; where boredom once resided it is pushed aside with zeal and genuine interest. If our schools were to make media literacy a priority, I believe there would be far fewer dropouts, far more citizens, and fewer *mediated consumers*.

NARRATIVE

Neil Postman said, "Without a narrative, life has no meaning. Without meaning, learning has no purpose."[62] Part of our constitution as individuals is an internal text— a continuous, conscious narrative—through which we cajole ourselves from one moment to the next about what we should do and why. Just as we perceive that somewhere about two inches behind our eyes is an autonomous "I" or something we call a self, we also seem to carry a summary of our judgment, a front page of consciousness, whose function it is to hold this self together. This self maintains the continuity of thought necessary to perceive of ourselves as individuals and to be the same person today that we perceived ourselves to be yesterday, last month, and last year. It all depends upon memory, which unfortunately proves to be a very corruptible resource.

Our internal narrative further enables us to form a political point of view, creating a measure by which we choose our friends and define our enemies. To be fully in control of our own narrative is critical to experiencing quality. As Michael Sandel puts it in *Democracy's Discontent*, "The loss of narrative would amount to the ultimate disempowering of the human subject, for without narrative there is no continuity between present and past, and therefore no responsibility, and therefore no possibility of acting together to govern ourselves."[63]

Recent findings in neuroscience indicate that because our neurological processes are in a constant state of interaction and change, each of us may actually be more of a "flux" than a single self. Even so, by supplying continuity, our narrative fuses into something we think of as perspective, and it becomes a keystone of our existence—the chief editor of our consciousness, the guardian of our identity. This may be why it is so hard to change our views on a grand scale and why we are so resistant to opposing views or to people who see the world differently. Being aware of these realties can help us work through issues without being overly hard on ourselves. It all boils down to perspective.

The cultural reality that we take for granted as individuals is itself the residue of a continuous societal narrative, albeit one that changes both subtly and in fits and starts. From psychology to local politics, what we learn to accept as normal is the result of a hard-fought polemical conflict, the origins of which may long ago have faded from sight. Just as the politics of left and right shift in pendulum fashion through time and space, to know with anything more than subjective bias who we are as a people and as individuals requires a vital sense of both history and world literature. In my view, a person cannot gain that level of understanding without experiencing a radical change in perspective.

In his book *Building a Bridge to the Eighteenth Century*, Neil Postman doesn't suggest that we emulate the eighteenth century, only that we mine its intellectual heritage for all its worth. During that era, Postman points out, the Enlightenment offered by thinkers like Thomas Paine, Thomas Jefferson, Benjamin Franklin, Goethe, Voltaire, Kant, and Adam Smith laid down the narratives that provided the foundation of American tradition. He writes,

"What is important about narratives is that human beings cannot live without them. We are burdened with a kind of consciousness that insists on having a purpose. Purposefulness requires a moral context, and moral context is a vital thread of social narrative. The construction of narratives is, therefore, a major business of our species; certainly, no group of humans has ever been found that did not have a story that defined for them how they ought to behave and why. That is the reason why there is nothing more disconcerting, to put it mildly, than to have one's story mocked, contradicted, refuted, held in contempt, or to be made to appear trivial."[64] A dismissal of our story triggers our bone-deep, existential dread of otherness and reminds us of our own mortality. Such reminders set in motion an escalation of the felt need to defend our worldviews.[65]

PERSPECTIVE

One remarkable feature of perspective is that when it changes, it really changes. This dynamic can be so forceful that, afterwards, little of the former outlook remains. For example, when a conservative reaches a critical mass of dissonance and suddenly becomes a liberal, or the reverse, the new perspective is so powerful that it overwhelms most of the former opinions. In the same way that we find it hard to remember what it's like not to know something after we've learned it, we also find it hard not to agree with ourselves completely once we arrive at a new conclusion. The old reasons for having thought otherwise just won't hold up to the new perspective. So, it's not much of a stretch to say that taking on a new outlook is a transformation of the self.

This is where the importance of reading really kicks in. Reading proves to be the primary way most of us are influenced to change our perspective. It deepens our ability to understand and articulate to ourselves and to others intensely significant matters. It helps us relieve existential anxiety about life's complexities. Indeed, the hint of a new perspective is how most of us choose the next book to read. In his book *The Middle Mind*, Curtis White writes, "Reading is an expression not of 'loneliness' but of a very different emotion (if we must deal in primary human emotions): curiosity. Reading is a part of our desire for experience, a desire to know the world, to internalize the world, to prepare to judge the world, and even to be able to participate in the future construction of the world. With respect to art and intellect, it's not so much that one is afraid of dying but that one is afraid of dying *empty*."[66]

Look back to that time when we were children. We've changed physically, of course, but what fills the gap of time for us mentally except perspective derived largely from the internal narrative of our life story? Our view of our first day of school is quite different now from our view of it in childhood, and our ability to describe the experience has no doubt changed profoundly. The same holds for other events in our past—our first job, our marriage, our first experience of birth, or the death of someone close to us. Reading opens our eyes to the ways that other individuals have regarded and endured the same kinds of occasions. It deepens our ability to think on these matters and come to thoughtful conclusions. By reading we can enrich our understanding of events, enhance our sense of self-creation, and edit our own narrative. The resulting change in perspective forms an avenue for improving relationships with others and for experiencing aesthetic enjoyment.

Indeed, what is art but association without the necessity of the presence of another? Art is about communication. Art brings people together through experience. Art is a method of reaching out for the things that matter in life. Art signals cultural longing and yearning for change. The creation of art, whether it is great literature or a painted canvas, comes about because the artist brings something special to our attention. He or she creates something that requires a psychic investment of appreciation on our part. If we find the work appealing, then we have shared an experience that gives us something in common. Art is aspiration. Art is a gesture of goodwill, an act of dissent, and many other cultural messages all rolled into one. In this way, then, art is a secret code, an open secret, but a secret and a code just the same. Art is thoughtfulness objectified. Moreover, art is not so much a product of leisure as one of stress and a need for speaking out. William F. Allman quotes Randall White in *The Stone Age Present* saying, "There is no question that art is not being produced as a result of people having more spare time; it is being produced when all hell is breaking loose and people don't have enough to eat." He goes on to say that "art is the equivalent of mutation."[67]

In the final analysis, perspective is not only who we are and what makes our lives the way they are, it's also the essence of what's left of us after we're gone. All of the positive illusions and embellishments we bring to life will die when we do. When our lives are over, we will continue to exist only as a memory (not a movie or stage play) in the minds of others, and only from their own perspective. This is a sobering thought. How do we want them to remember us? Reading, thinking, reflecting, and trying to develop a better-informed worldview are among the most important things we can do to set a memorable example for those who succeed us.

A better quality of life in fall and winter for one generation can, and should, lead to a better spring for the next. It's the seed that allows posterity to flourish. But to plant that seed requires that we understand the social soil in which it will have to grow. The stories about ourselves have to make sense in comparison to the stories of others. Our lives make no sense without cultural context. Genuine civilization, in my view, requires that we resolve cultural differences, move beyond us and them, and rise above truths that are accepted because they're imposed. It calls on us to communicate effectively across generations, respect the needs of each aging generation, and appreciate the aesthetic bonds that bind humanity.

SIX

THE AESTHETICS
OF LEGACY

*Life is no brief candle to me. It is a sort of splendid torch
which I have got a hold of for the moment, and I want
to make it burn as brightly as possible before
handing it on to future generations.*

GEORGE BERNARD SHAW

The subject of legacy is complex. Our concerns about
matters of heritage are often unique and may be
understandable in a meaningful way only in our
own minds as individuals. For some people, legacy means
money or other tangible assets bequeathed to loved ones.
For some, it means accomplishments that leave a lasting
mark. But ultimately, for many of us, what is most important about legacy comes down to the relationships we've
had that are worth remembering. The older I get, the fonder
I grow of memories of my grandparents, and the more I'm
aware of how much influence my wife and I have over our
granddaughter's future recollections of her time spent with
us. This realization makes me mindful of the vital role of
sincere communication in experiencing quality in human
relations.

To deepen our understanding of how to live, we can
turn to literature. It's where we can gain an aesthetic

appreciation of the best life has to offer and at the same time learn from misfortune without needing to experience it personally. These works stand as a legacy to us from their authors. For those of us committed to the September University vision, the lives we lead and the relationships we form can likewise be works of art for those who survive us.

PASSING THE TORCH

Transferring culture from one generation to the next is one of the most important things people do. It's what holds society together. In *Socrates' Way,* Ronald Gross points out how crucial it is to get across to the next generation the idea of insightful ignition. He says, "In every generation and in every life we find 'carriers of the torch.' These are the people who fulfill Socrates' role by stimulating us to examine our lives, question our beliefs and values, and think more clearly."[68] What is even clearer, in my view, is that in far too many cases the torch is being passed without first being lit. If the wisdom of each past generation cannot be mined for use in the present and the future, then we are in danger of social disintegration. Failure in this regard is why ignorance-based bigotry is so ubiquitous. At the same time, communication across the generational divide can be difficult.

In *The Longevity Revolution,* an exhaustive tome that delves into all of the pertinent aspects of aging, Robert N. Butler puts the generational dilemma in lucid perspective: "The ultimate answer to all questions about generational inequity is the intergenerational contract—what parents do for their children, children must do for their parents—writ large. So long as we remember the natural cycle of the generations in all its profound and rich ramifications, we can deal with the necessarily creative ups and downs in intergenerational relations: the struggle by the young for identity and autonomy and the hopes of the old for a decent ending to life. Neither group need suffer."[69]

From the beginning of recorded history, people have been complaining about the difficulty of cross-generational communication. Every few years, new books are published to address the predicament, yet the problem persists and at times seems to get worse. Each generation acquires precise metaphors and symbols that have an abiding resonance of meaning and nearly universal connotation, but these can be mystifying to someone of a different age. Escalating sophistication in communication technology further compounds the problem.

A few years ago, at an isolated work camp far from home, I waited to use a telephone while the man ahead of me in line talked long-distance to his teenage son. The conversation grew loud, and the father began shouting into the phone, insisting that the son learn to save his money for a "rainy day." I tried to imagine what this young man must have been envisioning as a rainy day—a timeworn metaphor that to him obviously sounded absurd. As the conversation continued, the father grew ever angrier and the son more bewildered.

Later I spoke to the father, a man I knew vaguely from years with the same company. I pointed out that this metaphor he and I grew up with used to mean that people in an agricultural society couldn't earn money when it rained. When I tried to explain that the image wouldn't make much sense to someone of the current generation, he just looked at me as if I were even more out of touch than his son.

In her book *Another Country: Navigating the Emotional Terrain of Our Elders*, Mary Pipher showed us how generational differences can be so significant that members of the same family will feel as if they are literally from a different country. She said, "The old are segregated not only physically—by their living circumstances and their ill health—but also by their worldview. Language is different. The old may call oatmeal porridge and refrigerators iceboxes. Depression refers to a time when money was tight, not to a mental-health problem. Consumption refers to tuberculosis rather than spending. Metaphors come from communal life or from the war years."[70]

More recently, efforts to achieve insightful communication have focused almost entirely on the young. In *How to Say It to Seniors: Closing the Communication Gap with Our Elders*, David Solie, a medical advisor and an expert in geriatric psychology, points out that in any major city at any time there are scores of courses on child development but nothing on geriatric development. He asks, "Why do we have nearly infinite patience for a two-year-old's communication challenges—sometimes in the form of a tantrum—and almost no patience with a seventy-nine-year-old widow when she quietly changes her mind about a well-conceived plan to revise her financial statements, or our elderly relatives when they start repeating a story we've heard many times?"[71]

Why the double standard? This question has an easy answer when you think it through. Human evolution requires such patience of us for our children's sake. And for most of human history the problems that accompany advanced age have not surfaced. These days, I tend to think that most of us are subconscious members of the cult of youth, eager to avoid anything that reminds us of aging. Solie's excellent book is an effort to bridge the gap. He writes, "When we observe the way senior adults sometimes communicate—by repeating stories, or fretting about details, or forgetting things—we may think that they're becoming frail or losing their grip. Nothing is further from the truth. In fact, this communication style may indicate that seniors are responding to their developmental tasks (also called drivers or motivators) in a compelling and urgent way."[72]

Solie reminds us that a primary drive in advanced age is toward maintaining control over the simple events of everyday life that we have for so long taken for granted. More significantly, he adds, "Up until old age, our developmental drivers pushed us forward—relentlessly—to the next hurdle on the road to maturity. But in old age, the driver pushing us forward is actually bringing us to a retrospective phase that commands us to review our lives."[73] Indeed, I suspect it is just this conscious, life-reviewing reflection that prompted me to write *The Rapture of Maturity*.

Only by taking advantage of the wisdom of past generations, combined with the ingenuity of youth, are we likely to develop the intelligence to achieve a sustainable future. The next time you become frustrated when speaking with someone much older or younger than yourself, put yourself in that person's place and listen more carefully. Be aware that the symbols and metaphors you use may carry different meanings than what you expect.

Millions of us in the Sept-U generation are dealing with the issues of aging parents who are in varying stages of failing health that require assisted living or possibly complete care. In a short time our parents will be gone and the other shoe will drop: we will be the ones requiring assistance. Let us hope our experience with our own parents will help us communicate better with our children when we begin to appreciate firsthand the difficulty our parents had as they began losing control over their lives. Mental health counselor Wendy Lustbader has put the predicament into crystal-clear perspective. Her book *Counting on Kindness* was published in 1991, but it is even more significant now than it was then. Perhaps one of the great ironies about the demographics of aging is that books on the subject do not become dated, but actually grow in importance. Lustbader's work is rife with touching examples of people whose lives changed abruptly from "having" to "being"— about people who led active lives one day, but who were incapacitated for life in the next. They are suddenly subject to "other people's timing, to what helpers choose to give and to the rhythms they impose."[74] Lustbader tells of people waiting by the window all day because someone casually suggested that they might stop by.

Those of us who have not experienced extreme dependency have no idea how much our sense of self-worth stems from our ability to live independently. We are not likely to appreciate the degrading feelings of dependency, even if we are the helpers, unless we make a genuine effort to understand what it's like. Frailty, as Lustbader shows, invites invasion and abuse, if caregivers are not fully aware of the dynamics that occur when the power among individuals is so very far out of balance. She writes, "The one who gives help is more powerful than the one who receives it. The sheer acknowledgement of this inequality is a relief to those who have to occupy the inferior position. They no longer have to pretend that they are pleased, and they can insist upon forms of repayment other than compliance."[75]

Imagining ourselves as "walking a mile in another's shoes" is one of our most underutilized philosophical aspirations. As baby boomers age in ever greater numbers, the realities of physical hardship and incapacity are becoming increasingly significant. Luck and genes play a big role in our lives, but good genes do not protect us from catastrophe. Once we pass the half-century mark, our general physical condition becomes a very serious matter. Those of us whose good health enables us to enjoy our later years need to be constantly aware that in the blink of an eye everything can change and we can lose our independence.

If we expect our children and grandchildren to want to follow our example, we need to be thoughtful about the example we're setting. The kindness we offer to those who, for whatever reasons, have found themselves dependent upon the compassion of strangers is the social capital that binds us. Unlike monetary capital, the more of this we spend, the better off we are. Saving money is wise, but being generous with our understanding and compassion for those who have lost their independence is the bank account we can depend upon for withdrawal when we lose our ability to live without assistance. Kindness is contagious, and so is spreading it, not because we may need it some day, but because it is the right thing to do.

I suspect it will be another great awakening when we begin en masse to gain insight into the effects of the loss of control so soon after having witnessed our parents' anxiety during the same process. Perhaps having been so frustrated with our own parents when they resisted losing control over daily life, we will suddenly appreciate their anxiety with enough insight to communicate with our caregivers without the ill will that so often occurs during this kind of experience. Maybe, if we are thoughtful enough, the legacy we create will be aided in part by a venture into philosophy, objectivity, connectedness, and the wisdom to dig beneath the superficial issues that divide us.

LIFE LESSONS FROM ART

Art is a social summit—a meeting place—a rendezvous of sorts where all parties who participate can escape both tyranny and mediocrity. Literature offers panoramas of reality that change through time, with or without our participation as individuals. When we do participate and play a part, the narrative of our lives begins to heighten our awe and wonder at having had a chance to appear on the stage at all. If we buy into the premise that our lives are themselves works of art, how can we possibly come to the end of life without trying our best to write a memorable last act? If we feel drawn toward identifying something of ourselves worthy of leaving behind, how can we do it empty? How can we concoct a legacy if we do not understand what's compelling us to act?

Art is where we can come together as human beings and put the abyss in perspective at the same time. Eugene O'Neill is celebrated as one of America's greatest playwrights, in part because of his work expressing the tragedy of his own childhood and how it affected him and his family. Seemingly lost in this celebration is the fact that O'Neill walked out of two marriages, abandoning three children of his own. O'Neill's life and work illustrate that existential anxiety is much more complicated than simply being afraid of death. We human creatures are complicated because it is in our nature to be egocentric and never fully satisfied. I suspect, however, that these traits have played a big part in our survival as a species through the ages.

In O'Neill's most famous play, *Long Day's Journey into Night,* set in America in 1912 and based on his own family history, the father (his father) is a miserly stage actor who believes he could have been one of the greatest Shakespearean actors of all time had he not sought finan- cial security by playing a popular role for years without taking any creative risks. Now he laments and grieves for what could have been, if only he had had the courage to take chances and to pursue and thus live his dream. Taken at face value, that would seem to be the moral of the play. But we human beings are insatiable creatures. Experience tells me that if the father had been the great actor he had longed to be, and if his fame had not brought wealth (a real possibility in those days), he would be wishing and longing for that, still regretting the path he had taken.[76] Life pres- ents us with too many choices.

The mother in the play wanted to be a nun but married a dashing young actor instead. She lost a child for which she blames herself and one of her sons. She is addicted to morphine and is filled with regret. Both sons are too pre- occupied with guilt, love, hate, jealousy, and sibling rivalry to know with any confidence what they want to do with their lives. All of the characters are self-absorbed. The action takes place in a single day and gives the sense that the family has spent the whole of their lives battling one another and spouting endless recriminations for nothing more than a little respect and acknowledgment that they are indeed worthwhile as human beings. At the same time, it's clear that these people really care for each other.

Near the end of the play, one of the sons, Edmund, who has reason to believe he has tuberculosis, speaks of an aesthetic experience he had once while at sea. He tells about lying on the deck of a ship, watching the froth of ocean spray amid the majesty of shimmering white sails in moonlight. He claims to have become so drunk with the rhythm of his visual experience, that he momentarily lost himself, and, for a few seconds, discovered the real meaning of existence or, at least, something very close.[77] He goes on to tell of other times in his life when he had similar experiences, when he "became the sun," the "hot sand" on the beach, or "green seaweed anchored to a rock." Then, when the spell has ended, he says his being born a man was a mistake and that he would have been much more "successful as a seagull or a fish," that he has always felt like a stranger who has "never belonged," and that he has always been "a little in love with death." In one of the most moving and haunting bits of prose I have ever encountered, Edmund describes finding God for a brief moment in the beauty and wonder of existence.

O'Neill draws us into this self-absorbed and dysfunctional family in such a way that we not only sympathize with Edmund but also aspire to share his experience. We rummage though our own life's memories searching for similar sparks of aesthetic transcendence. In these moments, the abyss is obliterated and Schopenhauer's will dissolves in elated contemplation.

ART AND RELATIONSHIPS

Art is both inspirational and aspirational, and aspiration is what sustains us. The willingness to go to a great deal of trouble to invent, to innovate, and to modify our efforts relentlessly has, among other things, made possible the medical advances that enable us to live longer lives. And yet, art is but one aspect of our thirst for innovation, because it's also a very social phenomenon that both includes and excludes. You don't have to be an anthropologist to acknowledge the simple truth that the harder we strive to work at something, the more disdain we have for those who do not go to the same trouble to do as we have done. We find it easy to hold people in contempt who do not seem to take seriously the things we think should be taken seriously. Thus, art is power, and not in a small way.

Art is also a diversion, and the more sophisticated we become, the more it takes to capture our attention and inspire our interest. We assemble into groups, imagining ourselves as sharing artful objects and literary genres because we are the only ones who know the cipher of appreciation. These objects and genres are said to have special aesthetic appeal; by acknowledging it as a group, we perceive that we are thus special too. It is unfortunate, but still glaringly true, that with our Stone Age minds nothing brings us together more forcefully than being against others, regardless of the reasons for deciding that their differences qualify them as others.[78] We tend to attribute virtue to those who are perceived to get art's coded message. We don't recognize this habit, however, because our unconscious minds desire status and group affiliation—we need to belong to the *right* groups. A shared perspective seems right, and others seem wrong, if they do not perceive as we do.

Artistic expression can have a cathartic effect. In the case of O'Neill's play, one of the messages is that, no matter which path we choose in life, the ones not taken may haunt us forever if we allow ourselves to become too self-absorbed. We must take the time and exert the emotional effort to apply the art of narrative to our own lives if we want to be satisfied with the way our lives turn out. More importantly we learn from art that we are all fundamentally connected through a visceral aesthetic appreciation of life itself.

The ancient Greeks used the theater to bond themselves emotionally to one another through the genre of tragedy, even as it gave them a forum for examining the most puzzling aspects of life. On the one hand, it seems we use theater and film in the same way but with less lofty expectations for meaningful results. On the other hand, it appears we have made our cinematic illusions so real that we can now live in them.[79] In his book *Life: The Movie,* film critic Neal Gabler writes, "To compare life to a movie is not to say, as the cliché has it, that life imitates art, though surely there is truth to that. Nor is it to say that life has devised its own artistic methods and thus reversed the process—art imitates life—though that also is true, as one can see from the number of novels, movies and television programs that have been inspired by real-life events. Rather it is to say that after decades of public-relations contrivances and media hype, and after decades more of steady pounding by an array of social forces that have alerted each of us personally to the power of performance, life has *become* art, so that the two are now indistinguishable from each other."[80] Let us hope, for those of us in Sept-U, that such is not the case. If we lose the ability to think of our lives as works of art, and lose the reality that distinguishes it from entertainment, then we lose the ability to direct; we become lost in the cult of celebrity where people become famous for being famous.

O'Neill failed miserably as a husband and as a father; yet, we can gain valuable insights from his work and learn without the necessity of repeating his experience. Reading and the aesthetics of art enable us to make small course corrections as we navigate our way through life. Although we may seldom think of ourselves as having made dramatic changes as a result of such learning, the accumulated effects can be significant.

My point is that, regardless of whether we perceive that we have succeeded or failed, the possibilities in life bedevil us endlessly with what might have been or could have been. Art and literature have the capacity to ease our anxiety by giving us insight and enhancing our perspective to the point where we can afford every person on the planet the right to enough equity to exist. Every person, it seems, no matter how rich or poor, loved or rejected, carries emotional scars from childhood into old age. But, if our lives truly represent works of art, we should by middle age be able to reach a perspective that enables us to move on to concerns larger than ourselves.

As useful as it may be to think of our lives as works of art, we are not literally on stage and we are not in a 24/7 life movie. What's more, we need novelty; we need to look away at times. Sometimes distraction is good. Art and entertainment are both about power, and both are capable of distracting us or focusing our attention. The real menace in regard to art and entertainment is not the constant blather about whether or not they inspire us but whether they distract us from things to which we ought to pay attention. What we should hope to get from art and from entertainment is the insight and inspiration to think what needs to be thought, to see what needs to be seen, to act upon those things that require action, and to learn to appreciate how much thoughtfulness and contemplation is required to achieve our goals and live a life worthy of repeating. To accomplish this we have to take the subject of relating to levels beyond that of our immediate families. In other words, we have to discover how to think past us and them to an ethos of *we*.

SEVEN

GETTING BEYOND
US AND THEM

Civilization is an accumulation, a treasure-house of arts and wisdom, manners and morals, from which the individual, in his development, draws nourishment for his mental life; without that periodical reacquisition of a racial heritage by each generation, civilization would die a sudden death. It owes its life to education.

WILL AND ARIEL DURANT

Civilization is a controversial concept. There are many wise people who wonder whether civilization is really desirable; some even argue that civilization is what will eventually destroy us. But the image I have of civilization is a state in which we harness our best instincts and mitigate our worst. To achieve such a condition requires that we learn enough about our respective cultures to perpetually keep the narratives and stories about ourselves and others in context, without resorting to ethnocentric or class distinctions. Civilization is about the evolution of ideas. If our culture truly owes its life to education, then we can't begin to make a significant contribution toward a robust civilization until we make a serious effort to understand what it could and should be. We have to move beyond the superficiality of popular culture, and we have to know as much about the groups our culture deems as other as we do about the groups we readily identify with.

THE DIFFICULTIES INHERENT IN BETTER THAN

In the mid-1990s William Henry III published *In Defense of Elitism.* Henry, a Pulitzer Prize-winning cultural critic for *Time* magazine and a self-described liberal, nevertheless took an old-school conservative approach to the whole notion of superiority. He railed against the Left's nonjudgmental slide toward egalitarianism, which, in his view, often amounted to an anti-intellectual, know-nothing stance run amok. "In the pursuit of egalitarianism," he wrote, "an ideal wrenched far beyond what the founding fathers took to mean, we have willfully blinded ourselves to home truths those solons well understood, not least the simple fact that some people are better than others—smarter, harder working, more learned, more productive, harder to replace. Some ideas are better than others, some values more enduring, some works of art more universal. Some cultures, though we dare say it, are more accomplished than others and therefore more worthy of study."[81] Henry expressed admiration for the kind of striving by individuals that favors risking failure over being coddled. He was against grading on the curve and would rather flunk a whole class than render a degree meaningless. Henry decried an overemphasis on the call for equal opportunity, suggesting that any opportunity at all would be enough for the talented and motivated to move ahead. "The vital thing is not to maximize everyone's performance, but to ensure maximal performance from the most talented, the ones who can make a difference," he explained.[82] "The point of elitism is not, when all is said and done, to promote envy or to enlarge the numbers of society's losers. It is to provide sufficient rewards for winning, and sufficient support for ideas that have shaped past progress and that might aid future progress so that society as a whole wins—that is, gets richer, better educated, more productive, and healthier."[83]

There is much that I agree with in Henry's position, although a subtle but dangerous point in his book requires vigilance. I'm not even suggesting that Henry was being reckless, just that with regard to this subject the need for caution can't be overemphasized. That some people are smarter, harder working, more learned, more productive, harder to replace is without a doubt true, but the toxic element in his assertions lies hidden in the declaration of "better than" in measuring the intrinsic worth of individuals. Saying that some people are better than others, in a practical sense of any sort, is all that is necessary to appeal to our worst instincts. Like radiation, a small dose of better than is as lethal in human society as a handful of nuclear waste. Better than gives license to a malignant strain of bias; contempt and oppression follow naturally. Better than is so toxic that these two words may be the only words remembered from a paragraph regardless of how they are used.

Aristotle couched the predicament of human equality in terms of potentiality. Although he failed to make mention of slaves, the potential for doing something worthwhile exists in all human beings, and therefore individuals should be valued, not for their shortcomings per se, but for their potential. Immanuel Kant took it further, arguing that we should treat people as ends in themselves and not just as a means to an end. If there is a better argument than Kant's, I would like to hear it.[84] Examined in another light, I believe Kant's reasoning would also suggest that we should not write people off simply because we disagree with them politically. So, my proposal is to reconsider this concept every time we find ourselves confronted with notions of better than.

HARMONY AND COMMON GROUND

Language and art bind us together. Can there be any doubt that learning to use the former and appreciate the latter enhances our ability to function in society? For centuries writers, poets, and philosophers have argued passionately that aesthetic sensibility is critical to our quality of life. Indeed, everything we do, everything we feel, and everything we care about is filtered through our ability to derive comprehension from our experience. Language makes this possible. When you start thinking of your life as a labor of art, the license to create takes on a whole new meaning.

In the matter of meaningful experience we are totally dependent on our individual reservoir of knowledge; our ability to use language sets the tempo and quality of practically everything we do. That any mentally unimpaired child in America can attend twelve years of formal education and not be a master of language is a disgrace. It's an indictment worthy of punishment for those who've allowed such a shortcoming to emerge in institutions designed to teach.

Nothing in America is supposed to command our allegiance more than our affection for democracy, and yet too many of our citizens don't even know what the word really means. Most people have fuzzy ideas about the U.S. Constitution based not upon what it actually says or implies but on what they would like to think it means. In his book *First Democracy: The Challenge of an Ancient Idea*, Paul Woodruff points out that most Americans are not aware that majority rule is antithetical to the foundational notion of democracy.[85] How can we expect democracy to bring us together, if the participants don't even know how it is supposed to work? How can it help but keep us apart? While writing his historical book, Woodruff discovered that a key ingredient to holding the idea of democracy together is some kind of social harmony; otherwise there are nothing but factions—one against another.[86] Woodruff's harmony is a kind of pulling together that acknowledges differences but lives with them. The need for such cooperation is precisely the reason for this book, and I propose that no one group can do it more effectively than those of us with ample life experience.

This is not to suggest, however, that America was founded in a state of harmonious euphoria. Nothing could be further from the truth. But, unless we really understand the dynamics that divide us, we run the risk of letting democracy slip away beyond the point of redemption. And thus, it is necessary to critically examine our Stone Age tendencies for divisiveness.

US AND THEM

The first step in getting beyond us and them is deciding who we mean by *us*. Indeed, who are *we* and how much difference does it take to constitute *them*? How big is our group? Is it inclusive or exclusive? Are we nationalistic, idealistic, both, or neither? Does race matter? Does religion? Does history play a role? Does it matter what happened to our group a hundred years ago, a thousand? In other words, is our worldview dependent upon ethnocentric grudges? To whom are we loyal and why? Is our sense of allegiance deepened by shared aggression toward a common enemy? Do we take offense at the thought of being citizens of the world or do we aspire to it? Do we really believe in equality? Are we hiding unacknowledged ethnocentric leanings when we choose to downgrade a proposal for genuine equality to requirements for equal opportunity? And if you or I profess to belong to the one true religion or to the one high-quality culture most in touch with reality, how, then, do we explain our good fortune unless we have explored all of the others?

My personal perspective is that of a Caucasian American male in his sixties. I believe in inclusivity, regardless of race, religion, or ethnicity. But I didn't start out believing this way. Moreover, I have lived among people all of my life who have scorned the idea of being citizens of the world. These folks ascribe to the old "America, love it or leave it" ethos, spouted mostly by people who have only vague and pop-cinematic notions of history, people who apply black-and-white reasoning to matters about which they know so little that it may as well be said they know nothing at all. Simply put, superficial us-versus-them culture amounts to the acceptance of truth based upon association and opinion, which is itself borrowed on the basis of associa-tion. Us-versus-them culture produces one-dimensional, association-based relationships that can't stand the light of reason because they remain intellectually shallow, even at their deepest point.[87] Thus, in my view, improving culture requires a rigorous effort toward enhancing community relations through our best efforts at reasoning and relating to others.

Ever since Robert Putnam published *Bowling Alone* in 2000, examples abound of how we are increasingly estranged from our neighbors. I don't doubt the veracity of many of these observations. Still, actions always bear con-sequences, and alterations in the way we live frequently bring forth changes that we did not expect. Just as we appear to be withdrawing from those next door, we are being drawn toward those who live beyond our borders. While community relations may suffer on a local level, I can't help but think that the estrangement may be offset by the positive effects of a coming together in a global sense.[88] The salient point is this: Chances are, we already have much in common with our near neighbors and share sim-ilar politics and worldviews. But with those elsewhere around the globe we are likely to come together by nature of key points of common interest, even though our overall worldviews may differ radically.[89]

In the 1950s, psychologist Gordon Allport pioneered studies into the nature of bigotry and prejudice.[90] It was his conclusion that the best way to get beyond the differences we perceive we have with others is to come together as equals.[91] This is most easily accomplished, he suggested, by identifying our interests and the things we have in common.

To try out this theory, let's begin with a list of personal attributes: age, gender, class, height, weight, language, marital status, nationality or race, and occupation. These are similarities we can relate to: man to man, woman to woman, one married person to another, persons of the same age, one countryman to another, one cop, fireman, construction worker, nurse, accountant, or attorney to another, and so forth. Then consider a list reflecting affiliation: city, state, country, schools, clubs, fraternities, sororities, military units, political parties, places of worship, and sports teams. It's easy to relate to people from the same town, people who went to the same schools, belonged to the same church or club, and the like. Now a short list of interests: art, books, ethics, geography, history, sports, music, philosophy, science, and games. Imagine how many more categories can be added. Strong interests can compel people to join forces with infectious zeal. What really brings us together, though, as Allport observed, is a sense of common cause in matters of life and death, like war or a violent ideological clash.[92] Common cause has great potential for the expansion of community relations in both positive and negative traditions. This is what makes Internet communications technology rife with possibilities for both good and ill.

The number of ways people can come together using the similarity of attributes, affiliation, and specific interests is practically inexhaustible. These identifiers provide empathetic pathways for cultural connection. Only a few of these descriptors are traditionally flash points for disagreement; the rest simply categorize things we have in common or the ability to share an interest. Politics, religion, nationality, and race often beget conflict due to stereotypical assumptions.

Imagine what the world would be like if we navigated our way through life without ever being aware of the flash points. In other words, what if religion were strictly a private matter that we never revealed to anyone but ourselves? What if the only thing we did that suggested our political affiliation was accomplished in a voting booth? Chances are we already have friends whose religious and political affiliation we remain unaware of, and we have no plans to inquire. I use these examples not to suggest that we remain silent about important matters of belief that really do need to be discussed but to point out that the ideas in our heads do not have to match in order to live in peace with those who do not share our views.

The most important achievement for society at large, to my mind, must be to overcome the distinctions that divide us. Doing so requires getting beyond the divisive labels that pit one individual or group against another. Consider these categories of opposing groups: Left vs. Right, Democrat vs. Republican, urban vs. rural, blue state vs. red state, nonbelievers vs. believers, metro vs. homelander, gay vs. straight, matriarchal vs. patriarchal, liberal vs. conservative, dove vs. hawk, feminist vs. traditionalist, nurturing parent vs. strict father, evolutionist vs. creationist, and pro-choice vs. anti-abortion. How many of the descriptors from the attributes, affiliation, and interest lists are required to neutralize opposing camps? Indeed, can they? Can the interests we share have any influential effect at all on our ability to get along with people who see the world very differently from ourselves?

Common sense, or at least what we perceive as common sense, suggests that the more things we have in common, the more similar our worldviews are likely to be. Our geographically clustered political demographics prove this beyond doubt. The more one examines these lists of similarities and differences, the clearer it becomes that the things we share in common bind us together while differences play to our insecurities.

That we can have similar backgrounds, experiences and interests and still have sharply divergent worldviews is in part what makes the world interesting and why the wonder of existence is a subject we can relate to. Still, it can also make the world a dangerous place, rendering dialogue and a continuous effort for understanding one another critical to community. In his book *Welcome to the Homeland,* Brian Mann frames the contemporary divide between liberals and conservatives as *rural* versus *metro.* He expresses his frequent exasperation in understanding his brother, who grew up in the same house as he did but who views the world very differently than he does. But, of course, Brian loves his brother and they continue to talk, even though they disagree.[93]

My own life experience is similar, in that my brother, who was nine years my junior, also viewed the world in dramatically different ways than I. Our differences changed nothing in our relationship while he was alive, except that we did not discuss them. I characterize this practice as putting irreconcilable world views aside (IWVA) as a practical way to behave about one's beliefs if they cannot be resolved through dialogue.

This brings up a subject that both intrigues and troubles me. In his book *Conservatives Without Conscience,* John Dean calls our attention to an unprecedented study begun in 1969 with the specific intent of trying to discern the future political orientation of three- and four-year-olds. He wrote: "In brief, this research suggests that little girls who are indecisive, inhibited, shy, neat, compliant, distressed by life's ambiguity, and fearful will likely become conservative women. Likewise, little boys who are unadventurous, uncomfortable with' uncertainty, conformist, moralistic, and regularly telling others how to run their lives will then become conservatives as adults."[94] In comparison the children characterized as nonconforming, self-assertive, talkative, curious, willing to express negative feeling but yet capable of developing close relationships tended two decades later to be liberals.[95] Could it really be this simple? Could our existential feelings toward uncertainty predispose our fundamental political orientation? I'm both fascinated by this possibility and skeptical about being so deterministic, but I'm also aware of the many examples of adults whose personalities as children seemed already set and have remained unchanged.

I doubt that we will get definitive answers to these questions in my lifetime, if ever, yet I think this subject is worthy of serious investigation. If indeed there is truth to the notion that the forces of nature and nurture can predict our political views as adults, even if only for some, the implications are deep. It may be evolutionarily useful for us to split into fundamentally different political orientations at an early age, but it may also mean that our ability to change another's mind is even more limited than we already suspect.

My experience in self-education suggests that from Alaska to Florida, and from Hawaii to Maine, Americans represent a profusion of diverse views on the subjects of politics and religion and that while some groups are seemingly more objective than others, no one has a lock on the truth. What is clear to me, however, is that some folks in our midst are irrational and grievously out of touch with cause-and-effect issues of morality and appear both unable and unwilling to try to perceive a sense of reality from another's point of view. This ideological conundrum is, I believe, one of the greatest educational challenges of the present and future.

Freud identified what he characterized as the narcissism of minor differences—a frantic attempt on the part of people who live near national borders to find ways of differentiating themselves from their close neighbors.[96] He observed that each group was desperate to regard the neighbors as others in an effort to protect and preserve their own sense of being special. We are now living during a time in which the technological obliteration of borders may be likened to a frenzy of identity anxiety. The world appears to be coming together technologically and coming apart ethnocentrically at the same time. Otherness is hard to detect in cyberspace. This chaos is having the effect of blurring social class distinctions as never before. At the same time, it prompts us to grasp for some variances— something to set us apart—some semblance of identity with which we can still distinguish us from them.

I remind myself frequently that during my lifetime mass murder has become industrialized. It's hard to get one's mind around Laurence Rees' depiction of the empty baby carriages left behind from the children who were put to death at Auschwitz.[97] A procession of these carriages and strollers being pushed in rows of five abreast took an hour to pass by. Unfortunately there is nothing in my study of humankind and contemporary society that gives me reason to believe that the lessons from the Holocaust have been learned. I find no indicators offering hope that it won't happen again. Quite the contrary, as Samantha Power shows so clearly in her book *A Problem from Hell*, it seems genocide is here to stay. In *A World Ignited*, Martin and Susan Tolchin remind us that "Anti-Semitism is a very light sleeper" and is indeed on the rise globally.[98] So, to reiterate my arguments from earlier chapters, I ask, can there be a more important subject for Sept-U discussion than getting beyond us and them?

Contempt is the self-justifying yet invisible substance that enables one group to imagine that another group's misery is preferable to their own mild discomfort. And it goes downhill from there. Some recent work by anthropologists suggests that our Stone Age ancestors may have been so fierce and aggressive that it took thousands of years for them to simply move from small group affiliation to groups large enough to form viable organizations, then nation-states and the like.[99] Religion clearly played a role in furthering human culture by expanding affiliation beyond familial groups, but it has only brought us to a point where millions of people with one worldview now oppose millions of others with a different worldview based on religious dogma and unsupported, indefensible arguments left hanging in the air by people who have been dead for centuries. And we are fast approaching a future with the very real possibility of pitting Christians against Muslims in a way that could remind us of the Holocaust.

Getting beyond the natural ethnocentric contempt for others that comes ready-made and seeded in our culture is a major obstacle to getting at the wonder of existence. Somewhere on the periphery of the black hole of cultural contempt is a force of despair that prompts confusion over our ideas about freedom and our relationship with others. It's like a psychic disconnect, a short circuit, or a loose wire that blurs our objectivity when we ponder *our* freedom versus *theirs*.

What does it mean to be free today? Do we really know anything at all about democracy, and what, if anything, does it have to do with freedom? If experience offers any wisdom on this subject, it is that strenuous thinking is not a privilege in a democracy—it's an obligation. Critical thinking is the foundation for justice; thoughtlessness is the seedbed for immorality. In the context of September University, freedom is another word for "what is there left to do?" Existentialist philosopher Jean-Paul Sartre is said to have remarked that he had never in his life felt so free as during World War II when the Nazis occupied his native France. Freedom is about rising to occasion.

I still recall the 1950s and 1960s when my parents' generation was free with words about freedom and equality, but did not apply them to anyone other than their own group. They had black-or-white, right-or-wrong answers for every occasion, and some of their rationale implied rigid expectations for perfection that were wholly out of line with the reality of how democracy works. As Paul Woodruff writes, "You can't kill democracy by killing its defenders, but you can kill it by insisting on perfection, by rejecting everything that is human and flawed."[100] What I saw reflected in my parents was an attitude that said the solutions offered to right wrongs were not perfect so there was no point in trying to fix problems of inequality that badly needed attention. It seemed that anything that couldn't be fixed completely was in fact not repairable. This kind of thinking eliminates democracy as a means for addressing problems. Coming together requires a thorough understanding of our body politic, and it means radically enlarging our outlook.

My early life experience contrasted with my self-education weighs very heavily on my worldview. I was born in Oklahoma in 1943 and grew up there and in Texas. I spent my first two years of school, and then every summer thereafter, with my grandparents. We lived a very stable life. My grandparents were church members; my parents were not. Compared to today's fast-paced technological times, those years in the 1940s and 1950s seem simple, stable, and desirable in many ways. Yet I'm very much aware that in terms of civil rights and women's rights those years were rife with overt prejudice—a form of injustice wholly accepted as common sense, the way things are, the way things should be. To those who were not negatively oppressed by such thinking, the slightest mention that unfairness existed in any form of social relations would incur the wrath of people who had no idea what they were talking about but who would willingly and without compunction use force to still dissent.

When I was about twelve years old my father bought a service station in Dallas, although our home was in Irving. At the time, Irving was one of the fastest-growing communities in the country. It was white throughout except for Bear Creek, a section outside of town reserved for Negroes. I don't recall "colored" restrooms in Irving, but they were ubiquitous in Dallas. Since our community was all white, the subject of race rarely came up, but when it did, any and every adult I encountered felt free to enter into a tirade of clichés or a stereotypical monologue about how Negroes should know their place in society and remain there, and so on. That place was never precisely defined, but there was no question that it was far away from us.

I remember hearing about signs around town that said "Nigger, Don't Let the Sun Set on You Here." I don't recall actually seeing them, but I don't doubt that they existed somewhere nearby. For some of the boys in high school it was considered something of a rite of passage to go to Bear Creek late at night and "rock" houses. These were the sons of Tom Brokaw's Greatest Generation acting out the verbal tirades of their parents in Stone Age fashion; by enforcing the boundaries of place, they were ensuring these metaphorical boundaries exist. It was a psychic breakdown in reasoning that suggested our freedom was more important than theirs.

The differences that our parents pointed out about minorities, and that we accepted, were not differences we discovered; they were differences that they and their predecessors had created, and we helped keep them in play. My point in calling up disturbing memories of times past is to make it clear that the concept of freedom requires rigorous vigilance. Without a visceral understanding of how association skews our judgment, we are incapable of determining fairness or defining justice. In order to do so, we need to take a hard look at who we think we are and why we take the stance that we do toward others.

EIGHT

IDENTITY

*What is not good for the swarm
is not good for the bee.*

MARCUS AURELIUS

THE DYNAMICS OF RELATING

Understanding the dynamics of us and them in a moral context takes us back to Kant and the compelling argument that it's immoral to view our fellow human beings as merely a means to an end. In 1923 Martin Buber published *I and Thou*, a book showing precisely how we relate and misrelate to others in terms of Kant's dictum. It's easy to appreciate that an I-You kind of relating puts others on a near equal footing with us as individuals. Buber wrote: "The world as experience belongs to the basic word I-It. The basic word I-You establishes the world of relation."[101]

Living solely through identifying with an ideology or a group is a misappropriation of I-You relating. Treating another as an equal is one thing, but basing our opinion about what must be done in the world on someone else's group identity, and not on what that person might really think or do, is not only an abdication of the responsibility of citizenship, it is also disrespectful to those with whom we wish to identify.

Standards for moral behavior in relational politics are missing by design. In identity politics you are either with us or against us, regardless of whether we represent good or evil. These qualities are now beside the point because we cannot see ourselves as being anything other than good in such a bargain, our deeds notwithstanding. When we are with those with whom we identify, we engage in I-You relating, but for all others outside our group our stance becomes an I-It orientation. This manner of relating is tribal. A perceived attack on one member is interpreted as an assault on the whole group. Criticize George Bush, Bill Clinton, or any politician, regardless of the reason or issue at hand, and those who identify with them will take offense and in many cases will offer a defense using irrational arguments when they run out of anything else to say.

This is easier to appreciate with some distance. Imagine what it would have been like ten thousand years ago when tribal communities were predominant. Does it seem probable that members of a given tribe would take sides against another outside their own territory based upon any criteria other than the question of identity? Not likely. When identity is the basis for allegiance, then policies, ideas, and facts mean nothing because they have no standing against *us*. The issues of identity and tribal-like behavior do not represent simple phenomena, but I doubt any of us is exempt or immune from depending upon identity politics in particular circumstances. So, in point of fact, it might be best to think of identity politics as something we experience and participate in as a matter of degree.

In every culture, there exists a code of behavior recognized as being honorable. An I–It relation, however, excludes the possibility of one's having honor. Absent such respect, those relegated to the status of an I-It relation are acknowledged as having value barely above that of lifeless objects, leaving little ground for empathy. In *Social Intelligence,* Daniel Goleman uses Buber's portrayal of relating to illustrate that it is commonplace for people to relate to others not as equals, but as objects without moral standing as human beings. Whereas I-You represents a near equal footing, an I-It form of relating is completely one-sided. Goleman writes, "The emotional indifference and remoteness of an I-It relationship stands in direct contrast to the attuned I-You. When we are in the I-It mode, we treat other people as means to some other end. By contrast, in the I-You mode our relationship with them becomes an end in itself."[102] Indeed, when we examine this fracturing point in human relations and give it serious thought, all sorts of epiphanies arise. It's easy to observe that I-You relations dominate at the family level, but as we extend beyond those close ties, we use our empathy sparingly. It shouldn't surprise us that political parties increasingly use metaphoric signals to encourage party members to engage in I-It relating with regard to those viewed as opponents. Ultimately the result is a posture of us against them or, when couched in religious terms, good against evil.

When you think about corporations in the context of I-You relating, it becomes immediately clear that only those employees in the top echelons are treated with I-You consideration. During reorganizations, top echelon executives get millions in golden parachutes, while those in the lower levels get a few weeks of meager severance, if that. What enables us to view others as objects is an abiding lack of respect that fosters contempt and an inability to empathize with them. It's a flaring-up of *better than*. Thus we can eat fresh vegetables picked by workers paid slave wages and not get indigestion. Because they do not have our admiration and respect, we are not predisposed to relate to them at the I-You level.

The treacherous political reality of I-It relating is that it's not that much further to the abyss. In *Faces of the Enemy*, Sam Keen said, "To mass produce hatred, the body politic must remain unconscious of its own paranoia, projection, and propaganda. 'The enemy' is thus considered as real and objective as a rock or a mad dog."[103] So when our regard for others is that of an I-It relationship, we're near-ing the point of ranking them with inanimate objects or crazed animals. Indeed, a world that consisted of nothing but I-It relating would be a world made up only of psy-chopaths and sociopaths.

Buber's model highlights how urgently we need to stop the politics of us and them and come together as equals in search of the better argument. As Buber said, "When a cul-ture is no longer centered in a living and continually renewed relational process, it freezes into the It-world which is broken only intermittently by the eruptive, glow-ing deeds of solitary spirits."[104] We need to talk, especially with people who see the world differently than we do, and we need to come to some kind of agreement about finding common ground and a common good. This is the kind of cordiality that I hope the Sept-U generation will come to represent.

TRUTH BY ASSOCIATION

In a nutshell, identity politics can best be described as experiencing "truth by association." Unfortunately, repre-sentative democracy as a foundational principle for a republic form of government sets up the appearance of a respectable charter for truth by association. In other words, those of us who do not do the intellectual work required by citizenship in a democracy may simply depend upon the ideas of those we deem wise enough to think for us. If, instead of simply voting our identity (which is too often the case), we decide to vote for someone we assume will do the reasoning required, then we have still failed to meet our obligation as citizens of a democracy.[105] This prac-tice may seem expedient and logical, but it undermines the very quality of our form of government. Granted, a group of enlightened representatives should be more capable of making wiser decisions than an uninformed public, and in this respect we should be grateful when only informed citizens vote. But what happens when our elected representatives no longer represent the interests of the people, but are solely responsible to special interest lobbyists? There must be a level of public sentiment that demands better of our elected officials, or our democracy is a sham.

There are thresholds of public opinion that politicians will not dare breach. No representative today is going to advocate a return to slavery, for example. But contrast this reality with two hundred years ago. No politician today is going to propose legislation to add pets to the list of exports to other nations for use as food commodities. Some such things don't require a second thought to deduce where the public would stand on the issue. But our general way of life and the alertness of the public at large are what create and sustain this sensibility. The requirement of a genuine democracy is not to limit our response to only those issues that make us feel a sense of outrage. We need to reason our way through difficult matters, or else we must live with what's left over after the demands of special interest groups have been met.

Democracy requires intelligence and fully developed but divergent opinions from a wide range of citizens, forcefully argued, as surely as fire needs oxygen. It doesn't take but a glance at the state of the world to discern that reasoning above a level of tribal relations is necessary for planetary peace. Furthermore, democracy seems so natural to us— we are so heavily dependent upon our actions as individuals for our own self-interest—we assume we are hard-wired for a democratic system. This is an illusion based upon what we are taught to expect of American ideals. Democracy is not natural. To the contrary, we are in fact hard-wired for tribalistic behavior, which explains in part why, with regard to politics, we so often say one thing and do another. Too often we imagine ourselves as reasoning when our emotions are really speaking for us.

In 1976 Richard Dawkins published *The Selfish Gene,* where he introduced the concept of a meme as a means of correlating ideas with genes.[106] The book, which was largely misinterpreted, caused a backlash in the humanities. Social critics said that to make assertive statements, even metaphorically, about genetic selfishness and human beings was overly deterministic. The essence of their argument was that we are much more than our genes. But when we consider selfishness as a type of psychological behavior, it's clear that, at times, our selfish actions parallel and reinforce the predisposition of selfish genes. I would argue that human behavior mimics selfish genes in a very fundamental way. Our behavior leads to increased survival by fostering reproduction indirectly. The ubiquity of this dynamic looms so large that we don't see the transparent logic in our actions because we are too involved in the process.

Simply put, we are loyal to that with which we identify. Period. Loyalty, in a very real sense, amounts to an expression of getting one's genes into the future by preserving and protecting our respective identities. There are great social penalties for disloyalty. Indeed, is there anything we do that is thought worse than the sin of betrayal?[107] If not for loyalty, patriotism would not be thought of as a virtue.

Feelings of loyalty provide the key ingredient that justifies truth by association and enables people to feel proud of blind obedience. But when blind trust results in mistakes in judgment that threaten the survival of the object of loyalty, hasn't one committed a treasonous act? Isn't it intellectually irresponsible to have been relating when one should have been reasoning? Why should any person whose group or nation depends upon their citizenship not be held to a higher standard of accountability than blind obedience? Truth by association is an adolescent posture at best; at worst, it can lead to such shallow rationalization that the end result is genocide. Truth by association might have worked well in the Stone Age, but it is dangerous in the age of the atom.

Truth by association is what gives the feeling of legitimacy to comedian Steven Colbert's notion of "truthiness"—

a claim that whatever it is that we say is true, is true by nature of who we are and has little, if anything, to do with facts of the matter.[108] Richard Hofstadter broached this subject more than a half-century ago as "a politics of the gut."[109] I see this as the logical conclusion of identity politics—that whatever unreflective people feel is good must, in fact, be good. They believe it goes without saying that their claims for truthfulness should be given the benefit of the doubt because their intentions are pure. This helps to explain the frequent inarticulate, inconsistent, and contradictory arguments offered by conservative authoritarians, described in John Dean's *Conservatives without Conscience,* who feel totally justified in holding on to irrational beliefs that they are unable to elucidate.[110] This impetus might be summed up by the exclamation, "Who are we to be wrong!" Contrast this stance with that of Socrates who abhorred the mere appearance of truth and died fighting imitations.

Thus, patriotism is a concept best not left to children or unreasoning adults who act like them. Far too often nationalism is mistaken for patriotism. The ethos of loyalty misdirected and misunderstood, in my view, is central to why enlarging the group we identify with is so hard and why so many people cringe at the suggestion that they aspire to be a citizen of the world.

In his book *Loyalty*, George P. Fletcher wrote, "There is no easy response to the idealist who insists that all [six billion] people constitute one community, with one cause. The answer must begin with an understanding of how we as human beings are constituted and what our natural limits of sympathy may be."[111] No doubt, this task is a major purpose of Sept-U. Civilization is at stake, and it is imperative that we enlarge our concept of our geographical citizenship at least to the extent that we can live with our global differences. This requires asking more of ourselves than allegiance by association. If we don't maintain and exercise an independent sense of moral judgment, then immorality, as history demonstrates, will metastasize.

Loyalty, as Fletcher reminds us, leads us to suspend judgment and to often give the object of our loyalty the benefit of the doubt.[112] Moreover, this is not a bad thing, unless it is abused. Indeed, those unable to establish feelings of loyalty are deemed psychopaths, and those who go too far with blind obedience resemble Nazis. But relying strictly on truth by association is an abject form of abuse, and it's what gives the impetus for pathologies like Nazism to begin with. *Sieg Heil* genuflection is the antithesis of thoughtfulness.

What makes the issue of truth by association so critical in a Sept-U state of affairs is that aging moves us toward a posture where we think we have learned (and this may very well be an unconscious realization) what is truly important in life and what is worth preserving and maintaining. Sometimes we refer to this feeling as generativity. So, when we try, through our own example, to point out to our children and grandchildren what must be done and what rules should be obeyed, our efforts are really another way of ensuring survival by protecting our kind. Thus we also protect our identity and further the likelihood of projecting our genes into the future.

Truth by association binds us together in one sense and rips us apart in another. The only antidote is to rise to the occasion of reasoning that democracy requires: representatives should stand in for us and cast votes on our behalf, but not do all of the thinking for us. Depending on certain individuals to represent us because we perceive them to be one of us, but failing to do the work necessary to judge whether or not they are successful in their representation, is socially disrespectful and practically irresponsible. The very quality of our life depends upon reciprocated accountability. The whole basis of association has to be about something greater than blood and genetics, if we are ever to mature as a civilization.

People who live according to truth by association have a vested interest in avoiding the acquisition of knowledge of any kind or in any form that puts the illusion of their superiority in jeopardy. Like so many millions of others in the world, I grew up internalizing the notion that my group was the in-group, that we had reality pegged, and that all others were still searching for it. We heard the adults loud and clear who said we were better than Negroes. But Negroes is not the N-word that we or they used. A vast majority of people of my generation who lived in the South internalized a racist philosophy of life and felt free to speak about it openly.

In time, no matter where we live, our associations and the ideas we encounter become internalized into an inarticulate worldview composed of wide-ranging, misguided ideologies encoded in a maze of muddled metaphors, but we resist any suggestion that our opinions might be wrong. It's the fuel and motivation of zealots: "Take issue with what we say, and you take issue with us." In other words, *we* becomes the operative word. *Our kind* is self-justifying; right or wrong is of lesser importance. We prove dedication and loyalty to our groups by attacking the positions of those who are opposed to us, regardless of the reason. Thus, young men enthusiastically demonstrate their willingness to go to war without any idea, whatsoever, of the reasons for doing so. On the one hand, this can be thought of as a noble trait of self-sacrifice, but on the other, it is precisely the kind of attitude that feeds conflict and makes genocide possible.

It doesn't take a lot of imagination to consider the evolutionary advantage of taking on the perceived enemies of our parents as our own adversaries. Nor is it a stretch to consider how easily and subtly prejudice is passed from one generation to the next. In their book *Shadows of Forgotten Ancestors,* Carl Sagan and Ann Druyan wrote, "The existence of common enemies can make the social machinery purr. Those groups that incline to xenophobic paranoia might gain a cohesive advantage over groups that are initially more realistic and carefree. If you've exaggerated the threat, at least you've reduced internal tensions in your group; and if the external threat is more serious than you've privately estimated, your preparedness is higher. As long as the social costs stay within reasonable bounds, it may become a successful survival strategy. So there's a bit of contagion about xenophobia."[113] Keeping the ball of hatred in the air is a big part of the game.

One of the most prominent side effects of cultures who engage in ethnocentric bias is that they tend to live behind barriers of rigidity, where fear is the most common response to any kind of change and an eagerness to demonstrate patriotism is often a mask for bigotry.[114] Obvious examples of this during the 1950s in Irving, Texas, and throughout the South, were frequent public exhibitions of the Confederate flag. As psychologist Gordon Allport once said, "Extreme bigots are almost always super-patriots."[115] Hatred expressed openly and subtly is now ubiquitous in media, especially on talk radio. Sagan and Druyan put it thus, "So next time you hear a raving demagogue counseling hatred for other, slightly different groups of humans, for a moment at least see if you can understand his problem: He is heeding an ancient call that—however dangerous, obsolete, and maladaptive it may be today—once benefited our species."[116]

We are all affected by the phenomenon of truth by association, especially when it comes to politics. This is precisely why we wind up living with laws that do not reflect the genuine wishes of either party. We don't listen to one another. Instead we identify the issues with which we are in complete agreement and sometimes wind up making compromises that are worse than having taken no action at all. Moreover, few of us know our own political minds well enough to make a compelling case that our views should prevail.

Most of what passes for debate during elections is a taking of sides based on political affiliation. It's hard to imagine that things could be any other way, since only one party wins. But who is right about a particular issue is very often considered of less importance than getting the most votes, so the end justifies the means.

Truth by association is extraordinarily powerful because it derives from our biological predisposition to favor kin. Rarely does either political party explore the genealogy of their own political values, which would mean getting to the bedrock of our beliefs. It would mean deconstructing each paragraph of our argument to get beneath the metaphors that constitute our understanding of the issues at hand. Metaphors are the structural support beams that give rise to our ability to understand anything. We understand one thing from having understood another. So, if we don't comprehend the nature of the foundation that girds our beliefs, then we are both literally and figuratively on shaky ground. In his inspiring book *The Happiness Hypothesis,* moral psychologist Jonathan Haidt put it this way: "With the wrong metaphor we are deluded; with no metaphor we are blind."[117]

Far too often we spend more time looking for weakness in our opposition's position than in developing real, indepth knowledge about our own. Most of us do not know the intricacies or the origins of our own political opinions nearly as well as we think we do. People in all political parties engage in heated debate, oblivious to their own emotional attachment to the concepts under discussion. Unless we're mindful of these attachments, they can be used against us, whether by those who see the world differently than we do or because we're blinded from understanding our own position well enough to make it compelling to others. The metaphor for these emotional vulnerabilities is *hot button.* Such issues may reveal that our penchant for politics is little more than truth by association. Knowing our own minds means that we are aware of our own hot-button issues and what precisely makes them hot.

In *The Rapture of Maturity*, I described the notion of rapture as those brief moments of intellectual exhilaration when we are profoundly aware that our life is indeed worthwhile and that we would not in these instances trade places with anyone else on the planet. But there are also moments on the other side of life—the dark side—when our lives seem meaningless and devoid of quality. The dark side is where we want to begin adding some light. The best place to begin participation in September University is to make it a priority to learn about all of those people we grew up regarding as others, for whatever reason. We need to study their history, their literature, their philosophy and learn everything we can about them. We need to see how it squares with the bias we grew up with.

RELATIONAL BEHAVIOR

There is ample scientific evidence to suggest that getting beyond us-and-them thinking and truth by association may call for a serious look at the parallels between human behavior and that of our nearest primate relatives, notably chimpanzees and bonobos.[118] We've known for years that we share their DNA, but we rarely discuss the degree to which we share their behavior. All primates are subconsciously hyperaware of their status as individuals among others within a social group. Primates comprehend rank without needing to think about it. This trait may explain why we sometimes cast political votes for other than rational reasons.

All you have to do to verify this phenomenon is to become intentionally aware of body language. You might notice, for example, that, when gathered in a room for a meeting, a group of people, once seated, will adopt the body posture of the leader—legs crossed, hand under chin, slumped forward or back, and so on. Someone of high rank sets the style, even the tone of voice modulation, and the lower ranking individuals do the adjusting.[119] It's been reported that Bill Gates rocks back and forth in his chair, and it can be a bit startling to see a roomful of his subordinates doing the same thing. I've purposely been making these observations for years. Once in a while I forget about it, only to be reminded during a meeting when I find that I too am participating in the group posture without being aware of it.

More often than not we pay too much attention to our verbal arguments and not enough to our body language, even though the body language often betrays thoughts we are unaware that we hold.[120] Sitting with arms folded or fists clenched can represent a posture of opposition, regardless of the words spoken. Sometimes we get the feeling we like or dislike someone long before we can give reasons for our feelings. By extension, then, we are capable of achieving harmonious or hostile bonds with members of our own or any other society at levels beneath consciousness.

At the very center of our being as individuals, of society at large, and even among other species of animals is our connectedness through emotional contagion. For example, we are stressed at the sight of an animal in distress, and the reverse is true for many animals when they observe humans in distress. Dutch primatologist Frans de Waal makes the point succinctly: "Emotions trump rules."[121] He reminds us that the psychologies of our feelings predate religion and that a key to understanding ourselves lies in understanding the nature of empathy. In *Our Inner Ape*, de Waal writes, "Empathy is the one weapon in the human repertoire able to rid us of the curse of xenophobia." He argues that, "We are stuck with a human psychology shaped by millions of years of life in small communities so that we somehow need to structure the world around us in a way recognizable to this psychology. If we could manage to see people on other continents as part of us, drawing them into our circle of reciprocity and empathy, we would be building upon, rather than going against, our nature."[122]

De Waal tells us that "our evolutionary design makes it hard to identify with outsiders" and that "empathy is fragile." This should not come as news to those of us in the Sept-U phase of life. We know from our intuition and our experience to be careful that what we say matches our feelings. We also know from experience the reality of Daniel

Goleman's assertion that "empathy lubricates sociability."[123] Indeed, a society where truth by association prevails can still delude itself into believing that it aspires to high human ideals, even when it has splintered into hostile groups who have partitioned themselves off from others and who find themselves increasingly driven by paranoia and a sociopathic disregard for outsiders. If we are to have any hope of getting beyond us and them or beyond truth by association, we must be ever alert to aspects of our behavior that reveal why we say one thing and do another.

The field of neuroscience has been set ablaze by the recent discovery of mirror neurons. Now, perhaps for the first time, we are on the threshold of putting the human predicament into a more refined and pragmatic perspective that will help foster better relations among diverse groups of people. Mirror neurons are simply groups of cells residing within our brains that fire when we see others doing what we are familiar with doing ourselves. We are thus wired for empathy. We are social creatures. We relate. And we do it all of the time. There is a core truth in the old saying "Monkey see, monkey do."[124] When we see a pained expression on the face of others, we are wired to feel their pain, or we feel their joy when they laugh and smile. Neuroscientist Marco Iacoboni, a leader in the research that led to the discovery, says that "vicarious is not a strong enough word to describe the effect of mirror neurons."[125]

Consider what this suggests about our temperament in a historical context. We can only guess how many thousands of years it took for our ancient ancestors to develop language, but clearly they were relating for eons before, during, and after language. They were literally enveloped in emotional relating long before they could speak and be quickly understood. They mirrored one another's behavior, and it solidified their kinship. Imagine going through life without ever speaking and relying instead on the facial expressions and gestures of others. Clearly, imitation is more than a sincere form of flattery.

Here is another way to illustrate our evolution. Let's say that beneath the software of the latest state-of-the-art operating system for computers is an old, fully functioning MS-DOS program. This program contains critical and crucial information for the well-being of the computer, but it is so overridden by the new fancy program codes that no one pays much attention to it anymore. Worse, no one really knows how to read the data. Even so, this information is vital to the very stability of the system, and overlooking its importance portends serious danger for computing. This is perfectly analogous to human behavior with regard to mirror neurons and the fact that we so readily relate to others beneath consciousness. When we are all sitting around the conference table in our respective organizations and we see others with their arms folded in the same manner as others, what we are seeing is the old MS-DOS program attending to our relating as it has done for thousands of years. Chances are we like the folks we are imitating and we are saying so with our actions, even if we no longer recall consciously that that is indeed what we are doing.[126] We are, so to speak, aware yet unaware of our awareness. So profound is our hard wiring for imitation that, given time, all of us begin to speak with the accents of our geographic region.

Iacoboni characterizes his branch of study as "existential neuroscience," noting that it literally invites us to "embrace meaning."[127] In his book *Mirroring People*, he suggests that existentialism has historically received bad press, because it has been associated with anxiety and dread, but that the real promise it offers is its hope and optimism for creating a more caring society. He argues that studying mirror neurons "will force us to rethink radically the deepest aspects of our social relations."[128] This adjustment to our thinking is a driving aspiration of Sept-U.

Nothing brightens the future better than setting aside ignorant assumptions, and nothing is as effective for arriving at conclusions that support equity for all. Achieving social harmony in an artful manner requires a willingness to be truthful with ourselves about the biases we grew up with, no matter how painful those memories are or how much we would rather not revisit such a past. The future depends on our ability to pass on the ethos of *we* to those who will live on after our demise. In short, we have to learn to talk to one another.

NINE

GROUNDS FOR COMMUNICATION

Communication leads to community, that is, to
understanding, intimacy and mutual valuing.

ROLLO MAY

TOOLS FOR SOCIAL DIALOGUE

Putting aside contempt for others in favor of bettering our relations with them requires nothing more complicated than learning to believe things for very good reasons and to doubt those things that can't stand up to the light of reason. In his book *Darwin's Dangerous Idea*, Daniel Dennett provides an excellent example through the use of metaphorical tools: cranes and skyhooks. A crane argument is one that is supported by reasoned explanation, factual data and/or logic. A skyhook argument simply hangs in the air because someone wishes it to be there. A skyhook is a claim that rests on conjecture or faith. All supernatural claims rest on skyhook arguments.

Using crane and skyhook logic is not as simple as it first seems. The ability to recognize skyhooks takes both practice and a determination to accept truth based upon evidence instead of dogma. Depending upon evidence instead of authority for deciding what to believe may seem to make the world appear less stable, but this is an illusion. I'm hopeful that if enough people can learn to accept the need to believe what they believe based purely upon thoughtful reasoning, then perhaps some of the contempt for people who see the world differently will evaporate. Even if these efforts are not fully successful, perhaps at least there will be a greater chance for finding common ground than can arise from fighting over seemingly irreconcilable differences. As anthropologist Lionel Tiger puts it, "The function of learning is to reduce social differentiation not to increase it."[129]

On the one hand, a crane-based argument isn't true by the nature of its construction; it simply has reasons for supporting its existence. A crane-based argument may be totally false, but it can be proven false only by another crane. A skyhook argument, on the other hand, could be true, but can't be proven either true or false without the use of a crane.

I know from personal experience that the more your worldview depends upon the existence of skyhooks, the more threatened you are by people who see the world differently, especially if they use cranes to make their point. People en masse belong to groups whose religious beliefs cannot be proven. Their usage of skyhooks is a part of the process that bonds their association. They can neither prove nor disprove their claims. If another group challenges their beliefs with a skyhook or a crane of their own, no amount of discourse is likely to persuade one side to abandon their belief and switch to the other side, unless both parties can be persuaded to accept a better argument.

Now, here is where we really get into difficulty: the most divisive kind of skyhook beliefs come not from the nature of the religion itself, but from the shadow concerns about how people are to behave in general. Views on abortion, homosexuality, and other subjects on the periphery of a major skyhook premise become smaller versions of the same argument taken as absolute fact. Such opinions are frequently expressed among like-minded participants, and they are accepted as truths simply because so-and-so says they're true without offering good reasons for that belief. The reason that controversial issues like stem cell research seem to matter so much is grossly misunderstood, in my view. These subjects become hot-button issues, not for genuine debate, but rather to foment ire. What's at stake here is not what it seems. These kinds of issues threaten the identity of people whose self-image is heavily invested in their ideological worldview. In other words, if it becomes acceptable for the majority of the population to behave as if what someone believes is unimportant, then that person's religion could be wrong and that person's identity is thus at risk. Simply stated: for purposes of identity, perceptions of reality matter at a deeply visceral level. As mentioned earlier, threats against one's identity are often perceived as mortal threats at a subconscious level.[130] Some degree of societal support or acceptance seems necessary for maintaining cherished views that reinforce notions of selfhood and group identity. Just imagine what would happen emotionally to the remaining members of a religious congregation if all but a few members suddenly renounced their belief one day and fled.

There appears to be a direct relationship between the credulity required for holding a belief and the hostility directed toward those willing to cast doubts. It shouldn't surprise us that some of the hardest things to believe in religious dogma are things that true believers are willing to kill and die for. The big trouble, of course, starts when people try to use cranes to take down other people's skyhooks. The most elegant crane possible can do nothing but reach for the skyhook, since nothing is there to fasten onto. The crane can make a devastating case that a skyhook is only an illusion, but no amount of evidence will be accepted as proof without a prior agreement to use reason as a means of discourse. The disconnect becomes clear when we realize that the things we come to believe at an emotional level as we are growing up do not lend themselves so easily to unraveling through rationality. That which has not been accepted through reason is unlikely to yield to reason without a significant emotional event or an unrelenting dedication to getting to the truth of matters without regard for whose side one is taking. Put another way, perhaps beliefs accepted emotionally can only be changed emotionally.

My point is simply this: If you are going to argue about anything, especially politics or religion, when you get to a skyhook, identify it as such and then leave it be. The only way to engage in political discussion and reach reasonable agreement is to match cranes with cranes and to understand that skyhooks are virtually unmovable, unless you can get all parties to agree that that is indeed what they are. You can't expect others to accept your skyhook argument as absolute truth simply because you hang it in the air.

It seems an inbred form of arrogance that majority populations automatically see their opinions as objective, believing that the way they see the world should be binding on minorities. So, when significant numbers of people begin to behave as if majority opinion doesn't matter, the result shows itself in frequent expressions of contempt and outbursts of hatred, especially on the part of the majority.[131]

Very often the general public does not appreciate the difficulty involved in establishing absolute rules for behavior. Even when we address moral dilemmas aggressively, we can still encounter David Hume's moral conundrum about arriving at an ought from an is.[132] This doesn't mean you can't use cranes to discuss morality, only that sooner or later you'll run up against a crane that dead-ends into a skyhook.

A PREFERENCE FOR THE BETTER ARGUMENT

Getting to an agreement for the better argument also means that we must rise above clichés, slogans, and platitudes. Although it's easy to be cynical about ever finding the better argument, especially in the kind of political turmoil we find ourselves in today, a September University frame of mind gives the effort hope. I work at trying to listen for the better argument, and I believe lots of us still retain the ability to recognize one when we hear it. I think we would do well to try to find some kind of simple formula for political dialogue, something like a *Robert's Rules of Order*, which stipulates at the beginning that before the participants conclude, they must find three things about which they agree, three areas where they are close, and three points about which they are miles apart but have some idea or indication of what might be necessary to bring the sides closer to agreement.

To accomplish this, each party would need to know their own position to the bone, fully understanding the hot-button issues on both sides, and be willing to see the process through without hitting those buttons on cue. Any number of influential authors have tried to address the issue of loggerheads. John Stuart Mill said, "He who knows only his own side of the case knows little of that." Emerson said, "The wise man throws himself on the side of his assailants. It is more his interest than it is theirs to find his weak point." J. Krishnamurti said that a true example of working together can only come about when both sides really understand a problem.

A few years ago I watched a panel discussion featuring the late philosopher Mortimer Adler and several prominent thinkers in debate over an issue, the essence of which I've forgotten. What was memorable was the moment when Adler conceded that his opponent had made the better case and said that he would contact his book publisher immediately and attempt to change his own written opinion before his upcoming book was printed. What struck me most about this incident was how stunned everyone was by his willingness to publicly admit a mistake in his own reasoning.

Here was one of America's most opinionated thinkers discussing a subject he had been thinking about for more than half a century yet willing to surrender his position immediately upon hearing a superior argument. We forget that this is supposed to be the whole point of philosophy. In this regard, Adler walked his talk; the fact that it was mind-blowing to his audience should give us much pause for reflection. A part of our reflection might include imagining what kind of a society could result if our court system did not aim for discerning the better argument in matters of law. If indeed we admit that the better argument is the basis for our very existence as a nation of laws, then why do we not insist on it in every other meaningful avenue of our lives?

METAPHORS THAT STAND IN FOR REALITY

Have you noticed how much of the language we use for political dialogue carries connotations of combat? We fight and do battle; we go to war; we go for the jugular, in for the kill, to the mat, or even to the mattresses, as they say in the movies.[133] But since debate is supposed to be a way of getting to the better argument, think about how the whole phenomenon of discourse changes if you simply change the metaphor from war to something more constructive.[134] For example, what if we used a sewing metaphor and imagined the purpose of an argument as an effort to stitch our way to an agreement, one stitch at a time, until we reached a complete pattern of accord? There are many ways to use metaphors that completely change the context of the subject of discussion. We have been bogged down in war-like language for far too long, and the better argument is slipping away as a result.

The way we use language affects our behavior. Nearly every week I hear someone use the heart as a symbol for the foundation of human feelings. In all walks of life people claim that, no matter what a person might think about any subject of importance, the truth is to be found in the heart. To name the heart as the emotional center for humans is a lovely expression—it's poetic, romantic, and comforting. But, when the goal is to make the world a better place, I believe this image is a major distraction and an impediment to action. Matters of the heart often turn out to be the things most people feel helpless to change.

At its core the heart metaphor is viscerally anti-intellectual. True, emotion is the source of passion—it makes life worthwhile. But, in reality, the function of the heart is to pump blood to the brain and to the rest of the body. Regardless of what we say, or with how much passion we say it, matters of the heart occur in the head. To relegate emotion to an organ that cannot think makes no sense, unless we are trying to escape accountability for our deeds or for a failure to act.[135]

Understanding the influence of metaphor upon my own thinking has convinced me that if I want to have any real effect on the matters I deem important, I must change my metaphors. If I really want to do something about economic inequality in the world, I must recognize that applying the heart metaphor is where concern usually ends. To do something positive, I must acknowledge that my indignation is in my head, not my heart, and that I must think and act instead of merely commiserating. If I don't, I am powerless where matters of the heart are concerned.

Until we can truly appreciate the dynamics of *us* and *them* divisiveness, truth by association, I-You and I-It relating, and how we instinctively use art and entertainment as cultural weapons, then we will remain ill prepared to deal effectively with hot-button issues. So the next step is to understand the importance of our sources for news and information and the dynamics of spin.

We live in the strongest nation on earth, where the dominant religion advocates brotherly love and compassion for the less fortunate. Yet too often I observe people who claim their hearts go out to the poor and the starving, even as their heads fail to conceive of constructive ways to solve the problem. If we intend to shape the future, each of us must put our heads to work in matters of the heart and begin acting accordingly. Civilization requires it.

TEN

CONQUERING THE
BIAS-SPHERE

We are all captives of the picture in our head—
our belief that the world we have experienced
is the world that really exists.

WALTER LIPPMANN

REALITY MATTERS

Reality, however tenuous, technically abstract, or seemingly impossible to discern, is something we care about, something to be sought and deliberated. The source of the news and information we get is a matter of considerable importance in an increasingly mediated society. So far in this book, we've discussed the dynamics of reading and the phenomenon of being mediated, but little has been said about media sources. In this arena, rhetorical bias is spinning with more intensity than at any time in history. Practically every minute of every waking hour, we are deluged with skyhook arguments presented as cranes from every ideological bent imaginable. Instinctively we choose sides and tend to cluster into groups of shared beliefs and identities that delineate us and them. By doing this we further detract from our ability to remain objective about the things that matter most. Let me digress for a moment, and then I will come back to this view.

In his book *Bad News,* retired CBS News foreign correspondent Tom Fenton wrote: "We live in a time when, suddenly, it seems almost impossible to know the real facts about the most pivotal life-altering public events of our day."[136] Fenton goes on to express his sense of despair that the American news media failed miserably by not creating a sense of reality about the Mideast that would have enabled us to foresee the likelihood of an event like 9/11. Fenton experienced 9/11, as did many journalists, as a professional failure that could and should have been avoided if only for the will to view the world as it is. Fenton and his colleagues had been tracking al Qaeda for more than a decade, but, prior to 9/11, news executives did not think the subject was worthy of attention. According to Fenton, deregulation, an obsession with ratings, the demand for profits, the decline of industry standards, cost cutting, news packaging, and corporate ownership have eviscerated the major news networks in America.[137]

While I believe that Fenton is right about the decline in the quality of the news we get, it is important to keep a historical perspective about where we are in relation to news and information. That the American news media used to do a better job of investigative reporting seems obvious, but it's easy to miss the point that for a person to be a truly informed citizen, the news media have never been a totally reliable source of information. It's far too easy to misunderstand what's at hand. Take the Chautauqua movement of public lectures in the last quarter of the nineteenth century. That seems to have been a glorious time in our intellectual history, a high time for lecture halls and an interested public, and in many ways it was. In comparison to today, however, the amount of information available then was so paltry and access was so limited that it hardly seems worth mentioning. Yet we still (myself included) look back on it as a time of intense intellectual inspiration.[138]

Nowadays, on any given day, the number of serious lectures and intellectual discussions going on around the country dwarf anything that has ever happened in the past. From Holiday Inns to community centers, seminars are offered on every conceivable subject. Sure, some are foolish self-help remedies for problems that don't really exist, but many are cutting-edge discussions in their respective disciplines. To those of us fortunate enough to have the technological tools, much of our rich cultural heritage is but a few keystrokes away. The number of viewable or downloadable video lectures online is growing rapidly. The Internet provides a deluge of information that makes both our current activity and the Chautauqua era seem quaint.

The difficulty about news and information is that getting closer to the reality of what's really going on in the world has never been easy. It's hard to be objective unless one's desire for truth transcends politics and ideologies that distort public perception. The greatest challenge to getting a bias-free view of the world may lie in our own proclivity for groupthink, a trait sometimes characterized as cocooning.[139] Cocooning is simply self-selecting news that already fits with one's worldview.

The Internet, as *Infotopia* author Cass R. Sunstein explains, offers simultaneously great risk and extraordinary promise. He says, "Every day, like-minded people can and do sort themselves into echo chambers of their own design, leading to wild errors, undue confidence, and unjustified extremism. But every day, the Internet also offers exceedingly valuable exercises in information aggregation, as people learn a great deal from the dispersed bits of information that other people have. Many people are curious and they often seek out perspectives that run counter to their own."[140] Indeed, in my opinion, this reality outshines the Chautauqua era as sunlight outshines starlight. The value derived, though, depends upon a sustained effort to seek out and consider various points of view with a thirst for knowledge that matters more than one's sense of affiliation.

If we take the idea of freedom seriously, then becoming unmediated appears to be a requirement. As important as it is to be media literate, it is equally important to be media aware, and this requires being hyperaware of the news and information we are ingesting as well as its source. We think and talk about what we see and hear, which means that too often others manage the agenda of our attention. It's not an exaggeration to say that the source of our daily media ingestion sets the very tone and tempo of our day-to-day consciousness. So, setting about to recognize bias in all of its many forms and manifestations is critical for having any sense of what we might claim as objectivity.

It seems paradoxical in the extreme that we champion universal education and work tirelessly to convince others of the value of education even as many of us feel an equal sense of urgency to warn against the overinfluence of so-called experts, who very often tell us how to do something they themselves have not yet mastered. Sometimes it appears that experts are formed by group stress, similar to the way carbon is changed under pressure into diamonds. In the case of experts, however, group bias takes the place of brilliance and clarity.

The old saying that it's easier to ride a horse in the direction it's already going seems pretty easy to accept. But it's not so readily apparent that when like-minded groups come together to talk about subjects that matter to them, they are likely to vault ahead in the ideological direction they are already leaning.[141] Regardless of our ideological bent, when we join others in dialogue, most of us are under the illusion that we are open to the better argument. But the evidence is overwhelming that during a discussion, a group of liberals will likely bear harder to the left and conservatives will bear harder right with the same consistency simply because of the structure and nature of their group experience. Agreement tends to reinforce the bonds that bring groups of people together to begin with. People endear themselves to one another, often getting themselves worked up into a frenzy to do something that gives their connection a feeling of significance and that further solidifies their association. An extreme historical example that makes the point crystal clear is a lynch mob: it often begins with a few casual statements of agreement about getting justice and ends in an emotional and mutually felt rage.

This tendency for a kind of groupthink is what academics have begun to call *ideological amplification*. If we give it some thought, ideological amplification is not that puzzling, and this exposes the seriousness of the problem. If the search for the truth about any matter is for the common good, it has to be objectively beyond the contamination of identity politics. In other words, the desire to know has to outshine the politics of identity and truth by association. The method for discerning wisdom requires the consideration of many points of view. The fact that ideological amplification seems to be an esoteric subject to those who engage in the process should be a wake-up call to those of us who really want to find common ground. Otherwise, we will be tripped up by our own sincerity in failing to grasp that our good intentions for getting together with likeminded folks need safeguards to be truly objective.

Another notable shortcoming of group discussion is that not all of the knowledge present in any given group is likely to surface. For example, even though a group may represent an enormous amount of knowledge and expertise, too many experienced participants for untold reasons (some having to do with social dominance psychology) choose to remain silent. Worse still, there is a cascading effect that occurs when a powerful figure makes a claim and others accept it in unison. They go along, as the saying goes, to get along and adopt the same posture, even when they know that the course of action they are agreeing to is not the best option, only that it is the politically safe

thing to do.[142] Thus, the creeping effects of truth by association and the politics of identity return by default to primeval
behavioral tendencies that very often occur beneath conscious awareness.

When we choose sides, we come together in frenzied
agreement and become ever more convinced about what we
wanted to believe to begin with. We latch on to skyhooks,
esteem them as cranes, and let our association stand in the
way of warranted skepticism. In other words, we stop
thinking and start relating. We don't listen to opposing
viewpoints. Instead, too often, we deflect *their* cranes with
our skyhook arguments, and they reciprocate. Thus seldom, if ever, do we settle issues based upon the better
argument. We engage in tit-for-tat rebuttal, never listening
to the other side so much as concentrating on developing
our own counterpoints.

Having the discipline to engage in dialogue with people
whose views are very different from our own takes strong
resolve, very much like the psychological crutch necessary
to be successful in sales. Selling is filled with rejection, and
an old sales psychology secret for withstanding rejection is
to assume success while acknowledging the inevitability of
many negative results along the way. It's acceptance that
the world doesn't end if we don't make a sale today, or if
our dialogue fails to achieve consensus; there is always
tomorrow. The same principle applies to getting our own
points across if we fail today; there is time to rethink our
approach for the next opportunity.

I want to imagine the best of all possible futures for my
granddaughter's descendants. But I don't want my own
view of what it takes to accomplish such a positive future
to prevail unless it really is the best possible plan available.
In spite of the fact that I consider myself dedicated to discovering the right things to do, I have no reason to believe
that I can know what the right things are without an
extraordinary amount of help, especially in discerning subtle bias.

SPIN

Tom Fenton said this of media spin: "Americans are being served by a news media so beset by spin, from within and without, that we've lost all sense of what objective truth feels or sound like. Spin acts as the cutting edge of the dumbing down process that the rest of the entertainment media daily peddles: the substitution of fantasy for reality, and the conviction that the public cannot take too much truth—indeed is bored by it, especially in its most complex forms."[143] I would add that spin is possible because of the human capacity for making judgments, particularly snap judgments.

Bias, after all, is the lifeblood and grist of human culture. Bias enables us to define ourselves, and to tell one thing from another. It helps us to decide what to do next. Without bias we would be without a sense of identity or a sense of purpose. Nevertheless, cultural bias held close is a very real obstacle to individual freedom when it remains unacknowledged and misunderstood for what it is, and why it is. Bias, in the contemporary lexicon, is increasingly about politics, and each side views the other's politics as propaganda. We have become very accustomed to the idea that we should be quick to spot the bias of those who oppose our views, even while we remain slow and reluctant in discerning our own.

At the very crux of spin lies the fact that billions upon billions of dollars are spent each year by advertisers who, with a fervor of seriousness as urgently felt and funded as plans for international war, study the psychological aspects of identity, truth by association, I-It and I-You relating, and the concept of better than. It is hard to appreciate how having so much attention directed at us, with the specific intent to make us uncomfortable if we do not buy particular products or services, plays to our existential sense of insecurity. As a result we endure the equivalent of a constant nagging that appeals to our worst instincts, self-ishness, and an obsession with our status in relation to others.

Without a concentrated effort to avoid the chatter of modernity, Emersonian solitude, which once fostered daily refection upon the events of one's life, is lost to mediation. Spin is rampant in every avenue of our lives, even in calling our attention to the movies we watch, the books we read, the art we appreciate, and all of the other cultural products and services that we use. Book reviewers, movie critics, and art experts merely pretend to be independent of today's incestuous media conglomerate relationships: the parent companies, subsidiaries, sister companies, contractual affiliations, and alliances that, without much need for discussion or serious deliberation, subtly but powerfully direct their favorable attention to the films, books, and works of art that fund their limited universe. There is only so much space and time allotted for product attention. When a large publishing house or movie studio makes a substantial investment in a new book or film, the attention given by reviewers will mirror the outlay in scale. Even if the attention is negative, the publicity will translate into sales. Thus, without a great deal of critical awareness on our part as individuals, we are caught up in a maelstrom of purposeful commercial bias, which often plays into the spin of political partiality enthusiastically perpetuated by those blind to their own culpability—people who actually believe their own rhetoric about their autonomy and independence as critics.[144]

The influential power of corporate interests in both business and politics is analogous to the effect of gravity. The invisible force felt by employees to do that which best serves the interests of the corporation does not need to be consciously acknowledged in order to pull them in a certain direction. People are influenced by their paychecks and political donations in the same manner that the earth holds sway on the moon. Just because we can't see the compelling force doesn't mean it's not there. The critical point here is not that these effects are necessarily toxic in every case. Rather, the importance lies in the fact that economic amplification is analogous to ideological amplification.

In his classic work *The True Believer*, Eric Hoffer said, "The truth seems to be that propaganda on its own cannot force its way into unwilling minds; neither can it inculcate something wholly new; nor can it keep people persuaded once they have ceased to believe. It penetrates only into minds already open, and rather than instill opinion it articulates and justifies opinions already present in the minds of its recipients. The gifted propagandist brings to a boil ideas and passions already simmering in the minds of the hearers. He echoes their innermost feelings. Where opinion is not coerced, people can be made to believe only in what they already 'know.'"[145]

We are emotionally subject to spin because we are ever on the alert for assurance that our own worldview is safe and sound. This means we are also hypersensitive to signs of disrespect. Spin works because differences in worldviews or religion easily fester into grievances. A grievance thus gives way to hatred and contempt, lending credence to Hoffer's conclusion that "hatred is the most accessible and comprehensive of all unifying agents."[146] Add a little ethnocentric better than and a little I-It relating, and then all aggressive actions to rectify a group's or nation's sense of having been disrespected become automatically self-justifying. The more insecure said group becomes, the more aggressive they get, and the more virulent their hatred grows until the only alternative seems to be to convert the opposition to their views or destroy them.

People who lack confidence in their own knowledge of the world, and who feel insecure because of it, become fearful of opposing views. Thus they fear the future, and they fear change, in particular. A major part of their insecurity stems from the realization (which often occurs beneath consciousness) that they have done very little about subjecting their beliefs to critical scrutiny. This only increases their frustration and anxiety. In time, they learn to regard contrary opinions as personal attacks on themselves and their respective identity group. In short, the dynamics of spin can lead to destruction. Comprehending them should be among our highest educational priorities.

As I've said before, if I've learned anything at all in my many years of self-education, it's that things are not as they appear. Millions of well-meaning people, of every political stripe, who get their fundamental source of information from popular culture engage in what amounts to a passionate pursuit of ignorance, never coming close to understanding that they have actually made very little effort to know much at all about the very things they claim matter most. A surface view of everything offers little of worth about the depth of anything.

RELATIONAL DIALOGUE

During the 1980s I took some college courses at a local university. The students, who were much younger than I was at the time, were incredulous that I was taking some of the courses I had selected simply for enjoyment. In turn, I was disenchanted that so few of the students seemed to enjoy what they were doing or had any interest in the subject matter, except as a means for obtaining a future credential.

When I expressed my disappointment to a counselor about not having a more dynamic group of people to talk to, she said, "You need a forum." Indeed, don't we all? A forum is simply a place to engage in public discourse, a roundtable, a tribal council, a committee, a board, a team, an assembly, a public or private square, a meeting place in person or in cyberspace, where a Socratic dialogue or a sincere conversation can take place. For this purpose the Internet towers over the ancient public square in its possibilities.

So how do we engage in a genuinely democratic discourse? How and where do we get our news? How do we find our forum? *The World Café* by Juanita Brown provides a good beginning for starting our own, if we can't find one we would like to join.[147] Brown suggests the first stage is to set the context and clarify your purpose. Create a welcoming and psychologically safe environment. Focus attention on things that really matter. Encourage participation. Take advantage of diverse opinions. Listen for insights and ways to deepen the questions. And finally, share the collective discoveries; make them clear, and actionable.

Internet technologies increasingly enable us to be very selective in gathering news and information. The danger, though, is that we can too easily wall ourselves in from dissenting opinion, choosing only to read those views with which we already agree. In doing so we become further estranged from reality and more hostile to those who see the world differently than we do. We need to get our news from many different sources. The only way to bridge the chasm of social disconnect is to seek out differing views and engage in civil dialogue about the things we really care about. We must agree to disagree, live and let live, and set aside the things we can't resolve while we continue talking about the things for which there is hope of agreement or compromise.

Whereas a student requires a curriculum of some sort, those of us who consider ourselves Sept-U participants not only need a forum, we also need to pay particular attention to where we get our news and information and with whom we engage in dialogue. The personification of ideological amplification is easily observed when those who depend on Rush Limbaugh for their news and information become "ditto heads." Moreover, if a person watches Fox News all of the time and has to be reminded that their news is balanced, there is reason to suspect otherwise. The same can be said for media left of center if it is one's sole source of news and information. Balance, however, may not be necessary, or even the right choice of words, because one side may be egregiously wrong. More often than not there are more than two sides to an issue; there are so many points of view that they are practically inexhaustible.

A key to arriving at the best of all possible answers to the questions that matter most is to care deeply about the result. It means caring enough to consider new points of view and to be ready to seek them out when there are opportunities for doing so. It means taking the time to listen, really listen, to opposing views. This may be likened to a learned stance or an insatiable desire that simply defaults to wanting to learn the truth of any matter regardless of the source. In other words, when we really care about achieving something that seems very hard to accomplish, we are ever on the alert for opportunities and they tend to jump out at us when they are present.

Imagine for a moment that a member of your family is falsely accused of a serious crime and that you are appointed to defend your relative in court. Would you not be open to any and all ideas that might help prove innocence? Would you not be so alert that the mere hint of a useful concept would be all it would take for you to recognize it, no matter how subtle the presentation? Would there ever be a time short of victory when you were not interested in a new thread of information that might be helpful? Granted this hypothetical case is extreme, but you get the idea. To get to the truth of any matter requires this kind of vigilance and tenacity. In my experience a bias-free search for the truth is an aspiration that can become a habit when the resulting knowledge is always valued more than its source.

Democratically inspired dialogue is not about winning arguments; it's about finding common good through common ground, and it's about insightful relating. Dialogue is usually thought of as more desirable than debate, but debate among people determined to discover the better argument used to be a time-tested, honorable way of getting to the truth of a matter. Unfortunately, thanks to television, debate dedicated to finding truth has given way to choosing sides, and now the only thing we hear is the perpetual spinning of one party line after another. Media group spokesmen seldom ever give an inch; they rarely concede a point, no matter how big or small the issue at hand or how well their opponents address it. Political pundits are selected for television media based upon their ability to spin and screech the party line. The only likely result when they square off is further entrenchment into their already set-in-stone positions. Comedian Jon Stewart hit a nerve when he appeared on CNN's *Crossfire* and told the hosts that the show was hurting America. *Crossfire* was subsequently canceled, but the spin goes on.

The public learns little from mediated public debate, other than reinforcement for which side to be on. The exception is when discerning the better argument matters more than anything that stands in the way. Then debate can still be a rigorous exercise in getting to the heart of a matter. In most circumstances, however, the lesson is to drop the notion of debate and pick up on the need for perpetual dialogue. Social scientist Daniel Yankelovich, who has been surveying public opinion for half a century, has concluded that the need for dialogue is something deeply rooted in a fundamental condition of our society.[148]

Relational dialogue is what happens when two or more people engage in a search for the truth of a matter with less regard for whose side prevails than for getting the right solution for the problem at hand. Imagine two gold miners taking turns swishing a panful of streambed gravel, sloughing off rocks until the only thing left in the pan is gold. Contrast this with typical partisan debate tactics, where I take a rock out of the pan and you put it back in, proving we are less interested in finding gold than in finding fault with one another's methods. That we engage in this mindless, nonsensical bickering to such a degree that we never finish a pan, but start over endlessly, is a slap in the face of the very idea of democracy. Yankelovich presents the issue this way: "When in ordinary discussion sensitive assumptions are brought into the open, the atmosphere may or may not break down. It may later be recalled as a good or bad discussion, but—and this is the key point—it is not dialogue. The unique nature of dialogue requires that participants be uninhibited in bringing their own and other participants' assumptions into the open, where, within the safe confines of the dialogue, others can respond to them without challenging them or reacting to them judgmentally."[149]

Dialogue is an I-You enterprise, and as such it has to contain enough mutual respect to sustain itself or it is likely to end abruptly. One of the most profound and easily missed values of dialogue stems from the fact that we imagine ourselves engaging others in dialogue in order to discover their views and opinions about specific matters. But it is often the case that until we enter into a conversation with others we don't thoroughly understand our own position on the subjects of our interest. It's long past time for us to grow up as a nation and act as citizens of the same planet, rising above our imagined differences. We desperately need a relational dialogue with those who see the world differently than we do; it may be the only path to wisdom, maturity, and a civilized society.

ELEVEN

MATURING
TO WISDOM

*If a nation expects to be ignorant and free in a state of
civilization, it expects what never was and never will be.*

THOMAS JEFFERSON

PHILOSOPHY

Acquiring knowledge seems to be a fairly straightforward task, but there is something special about gaining wisdom. Wisdom often contains a little surprise or shock value from its clarity and appropriateness, as in the epigraph above. In a sense, wisdom is an artifact of perspective. One way to bring about a real change in perspective—one that results in a fresh, new way to experience life and the world—is to explore philosophy. Before we begin to speak about philosophy, however, it's useful to know something of what's already been said. Philosophy adds quality to life that's easily missed if we don't heed Socrates' advice and attend to some serious study and self-examination.

I still remember how completely swept away I was when I first read Will Durant's *The Story of Philosophy* in my late thirties. He wrote the book in 1926, seventeen years before I was born. In a note to the reader he said he was attempting to "humanize knowledge by centering the story of speculative thought around certain dominant personalities."[150] It worked for me. Durant wrote of Plato, Aristotle, Francis Bacon, Spinoza, Voltaire, Kant, Schopenhauer, Santayana, Friedrich Nietzsche, and others. He made their work so clear that their ideas seemed immediately accessible to anyone who could simply read a newspaper. Here were thoughts handed down through the ages that stretched my thinking in every direction with a force of logic that seemed nearly irrefutable to an untrained mind. Here was an avenue into the wonder of existence set out by those who had lived their lives infatuated by wonder.

I was so taken with philosophical discourse upon my first introduction to it that I read *The Story of Philosophy* three times in quick succession. Having studied on my own now for many years and having learned how to refute well presented arguments, I still bristle at the claim by both professional and amateur philosophers that there is little to gain in a practical sense from philosophy. Henry David Thoreau expressed my sentiments best, "To be a philosopher is not merely to have subtle thoughts, nor even to found a school, but so to love wisdom as to live, according to its dictates, a life of simplicity, independence, magnanimity, and trust."[151] If this is true, and I for one believe it is, then we should ask ourselves whether this kind of transformation of our own life stance would not represent a practical value.

In his book *Irrational Man*, William Barrett reminds us that in ancient times philosophers lived their work. Socrates, for example, was sentenced to death for upping the ante of public discourse. To Socrates, philosophy is dialogue between those trying to get to the heart of a matter, not the text of books. But, as Barrett makes clear, philosophy suffers today because it has become a specialty, confined within the walls of academia. About these philosophers Barrett writes, "To the degree that their existence has become specialized and academic, their importance beyond the university cloisters has declined. These disputes have become disputes themselves; and far from gaining the enthusiastic support needed for a strong popular movement, they now have little contact with whatever general intellectual elite still remain here outside the Academy."[152] It is no wonder so many philosophers cast doubt on the worth of their profession; specialization has emasculated academic philosophy.[153]

September University offers us an opportunity to resurrect the application of philosophy to everyday life. Barrett said, "Philosophers breed ideas; and if anything keeps them anchored to existence, it is not philosophy itself but something that comes from outside it—either religion, or the personal drama, anguish, or rebellion of the philosopher's own life."[154] The worth of philosophy is not in its presentation but in its inquisitiveness and its perpetual striving to comprehend, to understand, or to reunderstand what has merely been taken for granted.

In *The Truth about Everything,* Matthew Stewart offers a sobering perspective: "Philosophy is not the foundation of our thought. It is just a collection of peculiar, largely self-referential, mostly timeless, thoughts. . . . Philosophy is the practice of the liberation of thought: most importantly, a liberation from the tyranny of old revolutionaries."[155] Philosophy, in my view, is nothing more or less than a genuine desire to learn the truth about life and the mysteries inherent in existence. What makes philosophy worthwhile is that it can instill in us the kind of critical thinking that can enable us to penetrate the destructive illusions we've internalized through our respective cultures.

Philosophy has given me the intellectual wherewithal to analyze and deconstruct many of the narrow-minded assumptions that I grew up thinking were bulwarks of truth, but which were, in reality, biases and bigotries dressed up as common sense. Philosophy enabled me to reevaluate my life circumstances and change the things I really care about. In a nutshell, it radicalized my worldview, enabling me to reject the common but limited historically prevalent views of a southern geographical region of America. Philosophical reasoning helped me understand that many of the cultural assumptions that I had accepted as ramparts of reality during my youth were instead aspirations of misplaced loyalty. What I had thought was patriotism was bigotry in disguise. The practice of philosophy has been instrumental in helping me aspire to become a citizen of the world. It's taken me from George Wallace to Mahatma Gandhi. To suggest that this experience is without meaning is to misunderstand the concept of value and the elusive nature of good judgment, especially when it comes to popular culture and the notion of common sense.

WISDOM

Through philosophy we can reassess and revalue all of those aspects of life that we appreciate as having had value; we can rearrange and reprioritize them. Philosophy gives us the means to abandon unworthy goals and pursue something worthwhile. Philosophy, after all, is supposed to be the love of wisdom. Why, then, is not everyone a philosopher? And if philosophy is preparation for death, as Socrates proposed, then is it a denial of death not to pursue philosophy?

Neil Postman defined wisdom, in a very practical sense, as the capacity to know what "body of knowledge is relevant" to your problem.[156] He writes, "Any fool can have an opinion; to know what one needs to know to *have* an opinion is wisdom; which is another way of saying that wisdom means knowing what questions to ask about knowledge."[157] In his book *Spirituality for the Skeptic*, philosopher Robert Solomon coins the phrase "the thoughtful love of life" to capture the essence of spirituality. Wisdom, he suggests, is synonymous with spirituality.[158]

The philosopher who claims philosophy is of little value is of little value to himself or herself, much less to philosophy.

It's true that a person's wisdom may have no cash value. But let's look at this issue more closely. Increased knowledge does not guarantee wise decisions; neither does it hinder them. In some cases it makes all the difference in the world. Which is preferable for solving problems, knowledge or ignorance? Could it add something of value to your personal life if you could examine the recent past and have made wiser choices? Have you ever said, "If only I had known?" Could you make good financial decisions without the ability to do simple math? Could you make a trip around the world without any knowledge of geography? If a young person, age twenty, needs to make a life-altering decision, will the wise counsel come from a friend of the same age or from a grandparent?

Suppose that, while immersed in philosophy, a college student studying to be a business major discovers she is enthralled by ideas. She decides to become an English professor because she recognizes the value of continuing to explore the human condition. Has that insight been of value? It's not what we get from philosophy but what philosophy gets from us that makes a difference.

How does the attainment of wisdom affect our lives as individuals? Schopenhauer argued that life is an art to be developed by building upon one's strengths and that we should strive to understand our natural talents so as to fully develop them.[159] With this in mind, ask yourself these questions: What might your life have been like if our educational system operated as if this advice was truly important? What if it had been a primary goal of traditional education to discover our aptitudes, reveal our natural talents, and build on those strengths instead of overfocusing on our weaknesses? Would it have made a difference? Would it have produced saddle-horse complicity or leadership qualities? Would it have been a wise thing to do?

When someone goes in search of wise citizens, expecting to find wisdom, the natural inclination might be to look in educational institutions. A wiser course of action might be to seek out those people with a half-century or more of life experience. More than knowledge attained, wisdom is the grasp of a life stance where one's perception is acute enough to blunt the forces of a culture that would have us act with purely prescriptive thinking. People who know intuitively that a breach exists between knowledge and wisdom often balk at too much emphasis on the former for good reason. But I believe that the pursuit of knowledge is closely related to the perpetual questioning of one's circumstances, which gives rise to insight and provides the core of what we characterize as wisdom.

Wisdom can be the result of direct experience; no reading or study about the subject at hand can compare. Reading about war and death is not the same as being in a war or experiencing the death of a loved one. I suggest that a shortcut in the search for wisdom in the later years is to be found in an unyielding appeal for honesty, especially with ourselves, about significant social matters that were avoided in our youth. And if you also believe, as I do, that curiosity is the lifeblood of a meaningful life, then you know too that life is eminently more enjoyable when you are doing your very best to better understand it.

Achieving wisdom in critical mass may be our last hope for humanity. It is entirely conceivable that we will someday reach a global predicament where the application of wisdom is the only thing that truly matters. It's just as likely that, if this wisdom is available, it will be because of a sustained effort to achieve it. Mark Twain said, "The perfection of wisdom and the end of true philosophy is to proportion our wants to our possessions, our ambitions to our capacities."[160] For these reasons, practicing philosophy enables us to achieve a measure of impartiality, setting aside our penchant for truth by association and thus enabling us to move closer to the provenance of wisdom and objectivity.

OBJECTIVITY AND EQUILIBRIUM

I have learned that it is extremely difficult to attain anything resembling objectivity with regard to the nature of human beings without first achieving some imagined sense of detachment as a participant. Anthropologists have been struggling with this issue for decades. Total detachment is, of course, never really possible, but it helps if you can imagine arriving on the earth as a nonhuman creature with the agenda of making sense of human behavior—alien sense, that is. One has to venture only a short distance into the study of nation-states, tribes, and races of human beings to realize that each group comes to adulthood with the built-in assumption that their particular culture has reality pegged and that every other group on the planet is living with a diminished capacity for appreciating reality as it really is. It has never ceased to amaze me how anyone from any culture, upon learning and fully understanding this fact of human experience, cannot go reeling into retrospection on their own take on reality. To discover this ubiquitous trait of learned human behavior and not to be suspicious that some of our own cherished beliefs about the world may be arbitrary illusions, strikes me as being disingenuous to the extreme. Taking the posture of disinterested observance, as if we were indeed aliens from another world, allows us to see things about ourselves that we are normally too caught up in experience to detect.

One wintry day many years ago, I visited a college bookstore in Fairbanks, Alaska. Perusing the shelves, I noticed a small, odd-sized paperback that looked very much out of place. I picked it up, opened to the preface and read, "I have always been fascinated by the law of reversed effort. Sometimes I call it the 'backwards law.' When you try to stay on the surface of the water, you sink; but when you try to sink you float." The thoughts that followed from Alan Watts' *The Wisdom of Insecurity* struck me as so profound that I bought the book on the spot and continue to reread it regularly.[161]

Watts was a student of Eastern religion, particularly Zen Buddhism. What I've come to understand over years of reflection is that what Watts was talking about is not unique to Zen. Though rarely discussed or acknowledged, something similar to the backwards law exists in varying guises of Western experience. If we examine the subject closely, we will realize that there is an enormous amount of power in a position of uninvolvement or disinterestedness. It's an insight so subtle that sometimes only through advanced age can we make the connection. If we make our peace with insecurity, which is the goal of Watts' book, one result is diminishment of the tribalistic angst that we would otherwise default to when stressed.

Our culture is thrust upon us with such force at birth that decades can pass before we can imagine observing anything without having a stake in the outcome. Neil Postman maintained, as I've already mentioned, that education is a defense against culture. Regardless of the subject, he argued, education should move us closer to a perception of reality that's untainted by cultural biases. Understanding the backwards law gives us the freedom to see things not as the swimmer in fear of drowning but from the standpoint of what it really takes to float. Pioneering psychologist Gordon Allport observed, "Perception is more than a simple physical phenomenon; it is a psychic function from which we may draw the most far-going conclusions concerning the inner life."[162]

We may have moments in early adulthood when we begin to recognize that, in spite of our enthusiasm and ambition, there are limits to what we can achieve in life. At some point we wake up to the idea that we are not going to be president of the United States or superstars or whatever high-minded goals we thought possible when we were children. Then, over time, in momentary flashes of insight, we awaken to the understanding that, as we age and feel increasingly less powerful in affecting life's circumstances, a new kind of intelligence arises—an objectivity that's much more commanding because it's more detached. Almost any game is easier to comprehend at a higher level when you stop playing it yourself and simply watch others play.

From a comprehension of perceived incapacity we gain a force of wisdom. We realize that much of what we assumed we could control in early adulthood was only an illusion; we never had much of the power we so took for granted in our youth, and at the same time many of our fears were irrational. The good news is that a well-developed sense of detachment allows us the autonomy to see more clearly when it comes to separating the important things in life from a preoccupation with trivial matters. To the teenager invited to next Saturday night's party, the event is of extreme importance; if he or she can't go, it will seem like the end of the world. But those of us in the fall and winter of life know from experience that desperation over a single social event is an absurdity.

When we are so vested in the events of our lives that the whole of our psyche is caught up in their outcomes, we experience a special kind of powerlessness. We're like the fish so compelled by hunger that he focuses on the lure while remaining oblivious to the hook. We're like the owner so desperate to sell his house, car, or business that he doesn't maintain the control to walk away from a bad offer. And yet, having the control not to sink your teeth into a deceptive lure or to walk away from a bad deal is precisely the kind of power that matters most.

In the strain of apparent powerlessness lies the strength to listen to our own counsel, to our own conscience. With that comes the power to defy convention and take the road less traveled for no other reason than that's where we want to go. Alan Watts says, "You cannot understand life and its mysteries as long as you try to grasp it. Indeed, you cannot grasp it, just as you cannot walk off with a river in a bucket."[163]

Western society deals poorly with the topic of power and the backwards law. Watts warns us that our desire for security is in reality a wish to be separate from life. The more security we believe we have, the more of it we want, and this futile exercise, he says, is the antithesis of achieving any realistic control over life's circumstances.

I would add that, instead of dreading an inevitable loss of control as we age, we ought to welcome the objectivity it brings to our thinking. We can relish our newfound ability to ignore the crowd. There is both power and wisdom to gain in appreciating the river for what it is and letting the bucket be.

There may be no better example of reaping the rewards of thoughtfulness than in the work of American philosopher Ralph Waldo Emerson. More than 150 years ago, Emerson offered penetrating insights about cause-and-effect relationships and how the little things in life can lead to big things. It's sad that we do not learn to make these kinds of observations for ourselves before we reach adulthood.

Emerson was a great force for the idea of self-reliance in nineteenth-century America, and he may well deserve to be thought of as the inspirational founder of September University. The dynamics of balance and equilibrium in everyday experience were an aspect of living that fascinated Emerson. To him, the better part of existence is a kind of attitude, or bearing, akin to scholarship—experienced as an unquenchable thirst for knowledge—and every person is a scholar but for the effort required to think and attain an honors-level quality of life. There's no doubt that he thoroughly comprehended the backwards law. Understanding life's credits and debits represented to him the very fabric of wisdom. In his essay "Compensation," he observed, "Every excess causes a defect; every defect an excess. Every sweet hath its sour; every evil its good. Every faculty which is a receiver of pleasure has an equal penalty put on its abuse."[164] When we apply this wisdom to our lives today, we can gain a broader view about the things that really matter to us and ultimately rise above our petty concerns over the actions of others.

Emerson intuited our Stone Age predisposition. He was concerned that too many people in his community engaged in a kind of vengeful thinking—that is, relating to others with the expectation that they were due a comeuppance in the next life for their shortcomings in this one. To him it amounted to a thoughtless illusion, keeping his fellow citizens from seeing the world as it was. He said, "The exclusionist in religion does not see that he shuts the door of heaven on himself, in striving to shut out others."[165] You've only to ask yourself how much of this kind of thinking is going on today to realize Emerson's relevance.

Even in his time, Emerson was profoundly aware of the stultifying effects of popular culture and its ability to lull us into a kind of wakeful sleep, where we experience the world but do not learn from our experience. He had the insight to realize this long before the arrival of electronic media. "For every grain of wit there is a grain of folly," he observed. "For every thing you have missed, you have gained something else; and for every thing you gain, you lose something."[166] He further suggested that we cannot be cheated by another, but only by ourselves, and that a more accurate view of reality than the one conveyed by popular culture is available only to those who are open to finding it.[167]

In Emerson's view, not seeing the world as it is leads to an inauthentic existence, and we must be ever alert to how rewards are bestowed if we are to learn from our behavior. "As no man ever had a point of pride that was not injurious to him, so no man had ever a defect that was not somewhere made useful to him," he says in the essay on compensation. "The stag in the fable admired his horns and blamed his feet, but when the hunter came, his feet saved him, and afterwards, caught in the thicket, his horns destroyed him. Every man in his lifetime needs to thank his faults."[168] When you contrast this kind of reasoning to the "victim mentality" expressed today by so many differing groups of people, you have a new lens for viewing any predicament.

How ironic it is that, only a few years into the twenty-first century, the wisdom to make sense of our fast-paced, complex lives is found, not in looking forward, but back to a time when the pace of life invited reflection, back to the thoughts of someone who did not cover his eyes in despair. Emerson declared that the only chance we have to live an authentic life is not to hide from the abyss but to look directly into it without blinking. Whereas Schopenhauer compared life to a curse, Emerson viewed it as sacred. Thus, if sacredness is to be more useful to us than simply being an attitude toward objects of reverence, it could find no better expression than the thoughtfulness with which we pass our legacy from one generation to the next.

TWELVE

CONTEMPLATION

*The ultimate value of life depends upon
awareness and the power of contemplation
rather than upon mere survival.*

ARISTOTLE

THOUGHTFULNESS

What do we really mean when we say that someone is thoughtful? When I try to come up with a definition for thoughtfulness, words like attentiveness, consideration, introspection, cogitation, contemplation, self-examination, speculation, kindness, deliberateness, tactfulness, and meditation come to mind. Taken together, these concepts suggest that thoughtfulness represents the pinnacle of human experience. Thoughtfulness elicits all of our facilities for making sense of the world, from reading and observing to creating and re-creating the internal narrative that takes us from one moment to the next and gives us reason to compare our lives to works of art.

Thoughtfulness can reveal itself in simple gestures like remembering important anniversaries in another person's life or accommodating someone's personal needs when planning an event or a trip. At other times, thoughtfulness takes the form of quiet reflection, logical analysis, or the weighing of multiple alternatives. In essence, thoughtfulness

143

is a way of seeing, an act of caring, a way of assuming responsibility, an expression of compassion, and a method of inquiry all rolled into one. If philosophy is the love of wisdom and a product of wonder, then thoughtfulness must be the neurological mechanism that drives wonder and makes it possible to philosophize.

Thoughtfulness occurs when we strive to get beyond the superficial, to look underneath the table to ensure we know for certain what's holding it up. Consider the care and concern that occur naturally in Socratic dialogue. Socrates' love of thoughtfulness was so enduring that he was relentless in exposing the seething malignancy inherent in thoughtlessness. Indeed, bigotry and hatred are the antithesis of thoughtfulness, and thoughtfulness can overcome them both. It affords us the opportunity to move far beyond the collective consciousness of popular culture while it fuels our desire to add something of lasting quality to our society.

Thoughtfulness includes the ability to both engage and disengage the intellect. It provides the middle ground where the philosophies of East and West have an opportunity to meet and explore their similarities. Thoughtfulness is as integral to emptying one's mind in Zen fashion as it is to filling the mind with Plato, and it is as much a part of Buddhist compassion as it is of Western charity.

To no small extent, thoughtfulness is a barometer that measures the capacity we have for experiencing significance in our lives. It provides us with the facility to mine wisdom from the past and apply that wisdom toward the realization of a better future. It's the crux of a meaningful existence, and it serves as the societal adhesive that holds us together as a nation and as citizens of the world. In an effort to be gentle and kind, for example, we respond to victims of tragedy by taking the time to pose thoughtful questions or convey our compassion in some other considerate manner. Seen in this way, thoughtfulness becomes a force that both creates and sustains civilization.

Sometimes thoughtfulness can result in a measurable

breakthrough in relating to others that can help to shape our attitude for life. In *The Underground History of American Education*, John Taylor Gatto describes such an experience he had as a boy. One day he shot a bird with his new Daisy Red Ryder BB gun, only to have an old, gray-haired woman burst out of a nearby house in tears. As the dying bird fluttered about on the ground, the woman shouted that she knew who he was and asked why he would do such a thing. Picking up the injured bird, she ran back into the house sobbing. Gatto said that, to be honest with himself, he had, at the very least, to answer her question, if only in his own mind. Thinking about her question he revealed the disturbing fact that he had killed the bird simply because he wanted to. Reflecting thoughtfully on the matter prompted him to get rid of the BB gun a few days later and, when winter came, to shovel snow from the woman's driveway without being asked and without ever speaking to her.[169]

Lying at the heart of science and art, thoughtfulness may in fact be the very foundation for spirituality. Some of the contemporary authors I hold in greatest esteem are the ones I consider to be the most thoughtful, and the same applies to the creators of our greatest literature. The works of Plato, Shakespeare, Melville, Dickens, Twain, Tolstoy, Milton, Faulkner, Voltaire, Kafka, Keats, Poe, Hemingway, James, Wilde, Conrad, Camus, Austen, Woolf, Hawthorne, and Mann are so steeped in thoughtfulness that we recall these writers' identities by using only parts of their names. And, for me, the words of Emerson are so imbued with thoughtfulness that reading them can be almost intoxicating.

It's no surprise, then, that writing is another form of thoughtfulness. As such it becomes a defensive act that allows us to explore possibilities without reservation, and for intervals long enough to still our existential anxiety about our being in the world. Viewed in this light, thoughtfulness is even more of an expression of humanness than I first imagined. Other creatures may indeed experience mental activity, but humans alone can be characterized as being truly thoughtful. Only humans contemplate their own death and the death of the people who matter most to them. Do you suppose this is why we are thoughtful to begin with?

Some of the most thoughtful advice about navigating through daily life comes from Seneca. He warned us that unrealistic expectations lead to unnecessary anger and resentment. To maintain a sense of control over life's circumstances requires that we not be caught off guard by the developments we encounter. This may sound easy, but it is very hard to do in actual practice. Imagine driving your car to town, being cut off by another driver, and keeping your temper because you were expecting fools along the way. That this is so hard to do demonstrates again that we lead with our emotions and then offer what we think is a reasoned explanation of our actions.

Thoughtfulness is an art. More precisely, thoughtfulness is *the* art that sustains quality of life, human relationships, education, democracy, and all of the aspirations we hold dear. Without thoughtfulness we have no culture. And without art we have no striving, no revelation, no distraction, no authentic self, and nothing to inspire posterity. Aesthetics is in part another way of demonstrating that we are most like one another, not when we are contemplating something of value but by nature of being distracted. It is a back door to the Stone Age software code that we use in relating to others, and it offers a way to enlarge our group to include everyone.

CULTURAL CODE-BREAKING

John Keats said, "Beauty is truth, truth beauty,- that is all Ye know on earth, and all ye need to know."[170] This declaration offers a brief summary of what Schopenhauer felt is truly important in life. He believed art speaks to us as no other means can, in ways that impart truth as no other means are able.[171] To Schopenhauer the intellect is not the

captain of the will, but is instead nothing more than a
deckhand. Escaping the will in the Buddhist fashion is the
supreme goal in life to Schopenhauer, and aesthetic beauty
is a shortcut to asceticism—the denial of the will altogether. He believed the supreme good of life is to be found
in losing oneself in the immediacy of one's own experience
and in beauty and high art in particular.

Schopenhauer was the first published Western philosopher to study Eastern philosophy and achieve a measure of
celebrity. And while some may question his conclusions
about the will and his pessimism about the value of life, his
work is still worth reading. Schopenhauer was very influential in his views about art, even with those who differed
with him fundamentally both then and now. Although I
long ago recognized the similarity between his notion of
blotting the will and Buddhist meditation, it was only in
studying the aesthetics of art and neurology that I realized
I had achieved a useful insight: I had at least partially broken the code that helps explain the foundational divisiveness between education, art, and entertainment.

Think how enthralling the notion can be to a creature
that owes its very existence to its ability to discriminate,
that its own impression of aesthetic appreciation is literal
proof of its natural superiority over others in a hierarchical
world. Of course, classism has always been a subject of
written history, and arguments about the relationship
between truth and beauty have been with us since Plato,
but in the nineteenth century the idea that truth and
beauty were one and the same reached a crescendo among
the lettered class. It prompted Edgar Allan Poe to write,
"That pleasure which is most elevating and most intense,
is derived, I maintain, from the contemplation of the beau-
tiful." This sentiment coincided with an influx of immi-
grants and the rise of the university in America. It also
created a formidable foundation on which to base snobbery: that, the ethic of treating people as ends in themselves aside, the possession of knowledge is all of the

justification needed for an assumption of *better than*. This attractive realization enabled the economically better-off class to distance themselves with congratulatory self-justification from newcomers whom they deemed socially inferior. Still today, it is considered a common-sense assertion that beauty is in the eye of the beholder, as David Hume argued, but only in matters of relative unimportance. When it comes to distancing ourselves from those we deem to be outsiders, we assume our superiority in judgment instinctively, and we back it up with tomes of sophisticated literature that exaggerate our special status for possessing something essential that others, through some fault of their own, are missing.

Shared belief is an extraordinary grouping schema. In terms of evolutionary psychology, how could it be otherwise? Conformity can be an antidote to loneliness; thus we have an innate predisposition for sharing our goods and opinions with insiders because there is a risk of alienation in not doing so. But social codes that blindly favor our own respective groups, especially when greater moral principles are at risk simply because our interests are at cross-purposes with those we deem to be others, are contrary to the very concept of objectivity, to democracy, and to the possibility of achieving a society where justice prevails regardless of affiliation.

As mentioned in the previous chapter, Emerson has shown us how strengths unappreciated become weaknesses. The contemplation that enabled Emerson to grasp the issue of compensation so clearly is the same level of thoughtfulness required for breaking through the social biases that once were useful to us when our numbers were small but now threaten a heavily populated planet. Emerson didn't stop thinking when he witnessed jaw-dropping and mind-halting aesthetic beauty. He readily understood that to see things closer to the way they actually are, you have to be able to see beyond your own customs and aspirations, regardless of the identity of your group. To be limited to a worldview of only one culture, no matter how extensive the knowledge, does not constitute an education; it is more in keeping with indoctrination. And here is where the objectivity of an impartial observer is crucial, since by now we are acutely aware of how much our cultural perceptual biases obscure our vision.

Simply put, discerning whether we are reasoning or relating is much more difficult than it seems. When our interests collide with the interests of those whom we perceive to be outside of our respective identity groups, we eagerly accept skyhooks as cranes to justify the positions we take. We perceive that we are reasoning when we are in fact relating. This cuts to the quick our idealized notions of the nobility of human character.

For centuries, people have held profound beliefs about our nature that do not square with the revelations of neurological science. The breadth of world literature offers myriad accounts of gifted writers trying desperately to sort out who we are and why we do the things we do. We know that every generation imagines itself to be the most important to date and to have the best grip yet on reality. But, more often than not, history reveals this to be just another stunning example of mass delusion.

In 1990, Walter Truett Anderson published *Reality Isn't What It Used to Be,* a very insightful book that dealt with a growing suspicion about the frailty of all human belief systems. He attempted to make sense of the senselessness that appeared to be creeping about in the shadows of popular culture. At the time, the mania of deconstruction seemed about to override everything we had come to value. Anderson followed up with a very lucid examination of popular culture as editor of *The Truth about the Truth.* What's closer to the truth, however, is to say that reality has never been what we thought it was and isn't likely to be until we get a few fundamental things straight about human beings. First and foremost of these is the fact that our brains, which we celebrate as the most astounding creation in the universe, do not work as we have imagined. It is not a stretch to say that we are not who we like to think we are, nor have our aspirations ever been in precise alignment with our predispositions.

We aspire to noble ideals about our nature and what we assume to be the character of human beings, but for all practical purposes these are deceptive illusions. They undermine our ability to see things as they are and not simply as we wish them to be. And while our aspirations may be honorable in an ideological sense, the greatest obstacle in the way of achieving them resides in failing to understand that our neurological wiring short-circuits our cultural expectations *by design*. For example, we are taught to abhor gossip, bias, and prejudice for what seem to be good reasons, but most people are oblivious to the reality that this conduct also has a positive evolutionary side by helping us to identify, clarify, and reinforce what we deem is acceptable behavior and whom to trust. Until we can deconstruct our own predilection for bias and determine both its positive and negative effects, we are ill equipped for the kind of social harmony that is necessary to achieve a peaceful and sustainable civilization.

Scholars have been arguing about reason versus emotion for centuries, and we are still far from settling on a fundamental view about which is which and where one begins and the other ends. Strong conviction feels like reason precisely because of the emotional force with which we experience it. In *Proust Was a Neuroscientist,* Jonah Lehrer states the case succinctly: "Our human brain has been designed to believe itself, wired so that prejudices feel like facts, opinions are indistinguishable from the actual sensation. If we *think* a wine is cheap, it will taste cheap. And if we think we are tasting a Grand Cru, then it will taste like a Grand Cru."[172]

Robert A. Burton puts it this way in *On Being Certain*: "We know the nature and quality of our thoughts via feelings, not reason. Feelings such as certainty, conviction, rightness and wrongness, clarity, and faith arise out of involuntary mental sensory systems that are integral and inseparable components of the thoughts that they qualify."[173] But if certainty is not exactly as it seems, then, in my view, a belief is a belief is a belief. A belief is in part a relation, and as such it presents an obstacle to objectivity and a barrier to negotiating differences.

A conviction may depend less on the truth of a matter than on the relationships involved. If it feels right, it must be right. So, we believe what we need to in order to maintain the integrity of our respective identities. If we develop an aversion for information that conflicts with our identity, then so be it, because our default nature is automatically preset on self-justification, circumstances be damned. Thus, the bar of objectivity for modernity is raised too high for Stone Age thinking. No doubt, the postmodernists made too much of a fuss about the imprecise interpretation of texts in recent years, but their deep suspicions about something being amiss in our penchant for certitude deserves another look.

In reference to Malcolm Gladwell's bestselling book *Blink*, Burton argues that if we "mass market the belief that instinct can be the equivalent of months of scientific study," then we may reach a point where physicians practice medicine based on hunches, or worse on what they imagine their heart tells them to do. "With one blink we will be back in the Dark Ages."[174] But, then again, it is our neural wiring from before the Dark Ages that makes us feel that our hunches and aesthetic inclinations seem to be the embodiment of truth.

The notion that the feeling of certainty is a mental sensation that can simply happen to us flies in the face of all we have accepted for centuries as common sense, and yet it represents neurological reality.[175] When we understand this, really understand it, perhaps we are armed for the first time with the wherewithal to challenge the codes of bias that heretofore have been too prominent for us to recognize. This is much easier to appreciate when we begin to recall all of the times in the past when we were absolutely convinced that we were right about a particular matter but were, in fact, *wrong*.

It took a great deal of concentrated effort for me to be able to comprehend why Schopenhauer's notion of will-blotting was misplaced. At first I thought it was simply a skyhook argument in the place of a crane, but it's not. A good case can be made for aesthetic distraction—that being awestruck in our tracks, so to speak, is a socially relevant occurrence. But Schopenhauer misused it. Instead of discovering its real utility he used the idea to cover for his own disillusionment. He was too clever by half. He hid his anxiety from himself by simply pretending it didn't matter. That indeed nothing really matters. That life is truly absurd, and nonexistence is preferable. And yet, what is heralding will-blotting, but a bait-and-switch method of avoiding the abyss? His error is *our* error, yours and mine. When our aspirations collide with the perception of a reality of disenchantment—namely, that we are going to die soon—maintaining objectivity is exceptionally difficult.

This is hardest to appreciate when it comes to art and aesthetics because our sense of taste seems the most right-eous of all of our means of knowing. We think we know what we like, period. We perceive our likes and dislikes as pure objectivity, even though they are to a significant degree socially constructed. After all, we didn't come to believe what we suppose and appreciate all by ourselves. Schopenhauer's notion of the humanistic significance of will-blotting may offer us some aesthetic value as individuals, but its universal benefit to society is largely unappreciated for what it really represents. Our actions as individuals are much more dependent upon the context of our circumstances than our romantic notions of human character allow.[176]

FILLING THE EXISTENTIAL VOID

At the beginning of this book I discussed three main concerns that subvert our humanity by misdirecting our anxiety: the fear of death, fear of or an aversion to or intolerance of the other, and a lack of curiosity. All three coalesce into an existential triad where it is often difficult to tell which one is the cause of our angst. We fail to recognize that it is really these things that are bothering us and not simply external reminders of our fears. I submit that developing an awareness capable of social code-breaking is the best remedy for these maladies. It's the only surefire way to avoid the cumulative misunderstandings that come all too easily to a species with a thinking apparatus whose default settings have been rendered obsolete by the complexity of circumstance.

The concept of will-blotting was never accepted as the philosophical breakthrough that Schopenhauer intended, although it might be worthy of consideration on a parallel with Eastern meditation or perhaps Mihaly Csikszentmihalyi's concept of *flow*.[177] What did fill this existential void with a vengeance was achieving a level of *aesthetic appreciation* that makes one feel special for seeming to have understood what others don't yet get. This propensity for self-regard feeds our dread and apprehension because we are as perpetually alert for discerning the like-mindedness that enables us to form in-group and out-group differences as the NORAD radar system is for detecting incoming missiles. While we may seem to temporarily avoid the abyss through a sense of elated contemplation, existential reality has a way of roaring back with our fears looming ever larger.

In the paragraph above, what void am I referring to? Puzzled? Considering our formal educational system, that's not surprising. I'm talking about an egregious error within education so blatant and so severe that, for all practical purposes, its existence is unacknowledged. It's the idea (or lack of ideas) or conviction that suggests the core subjects regarding the behaviors and needs of human beings—the arts, anthropology, geography, literature, politics, psychology, philosophy, sociology, and religion (not one religion but all religions and belief systems)—are elective subjects that students can safely skip. As if the study of these fields of knowledge is irrelevant, or somehow the masses are exempt. It's the assumption that some humans don't need to think about what humans desperately need to think about. That the most intimate aspects of our lives are better left to experts. That most of us are excused from knowledge that uplifts our species and helps us avoid a life of perpetual frustration because we live in a world that has outgrown our primitive predispositions. That ordinary people don't need the kind of knowledge that can help them grapple with the fear of death, a lack of curiosity, and hostility directed toward otherness. To endorse as complete an education that omits the very knowledge necessary for enough existential equilibrium to cope effectively in a universe rife with chaos is patently absurd. Misplaced anxiety and mindless conflict inevitably follow from such ignorance. And that's exactly where we are.

We are programmed for distraction because too often, when it comes to human relations, we don't reason objectively; we relate selfishly, even to the extent that we use our distractions to separate ourselves from those we perceive as different. The core subjects that give us confidence as human beings, that assure us we are not oddballs or freaks of nature, cannot be considered elective subjects, unless the underlying and perhaps even unconscious intention is to keep the populace ignorant and commercially pliable. I don't think it's an accident that mass industrialization led us to an education system that is missing the ingredient, by design, that could nurture the Thomas Paines among us.[178]

This is not to suggest that knowledge gained in the humanities means that our lives will escape difficulties and the existential dread that comes with them. Psychologists still have emotional problems; marriage counselors still get divorced; and very often the people who write self-help books need them more than the people who buy them to read. But what a deep interest and knowledge of the human condition *can* lead to, if one has the will, is dissipation of culturally created contempt through a vast range of thoughtful considerations that ignorant people simply do not possess or have access to. An existential education grants one the possibility of developing a radicalized view, a counter-opinion to status quo culture.

Socrates feverishly advocated the need for an examined life. Although I've always thought he overstated the case a bit, I'm convinced that without a rigorous understanding of the social conditions that shape us, there is little to compare and hence nothing much to examine. Human beings without adequate knowledge of the humanities are too often indifferent and too readily inhuman. Neal Postman's assertion that education is "a defense against culture," any culture, as I stated earlier, is thus difficult to overemphasize, and it may also be a defense against our genes as well.[179]

Human civilization depends upon humans learning what we need to know, getting not what we want but what we need, and the shortcut to species maturity is making sure that we want what we need and that our willingness to learn is more powerful than our group loyalty. If it isn't, our efforts are likely to subvert our own best intentions as we destroy one another for selfish reasons. When we obsess about petty differences, we enter the onramp to the abyss. There is a sad bit of irony in the fact that people who do not learn to think critically become intuitively suspicious of people who do think deeply. And herein lies one of Emerson's examples of an unappreciated strength becoming a weakness: Our social need for connections with others is so strong that we act overtly against others to cement our own group bonds.

Everything we witness and experience in art, literature, music, meditation, computer simulation, sports, Masterpiece Theatre, and reality television—all can be argued to have aesthetic appeal. All of these activities can seem to stop the world and arrest the will, just as when we witness a sunset or lie on the deck of an ocean vessel watching white sails and sea-spray in the moonlight. Their effects, however, are directly related to the learning we have achieved in terms of furthering our ability for appreciation. Although it is crystal clear that some of these activities are superior in enabling us as individuals to enhance our understanding and therefore the conditions of our lives, they cannot, and do not, regardless of the millions of words of rhetoric in support of their superiority, demonstrate that one person is better than another because of them.

Schopenhauer's attribution of the aesthetic value of objects of art as being responsible for an elevated sense of appreciation amounts in some cases, no doubt, to a learned appreciation—a sophistication of one's capacity to derive meaning. For example, after we study classical music or opera, we increase our depth of appreciation and thus our capacity for future enjoyment of such music. But, in a practical sense, the result may amount to nothing more than an occasional minor difference in brainwave activity. So, even in the best case, it is learning and not the natural superiority of the individual that should be the major focus. In other words, this realization pulls the rug out from under the predominant reasons for snobbery. Absent the desperate need to separate ourselves into classes distinct from one another, the fact that every person has the capacity to increase their aesthetic appreciation of the arts should make it obvious that there should be more emphasis on learning than on class distinction. Moreover, aesthetic appreciation may be deeply rewarding and meaningful to the nth degree, but there is no objective way to prove that one person's experience is better than another's. Even though our predisposition to believe the contrary is one of nature's most compelling and seemingly self-evident notions, proving that one person is better than another because of what they perceive is a higher philosophical hurdle than getting an ought from an is.

Attributing aesthetic value comes after the contemplation of great beauty, when we embellish our experience as a way of justifying the sense of superiority we thought all along that we already had. We imagine ourselves seeing what others don't, won't, or seem unable to see, appreciate, or articulate. Mihaly Csikszentmihalyi captures something similar to the essence of this phenomenon when he describes optimal learning.[180] Here the process is just difficult enough to keep one interested but not so hard as to discourage the effort. Although one's learning and satisfaction increase with sophistication, the state of flow remains what it is, just as when we're dumbstruck by the beauty of a sunrise. And even this we do through a learned response of aesthetic comparisons to all of the other sunrises we have witnessed. Likewise with any and all kinds of infatuation: over time the devotee requires more input and greater amounts of a substance or activity to achieve the degree of bliss that makes the essence enchanting. But here again, when satiation is achieved, the feeling of being elevated is what it is, nothing more. To claim that one person's appreciative experience is better than another's is just untenable.

All of the attribution that we later apply to explain our superiority of taste is just arrogance dressed up as a wishful and wistful misreading. When we start trying to analyze the relative worth of individuals using aesthetics, we can't avoid the slippery slope of endless tit-for-tat comparisons, where one side offers the uneducated Marine who gives his life in service to his country against the MBA who goes to jail for embezzlement. It's a no-win argument, too foolish to consider entering into. It is likewise foolish to think that if every person of every social class suddenly gravitated toward high art, the old-school elites would not ratchet-up

the rhetoric of aesthetics to a level that no one but themselves could interpret. Even if they could not understand
their own pretentious illusions, they would never let on.

Simply stated, better off does not mean better than, no
matter how sophisticated the argument is for making it
seem obvious—even when it comes to an appreciation of
the arts. In his book *What Good Are the Arts?*, John Carey
writes, "Taste is so bound up with self-esteem, particularly
among devotees of high art, that a sense of superiority to
those with 'lower' tastes is almost impossible to relinquish
without risk of identity crisis."[181] Identity crisis, indeed.
Snobbery is the epitome of I-It relating, and it reeks of better than. The sacredness attributed to high art is embedded with a thinly veiled contempt, a malicious derision for
those who are thought to be excluded from its appreciation, and this is often expressed with breathtaking arrogance. Carey debunks the pretentiousness of those who
claim superiority because of aesthetic sensibility as easily
as one bursts a burgeoning balloon with a scalpel. But he
defends literature as art precisely because it is the only
form of art capable of criticizing itself, "the only art capable
of reasoning."[182]

The generative task of September University is to break
the self-selecting social codes we have erected for preserving a Stone Age mentality that should have stayed on the
plains of Africa. It's time to put aside the cultural contempt
that comes to us so easily. Think of it as excess psychological baggage that needs to be discarded with great care.
Appreciating arts and entertainment while giving up our
contemptuousness for the tastes of others is a lot like giving up smoking—it takes a lot of effort and persistence.
But, in the end, it is every bit as worthwhile because the
negative effect of cultural contempt is the moral equivalent
of cancer.

Let me be clear about this. I'm not saying that an uneducated opinion is as valid as an educated opinion when it
comes to aesthetics. What I'm suggesting is that the history

of our experience with art is more about status and distinguishing between us and them than it is about the true value of art. If we examine art from the perspective of evolutionary psychology, then it's clear that we have some serious work to do to make up for our archaic tendency to act as if we're still living in small tribes, fearing that the very continuation of people in other tribes threatens our existence.[183] We still use art and entertainment as obsessive cultural weapons to separate ourselves from all but the members of our own class or group.[184] The sooner we admit this and get this maladjustment out of the way, the sooner we may achieve something that deserves to call itself civilization and high culture.

To clarify further, neither am I saying that we should not strive to create and appreciate great art. On the contrary, we should pursue the arts with greater vigor than ever before, but we should substitute the natural contempt that comes to us so easily with the reality that it's our capacity for aesthetic appreciation that binds us as one people, not what we know specifically that others don't. Aesthetic sophistication dramatically enhances our ability to experience quality in all facets of life and art, but we are less connected by the acquisition of special knowledge than by the *capacity for appreciation*. If you watch Mark Johnson and Jonathan Walls' *Playing for Change* DVD, this position will become profoundly clear. The faculty for rapt attention—for being lost in time, in a state of mesmerizing awe and wonder—*this* is what makes us unique and in a sense human, not the knowledge or experience that brings it about per se, even though these things can reinforce our affiliation. If Schopenhauer had focused on this point instead of presenting aesthetic distraction as the Holy Grail of our species, I suspect he would not be thought of today as a philosopher of pessimism.

Many of the sophisticated ideas we have about the arts come to us from the Age of the Enlightenment. We tend to view that period as a time when thinking seemed a more rigorous activity. It is indeed ironic that we would need to go back that far to break a code of pretentiousness that still causes so much grief and misunderstanding. But we are smarter today. We know enough about human psychology to realize that our evolutionary baggage is sabotaging us through an inability to discern that people are people; it's simply self-justifying pretension to believe that so few deserve so much while so many have so little. Drop the animosity and contempt between the educated and uneducated, and the cultural barriers that perpetuate ignorance will dissolve as quickly as ice melts into water when the temperature rises. We know today without a shadow of doubt that learning increases our sophistication for aesthetic experience, so why do we still rely so heavily on class distinction by disparaging segments of our society as less than worthy instead of insisting on better access to education for everyone?[185]

I'm belaboring this social predicament because there is a parallel phenomenon that can be even more malevolent than misdirected hostility toward those we mistakenly blame for our anxiety: namely, the willingness and eagerness of undiscerning people to embrace simple-minded clichés, platitudes, and politically contrived distractions in order to avoid dealing with existential problems altogether. When we can face the abyss on our own, we are less vulnerable to manipulation by zealots, tyrants, and dogmatists. If we can put snobbery in perspective, once and for all, and embrace the compassion that our great religions preach but don't always practice, we can experience the wonder of existence through a new cultural awakening that begins by appreciating art for art's sake and the humanities for the sake of civilization. And if we can fully understand the human frailty that plays to our worst instincts, we can add a whole new dimension to the idea of thoughtfulness in the fall and winter of life.

The subject of art has been especially problematic in that the creativity that drives the process is often perceived by those fearful of change as something that's occurring near the edge of the abyss. In *The Creating Brain*, neuroscientist Nancy C. Andreasen reminds us that creative people are open to experience, tolerant of ambiguity, and relatively free of preconceptions—traits that make them seem odd and on the edge of mental illness to those who profess the need for a rigidly ordered society.[186] And, in *The Power of Art*, Simon Schama tells us that great art roughs up our sensibilities, shatters our complacency, and shifts our attention, often to matters we don't want to consider.[187]

So, it seems obvious to me that if we can embrace a little uncertainty and learn together without pretension, we can aspire to be citizens of the world, in no small part because the world of art is binding upon us. We can rethink our goals, light a fire in our minds as individuals, and achieve the kind of elitism that William Henry III aspired to—a passion-driven quest for mastery—a qualitative and joyful existence made possible by striving for excellence, for something worthwhile, for work and art for the sake of us all. But this is not to be confused with the sociopathic ethos of being a winner pathetically portrayed by reality television participants in trying to outmaneuver and outmanipulate one another in order to come out on top. In my view, human aesthetics realized have the potential to represent the idealization of I-You relating and offer a new opportunity for us to think of ourselves as better citizens, far better citizens than those portrayed by the caricatures of popular culture. Such potential represents the core value of existentialism, in that civilization is achieved, not through a herd mentality of conformity, but by and through the motivated intellectual pursuits of individuals en masse.

Sorting through the metaphysics of our human predispositions, our ideas about character, and the grave nature of the problems we face is a challenge worthy of those of us in the September of life. How do you want to live? What kind of world do you want to leave for your children and grandchildren? How do we help them learn to break the cultural codes that foster ethnocentrism, oppression, and debilitating anxiety? How do we help them to recognize hurtful illusions? How do we help our descendants bridge the existential divide among believers and nonbelievers? What can they learn from our failures that might lead to a just world?

THIRTEEN

SOCIAL JUSTICE

*Every college student should be able to
answer the following question: What is the relation
between science and the humanities, and how
is it important for human welfare?*

EDWARD O. WILSON

To everything there is a season. The last baby boomer will turn sixty-five in 2029, at which time many of the leading-edge boomers (those born in 1946) will still be alive. This means that members of this generation will be experiencing the fall and winter of life well into the second quarter of this century. What the baby-boom generation may have accomplished in the past pales in comparison to the possibilities for the future. My hope is that the Sept-U generation's contribution will have a lasting influence throughout that period.

In 1999, Marc Freedman published *Prime Time: How Baby Boomers Will Revolutionize Retirement and Transform America.* Since then, I have frequently heard doubts expressed about such enthusiastic predictions, but I believe it's premature to second guess the changes the aging baby-boom generation will initiate.[188] Freedman refers to the coming "long gray wave" as "a solution waiting to happen," and he founded Civic Ventures to help provide seniors with increasing involvement in their communities.[189]

163

The late Ernest Becker said that our human aspirations are mostly fiction and that our freedom is a fabrication for which we pay a price. At the same time, he thought the most wondrous thing about us is that we have come to understand our pretentiousness. That future historians would record this discovery as occurring in our lifetime would amount to one of the most liberating breakthroughs in history.[190] In other words, the ability to see ourselves as we really are is the only hope we have for a lasting legacy.

It's not clear to me whether every college student should have an answer to the question posed in the opening epigraph for this chapter, although I wish it were true. Every adult, however, who has reached the half-century mark in age on this planet should have an opinion, and the fact that many can't, don't, or won't, represents one of the greatest threats there is to humanity.

SOCIAL CONSCIENCE AND CIVIC RESPONSIBILITY

Mention civil disobedience, and most people think of Martin Luther King Jr. or Mahatma Gandhi. But, a hundred years before their time, Henry David Thoreau was its champion. Thoreau was very nearly an anarchist, and his scorn for government has caused him to be greatly misunderstood.

In his essay "Civil Disobedience," published in 1849, Thoreau argues that the government that governs best is the one that "governs not at all." People who misinterpret his work stop there, failing to recognize that what he really advocated was "better government." His notion of better government required superior constituents. King and Gandhi knew exactly what he meant. In a country made up of citizens like Thoreau, there would be no need for much government at all. And in such a society, institutions like slavery would be impossible.

Thoreau's essay was a clarion call for development of a social conscience by each and every member of society, not just by victims of oppression and injustice. He asks, "Must the citizen even for a moment, or in the least degree, resign his conscience to the legislator? Why has every man a conscience, then? . . . The only obligation which I have a right to assume is to do at any time what I think right."

Beyond the oppressors themselves, Thoreau also held accountable those who benefited from the oppression, regardless of whether they had anything to do with creating the injustice. By extension, the concept of nonviolence is first and foremost like that of the physician's oath: first to do the patient no harm. The first measure of nonviolence, then, is not to participate in oppression. If your bank discriminates against minorities, for example, move your account.

Thoreau's philosophy was about accepting responsibility. Beyond the evils inherent in government, he decried the lack of public awareness and of felt responsibility among the free citizens of his time. Little has changed. For example, turn your television to the financial news and you will hear about arbitrage, leveraged multiples, short selling, buyouts, derivatives, subprime, Alt-A, and option ARM loans discussed in jargon so complex as to defy comprehension. And yet, the majority of people who strain to understand these convoluted concepts cannot conceive that people who enjoy the advantage of this system bear any responsibility for setting it right. In a further illustration, anyone who thinks that slavery and the legal segregation that followed it has not had lasting negative effects on subsequent generations of African-Americans has not given it enough thought. Economic justice requires thinking about fairness with as much intellectual rigor and enthusiasm as should have been applied to Wall Street investments before public indifference led to a financial meltdown. It requires slicing the pie without knowing which piece we will get.

Thoreau allowed that each of us might pursue legitimate interests without taking up the banner of a particular injustice.[191] At the very least, he argued, we have a duty to stop benefiting from the disadvantage of others. Simply put, he holds each of us responsible for the society we live in today. It matters not a whit to Thoreau that you and I weren't a party to establishing the institutions that continue to perpetuate injustices through discrimination and exclusion. That we benefit from them today, in ignorance of our own culpability, is not an excuse. King and Gandhi understood the power of injustice brought to light. They knew that nonviolent protest—especially when those who protest are mistreated—will rekindle social conscience in anyone who harbors any semblance of honesty.

More than a century has passed since Thoreau published "Civil Disobedience," yet millions of Americans remain unmoved to figure out for themselves what is just and unjust. The sophomoric sense of citizenship embraced by too many for too long is a freedom *from*—a poverty-stricken sense of freedom which focuses on what each of us has a right to escape at the expense of responsibility we should own. People who deny their culpability for slavery, because they were not yet born when it was practiced, find it hard to comprehend that they, as citizens, are responsible for what's extant today. If injustices are still present as a result of the institution of slavery, then each of us has the duty to discover the cause, the effect, and the remedy.

The Sept-U generation of aging adults has the demographic muscle to set an agenda for a sophisticated review of human welfare not just in America but for the planet. As a fourth culture we have the power to influence what media pundits will want to tell us about. We don't have to wait each day for news networks to tell us what is important. We have the power to choose the subject matter and to change it at will. Demographically we are in the catbird seat, and through our progeny we have an enormous investment at stake. We need to make long-term decisions now to ensure that our children and grandchildren will have a qualitative future. For us this goal means everything and nothing—

everything because the lives of our progeny depend upon what we do; nothing because we will not live to see all of the results of our efforts. This disengagement can help us discuss the issues rationally. Perhaps in the process we can also help bring about a more civil society.

CULTURE KEEPING

It's often said that psychology was the theology of the twentieth century. What I hope might be said someday of the twenty-first century is that it was a time when the world awakened to the idea that every person who has a psyche needs to be familiar with the latest theories about human behavior. During my lifetime, fundamental assumptions about human behavior have been kicked around like a soccer ball—from one goalpost to the next. New theories often bear little resemblance or relation to the ones they replace.

Throughout my years of self-study, I've been drawn over and over to the deeply integral function of human emotions and their visceral connection to the intellect. Spinoza once said that "a passion is an inadequate idea."[192] In *How the Mind Works*, Steven Pinker writes about the emotions from the perspective of the evolution theory and reverse engineering. He argues that "emotions are adaptations, well-engineered software modules that work in harmony with the intellect and are indispensable to the functioning of the whole mind."[193]

Despite our increasingly technologically capable society, we are still inherently tribalistic in a psychological sense. We learn so much about the world in scientific terms that it's easy to forget what our psychic apparatus was designed for—and how it distorts reality and our relationship to others. Even in practical matters, we don't really seem to understand how our penchant for keeping our culture operates or how best to use it. When I'm driving and see another car enter an intersection erratically, and then notice the driver is talking on a cell phone, it makes me angry.[194] Likewise, I feel the same way when I witness someone speeding in a residential area, passing illegally, or going too slowly in the fast lane. It's not just because I'm a former police officer that someone running a red light in a flagrant manner makes me want to follow and stop them. There are rules for behavior that must be followed, or the rest of us are put in jeopardy. My feelings are similar when I encounter reality shows on TV, or public humiliation for profit, as I tend to regard it. Reality television, in my view, is the psychological equivalent of putting people in cages and poking them with sharp objects.

Increasingly I hear the term *aggressive altruism* used to describe what I'm feeling when I experience this kind of anger. David Berreby says, "The desire to transmit regulations appears to be a universal human trait, found in all societies."[195] In terms of psychological evolution, this tendency seems to be a necessary ingredient for keeping, shaping, and conserving culture. I might go so far as to suggest that this kind of behavior is where the term conservative originates. Unfortunately it is difficult or sometimes dangerous to express criticism in public. Within a family or a small group, a raised eyebrow or a stern look by a parent or an elder is often all that is necessary to change or modify the behavior of individuals. But in a multicultural society, people even refrain from making eye-contact in public places. I suspect that part of the fascination with reality television is that it puts strangers in awkward situations that are uncommon to everyday experience. Perhaps most of us know intuitively that public criticism is a Stone Age remnant integral to the keeping of culture. Where do we draw the line for criticism?

Perhaps we could change the nature of the inquiry. Instead of complaining about something someone does to endanger our safety, like talking on a cell phone while driving, what if we took issue with something they don't do, like vote or take their civic responsibility seriously? What if they spend all of their leisure hours watching soap operas, wrestling, golf, or NASCAR races? Should this kind of behavior raise our ire? Don't people need to fulfill their duty as citizens? When comedians interview people on the street who seem ignorant beyond belief, should we be angry? Don't people need to be knowledgeable about what is going on in their community and the world? How do we contain our annoyance and withhold contempt for people who fail to do what we think they are supposed to do? We're troubled not about what they are doing but about what they are failing to do. Where do we look for guidance for sorting out this kind disconnect with our fellow citizens?

I suggest we need to look no further than our own families for the answer to these questions. Until we can extend to people we consider others the same consideration as we do our next of kin for being acceptable and worthy of enough equity to live, regardless of what they do or fail to do, then we will be unsuccessful at transforming our annoyance and our anger into a form of disapproval that's constructive. We may be disappointed in our family members or our close friends and associates when they do not live up to our standards of what we believe people should and should not do, but we readily forgive their faults and repeatedly provide them with the benefit of the doubt. Of course, some indiscretions require that we maintain our anger without concession. Commission of a crime, for example, is not so easily forgiven. But it doesn't take a lot of reflection to acknowledge the slack we apply to those who are close to us nor to realize how inconsistent we are with regard to those we view as others.

I propose that a primary goal for Sept-U participants is to figure out how to encourage people to obey the laws and rules necessary for navigating our way through everyday life without escalating these incidents into psychosocial altercations. How do we appeal to our fellow citizens to use common courtesy and return to civility? Perhaps we should apply some more work on ourselves first.

SENIORS AND CIVILITY

Ever since it was first built, the post office in the small community where I live has been plagued by inadequate parking space. Traffic has increased exponentially over the years, and yet each day as cars line up, people already in the parking lot sit in their cars reading their mail. They remain all but oblivious that traffic is backing up, even though a short time earlier they were also waiting. Perhaps it's just an artifact of my age, and I could be mistaken, but forty or fifty years ago I don't think people were this inconsiderate. It gets worse. Inside the post office, it's now routine to expect that at any moment someone will begin talking on a cell phone in a voice loud enough to be heard a half-block away, often discussing intimate matters. Again, I'm perplexed to understand where such lack of consideration comes from. To me it's an extreme intrusion on my privacy to be included in the details of another's personal life, especially when I'm in a place where I cannot escape without losing something, such as my place in line.

In another example, I've always hurried up whenever I've noticed I'm blocking the way, whether I'm in a vehicle or on foot. I was taught that it's just common courtesy. I don't, however, think it's my imagination these days that occasionally, when I pull up to an intersection, the person crossing the street in front of me downshifts into a purposefully slower walk. It makes me wish I had a horn capable of blasting them out of their shoes.[196] But then, that wouldn't likely do much for civility's sake.

Looking back a half-century, I can recall a time when it seemed people went to extraordinary efforts to avoid being rude. Common courtesy used to be a fundamental element of child-rearing. Parents, grandparents, and even strangers would remind young people when they forgot to mind their manners. How did common courtesy skip so many generations? (Then again, the last person I recall who used her cell phone as if she were the only person within earshot must have been fifty.)

Mark Twain once said that a prerequisite for courtesy was that we must "admire the human race." What will it take to restore our mutual admiration? And what can we do to regain the civility lost? Put up billboards? Use bumper stickers? Ask for legislation? As tempting as such ideas sound, I think the answer rests instead with the groundswell of Sept-U participants who have the will to revitalize retirement and transform society.

Here are some possibilities: Whenever we find ourselves in any situation where our actions will affect others, imagine that our grandparents, or even great-grandparents, are watching us. If we listen hard, I suspect we can hear them offer bits of wisdom: something about common courtesy, politeness, the golden rule. As we cross the road, we may imagine that they whisper, "Hurry along." And as we begin talking on our cell phone, they will murmur, "Lower your voice; it's not polite to speak as if you are alone when others are present." Could restoring civility be so easy? I believe the process works similarly to priming a pump, meaning that you have to do something to get it started. Like set a good example.

I'm hopeful because Sept-U members have already discovered the notion of random acts of kindness. Purposeful acts of courtesy can produce the same kind of result. I daresay that all of us will find it easier to admire the human race if the people crossing the road acquire a spring in their step as they get out of our way and talk on their cell phones as if what they have to say is a secret. Civility seems like such a small thing, and yet, without it the whole world seems so hostile that we are ill disposed to be ourselves.

Elsewhere I've written that in many ways we are a more moral society than ever before in history.[197] The current lack of civility, in my view, stems from two primary reasons. The first is that people exhibit rude behavior simply from a lack of awareness of and consideration for other people. This is the case with most of the examples above, and they are the easiest to fix. The second is a much more difficult problem rising from the rippling waves of disrespect that reverberate throughout the hierarchical echelons of societies with too much of a gap between rich and poor. These stressful expressions play out stereotypically as someone at the top level of an organization who lashes out at a subordinate, who passes it on to those beneath him until someone who is without power at the bottom winds up kicking a dog. Addressing this kind of societal stress requires a long-term approach aimed at increasing the equity for those at the bottom of society. The wisest philosophers and theologians among us have long argued that the virtue and moral good of any nation can be judged by how it treats its poor. Thus civility is a precursor to genuine civilization.

Perhaps the most important thing to keep in mind about civility and posterity is that the kind of I-You relating that best results in civility is established as an integral part of childhood education. Respect for others provides the very grounds for I-You relating, and when it receives enough emphasis, it has the power to set one generation after another on a path to maturity through meaningful and mutually respectful relationships. Civility, in other words, is social experience akin to quality.

FOURTEEN

MEANING AND POTENTIAL

To live only for some future goal is shallow.
It's the sides of the mountain
that sustain life, not the top.

ROBERT M. PIRSIG

MATURITY AND QUALITY

The late Viktor Frankl, a psychotherapist and survivor of three Nazi concentration camps, dedicated his life to the subject of meaning in terms of human experience and perspective. Long ago he asserted that it is in the very nature of human beings to search for meaning and that we have hope of finding it right up until the moment of our last breath. Frankl's book *Man's Search for Meaning* has sold millions of copies since World War II, but it's a mistake to assume that it was strictly his imprisonment that fostered his interest in the subject of ultimate meaning and the wonder of existence. Frankl was intrigued by the subject even as a child. I've read nearly all of his books, and it is my impression that the heart of his whole enterprise of logotherapy (or meaning therapy) lies in simply helping people become genuinely interested in their own lives—not in a sense of self-absorption but rather in the context of society, in a world of societies.

Frankl thought it was the duty of psychologists to help people find meaning. He often used the analogy of a dwarf standing on the shoulder of a giant to make the point that in doing so the dwarf can still see farther than the giant. Indeed, from more than 2,000 years of recorded history we have a wide variety of giants onto whose shoulders we can easily climb if we so choose. If you haven't already begun, there is no better time to begin than at the point in life when your life experience beckons examination from its sheer weight.

Long before it became popular to speak of family values, Frankl addressed the subject in the context of three chief groups: The first is what we *give* the world in terms of our creation; the second is what we *take*; and the third is in the *stands we take*.[198] September University is a setting for taking a stand, and enrollment, as we've seen, comes automatically with age. On a large enough scale, a September University frame of mind could amount to a re-enlightenment in the twenty-first century that matches or surpasses that of the rigorous intellectual contribution of the eighteenth century.

What I have come to understand as two of life's greatest lessons are both simple and complex contradictions. The first lesson is that life is not now, never has been, nor likely ever will be *fair*. Even reaching a consensus on the definition of fairness can be difficult. Nevertheless, we must devote our lives, our ideas, and our actions toward making it fair. For the sake of all humans, now and in the future, this is necessary and even critical. The second lesson is that, no matter how much we learn, we are fated to a life that future generations will describe as ignorant in some fashion. We will not succeed in nailing reality to the wall no matter how hard we try. We will never learn with confidence everything that we need to know. And yet, in the style of the first lesson, the very quality of our lives as individuals and as a society depends upon our acting and behaving as if those achievements are possible.

It is common practice for millions of people to spend a fortune learning what is free for anyone to learn whose desire is strong enough to settle for nothing less than a meaningful existence. Careers aside, it is an open secret that the learning most critical to life is free for the taking, if one is resolute about doing so. Still, large numbers of people behave as if this isn't true.

Many years ago, Robert M. Pirsig wrote *Zen and the Art of Motorcycle Maintenance,* a philosophical road trip of sorts that dealt with ideas of ultimate value and the metaphysics of human aspirations. Pirsig observed that the quality of our existence is, in part, a measure of our appreciation for complexity and our ability to achieve a method of mindfulness that enables us to be alive in the moment and thus derive Quality from experience. I've pondered the underlying thesis of Pirsig's book for years, and I think I've come up with an explanation in parallel with the notion of maturity that I hope is much clearer and more useful. Bear with me for a moment, and I will return to this idea.

Every living creature on our planet is faced with the same dilemma: survival. Every living being has a DNA blueprint that limits its potential, and very few earth creatures reach their full maturity. It may be worse than very few; it may be closer to none, because the reality is that conditions have to be very nearly perfect for each living entity to achieve the full realization of its capacity for development. In this sense, life represents an aspirational trajectory. For example, for a plant to reach the apex of its physical maturity, it has to have precisely the right amount of nutrients, oxygen, water, and sunshine, and it has to receive them at the right time. Clearly it's difficult for a plant to live up fully to its design. Living sentient creatures not only have to meet the criteria above, but they also have windows of opportunity for multiple types of learning, some of which, if not opened at precisely the right time, may remain closed forever. Learning language is but one example; it's far easier for children to learn a new language than it is for adults. In cases where infants are not able to see during the early stages of life, a lifetime of blindness is often the result, even if later nothing is physically wrong with their eyes.

Life in all its manifestations is an effort to *be*, a strain to exist, and although the quest for power is an ingredient, at times power is beside the point.[199] Sometimes what one needs most is not power but the essential substances that make our lives possible.

Maturity and Pirsig's notion of seeking Quality are parallel drives for strength, faultlessness, purity, and the intellectual appreciation of these things, all rolled into one. Maturity and Quality are both expressed in matters of degree, as each and every creature begins life with a path toward adulthood, but few if any achieve what is possible in absolute terms of their potential. Nietzsche's "will to power" pales in comparison to being what one can, could, and would be, if only one could truly be what one was designed to be.[200] To my mind, this quirky aspiration lies at the heart of the exhilaration that millions of people felt the first time they read *Zen and the Art of Motorcycle Maintenance*. The story merely hinted at greater aspirations for being and thinking in the world, but it hit a nerve. It still reverberates among people who are grasping for something meaningful—something beyond the mediocrity of culturally induced daily existence. This aspirational quest is also to be found in Plato's theory of forms, which David Denby likened in *Great Books* to a "longing for God."[201]

In my view, Pirsig's notion of Quality is simply mindfulness and aspiration bound together by a straining for comprehension that enables one to experience a measure of excellence. It's too bad that so many people who were awakened by Pirsig went back to sleep before they realized that they were on the trail of the quest for maturity. Quality, maturity, and a sense of having mattered are, I suspect, all components of the same thing.

Human culture professes to promote maturity but in fact

impedes it. It often takes an extraordinary level of contrariness to see what we might see naturally without the force of cultural officialdom that envelops us. For centuries the evidence for evolution was everywhere humans looked, and yet it took Charles Darwin to explain what his contemporaries could not see. Likewise the theory of plate tectonics: once it has been explained and you look at a globe of the earth with its puzzle-piece characteristics, you can't imagine why you didn't see it before. Or take Jared Diamond's theory of the development of human culture and why some cultures are wealthy and some are poor.[202] Once you've heard professor Diamond's thesis, you regret that someone had to point out what seems always to have been so obvious.

There are limits to our physical development and perhaps to the parameters of our intelligence, but for all practical purposes our capacity for furthering our understanding and comprehension of all matters of importance is very nearly infinite. A better view is always to be had for those who go to the trouble to look. In human terms this is why maturity is a matter of degree and why it and the metaphysics of Quality are forever aspirations. Humankind has moved through the centuries in fits and starts with countless wars, senseless destruction, and often with little regard for the generations to follow. So many of us fall so far short in our intellectual efforts to better understand the world that society as a whole suffers needlessly from our collective ignorance. Ignorance at best is corrosive to character; at worst it's cancerous. One of life's greatest paradoxes is how creatures with the capacity to be so thoughtful can be so thoughtless. The purpose of September University is to reverse these trends.

ON THE CUSP OF PROBLEM SOLVING

So, how do we use our maturity and our understanding of the concept of Quality to ensure a culture of thoughtfulness? How do we turn the ship of thoughtfulness into the wind so that we can launch an effort to apply intelligence where it is needed so badly? In a nutshell, it's time to admit we need to start thinking for ourselves with sufficient effort to break the primitive Stone Age codes we use automatically for purposes of group selection. None of us as individuals are so smart or well educated that we can't learn from other people and other cultures. We need to engage in a vigorous dialogue with others that can and will yield affection for conversation. Moreover, since our stake in the long-term future will be realized only after we are long gone, we should be able to learn how to negotiate our way to the better argument by putting hot-button issues into a perspective that will enable us to discuss them rationally, compassionately, and with some semblance of ethical objectivity.

A lucid discussion with those whose worldviews differ radically from our own is critical to the notion of maturity and quality. Granted, reaching a consensus to accept the authority of the better argument is both ambitious and, in many cases, overly idealistic. Even so, I believe we can live together peacefully in a world where we understand one another without the need for being in agreement or condoning one another's views. First, though, we have to talk. In his book *Cosmopolitanism*, philosopher Kwame Anthony Appiah puts it like this: "Conversations across boundaries of identity—whether national, religious, or something else—begin with the sort of imaginative engagement you may get when you read a novel or watch a movie or attend to a work of art that speaks from some place other than your own. . . . Conversation doesn't have to lead to consensus about anything, especially not values; it's enough that it helps people get used to one another."[203] Appiah uses the word *conversation* in both a literal and a metaphorical sense for engaging others, reinforcing the concept of thinking of art as a social summit. Simply put, art contains the commutative power to transcend cultural differences.

Say we push our differences and ideological boundaries to the extreme, to the farthest reaches of us and them, all the way to the kind of clash that results in acts of terrorism. What then, in the face of irresolvable conflict, is the value of the better argument? It's still critical and practical, in my view. The idea put forth by some politicians that terrorists hate us for our freedom is too simplistic.[204] Terrorists are terrorists because they have been radicalized by their perception of injustice of one kind or another.[205] Their reasons for believing and behaving as they do may seem illogical, even bizarre, and we may never be able to have a rational dialogue with them. But if we do not know what they believe and why they believe as they do, then we have no means to begin a conversation or the means with which to stem the tide of new converts to their beliefs.

To respond to acts of terrorism with a resolve to declare a "war on terrorism" is a grave error; it amounts to an egregious misuse of metaphor. All of the terrorists associated with 9/11 should have been hunted down as criminals. Declaring a war on their behalf adds to their importance, giving them prestige they are not due. They are not warriors; they are thugs and criminals. Worse still, declaring war on a tactic guarantees failure because it sets up a contest that cannot, by its very nature, be won. Declaring a war on terror is like declaring a war on tornados. Tornados, like acts of terror, occur when conditions are ripe for their development. The best defense against both is intelligence and a complete understanding of what causes them, because it allows for time to warn the public of the former and offers time for intervention in the case of the latter. It's not necessary to wait for a crime to occur to take preemptive action against criminals. Terrorists are criminals. Period. Try as we might, with all of the reason and resolve we can muster, there are human conflicts that cannot be addressed without returning to the abyss and resorting to the annihilation of enemies. But when this occurs, the only way to cease the destruction is through a resumption of dialogue.

It may seem to be a stretch, but engaging in a meaningful dialogue with those with opposing worldviews reaches all

of the way back to the exhilaration of the wonder of existence. The reason is simple yet intricate. It's not our similarities and common needs that kindle our humanity so much
as our capacity for continuing our interactive conversation
and the realization that this narrative is essential to our
imagination. The friction generated by our storylines is the
art that keeps the turnstiles of history moving. We may not
appreciate each other's stories for what they say, but we can
value and fully comprehend that the need for these accounts
is deep enough that we're willing to stop short of settling our
disagreements with violence. There follows the realization
that the novelty and variation in our historical narratives are
what sustain our imagination. From this arises the interior
craving that drives our desire for knowledge and education.

In a C-Span2 television appearance on *Book TV*, religious scholar Karen Armstrong spoke of an ancient Indian
tradition in which priests engaged in a competitive dialogue
using formulaic riddles in an attempt to describe ultimate
reality. One would speak, followed by another, until the
profundity of what was said reduced the participants to
silence. And thus, Armstrong suggests, dialogue should
lead to "silence, awe, and appreciation," because it's in the
moments of stillness when we really learn about the values
we have in common.[206] Simply put, it is not violence but
conversation and the thoughtfulness achieved through dialogue that can produce knowledge, reflection, and feelings
of commonality that move us toward civilization. Common
good is derived from common ground, which is itself a
result of an I-Thou-I-You kind of relating that overrides I-It
and inspires the becoming of *us*. One need look no further
than the confederation for Internet neutrality to observe a
side-by-side alliance of groups as diverse as the Christian
Coalition, the ACLU, and Moveon.org.[207]

At a most fundamental level, the way I envision a
September University movement getting underway is
threefold: First, we get the message across to media about
what is and is not worthy of our attention. The second goal

is breaking the codes to identify the Stone Age biases that are still presented and represented in literature, cinema, and art in all of its forms. And finally, we engage as many Sept-U participants with as many divergent points of view as possible in an ongoing public dialogue in order to get to and fine-tune the discussion. John Adams and Thomas Jefferson, our second and third presidents respectively, were political rivals, but they corresponded for a half-century in a dialogue to further their ideas about what was best for America. In 1813 Adams wrote to Jefferson saying that they should not die before explaining themselves to one another.[208] There are no good reasons why we cannot do so as well. Sept-U is an opportunity to redefine the role of senior citizens.

In the movie classic *Doctor Zhivago*, set during the Russian Revolution, Julie Christie, who plays Lara, at one point expresses the sorrowful sentiment that it "is an awful time to be alive." The same could be said today for people around the world who have suffered severe economic hardship, people who live in the embattled Middle East, or those in any number of countries on the African continent ravaged by war and famine. But if a person is fortunate enough to be economically well off, live in a prosperous developed nation, be well-educated, and have good health, it is truly an exciting time to live. While I don't pretend that technology will solve all of our most pressing problems, I do have tremendous respect and expectations for the future of technology. From biology and medicine to computer and rocket science, we are on the cusp of profound innovation.

That it is still an awful time to be alive for so many of our fellow citizens on this planet is a moral quandary of epic proportions, one that threatens every cultural pretension in every developed nation that does not acknowledge it as such. It's time to see past our artful aspirations and take a hard look at the footprint we are leaving behind. In his book *American Mania*, Peter C. Whybrow offers a powerful reminder: "Unwittingly, in our relentless pursuit of

happiness we have overshot the target and spawned a
manic society with an insatiable appetite for more.
America's dream of a Utopian social order—fueled from the
beginning by the twin beliefs that material success equates
with personal satisfaction (a notion that is embellished now
by a commercially contrived illusion of infinite opportunity)
and that technical advance is the key to social progress—
has become mired in a confusing mix of manic desire and
depressive discomfort."[209]

We have cracked the code of human DNA, and we are
tinkering near the point of significantly prolonging human
life. Our communication technologies have made the world
a very small place. Marshall McLuhan's global village may
be close to becoming a reality. We have broken the barrier
of species communication, having succeeded in teaching a
gorilla more than two thousand words in sign language.[210]
We have erected listening posts for alien civilizations in the
cosmos. We understand now, perhaps for the first time,
that our unmindful living excesses are polluting the global
environment, and we have made impressive technological
progress in lessening our destructive environmental footprint. If we had the will to do so, perhaps the most we can
get from technology now is to clean up the mess we have
already made. In practical reality we have the technological
wherewithal to deflect an asteroid headed for a collision
with the earth—something thought possible only through
intervention by the gods a short time ago. We dream of
terraforming other planets to make them earthlike in order
to send our kind among the stars.

Still, amid all of this aspiration, anticipation, and wonder, we continue to live in a world where poverty reigns
supreme for most of the people on the earth. The bottom
twenty percent of the earth's population are desperately
poor, just a few meals short of starvation, living on garbage
piles and drinking water so foul that just to imagine it is
nauseating. Professor Bjørn Lomborg of Denmark makes a
compelling case that in the developed world our highest

priorities should first be to do those things that cost the least and can do the most good, like helping developing countries with clean water, food production, and conquering disease.[211] These are matters of life and death. Remember the abyss? For as long as we are fearful of death and the existential nature of the human predicament, we will likewise remain unaware of the malignant nature of global poverty, and this unmindfulness will stand as a formidable barrier to both civilization and experiencing the wonder of existence.

My point is not to depress but to suggest, in the strongest terms possible, that to have any pretense of getting closer to our highest aspirations we cannot remain oblivious to the reality of suffering in the world or fail to attempt resolution. And for that to happen, to the extent that anything worthwhile comes of it, will require a re-ignition of curiosity among the members of Sept-U.

EQUITY AND TECHNOLOGY

Throughout history, moral leaders, both religious and secular, have argued persuasively that human beings are not to be used simply as a means to an end, but are in fact ends in themselves, and no one made a better case than Kant. In other words, we humans should be considered more important than our tools. So far, however, the engine of global capitalism is a transparent demonstration of the reverse. The thrall of money as the valuation of all values long ago surpassed religion as an ethos of ultimate value. Study the history of economics in America, and you will learn that capitalism in its present form is not a moral template that fell from the heavens to embellish virtuous behavior. Capitalism is instead an incredibly powerful system analogous to chemotherapy and radiation—powerful substances that can both cure and kill—but capitalism is arbitrarily maintained and manipulated by those already deemed winners within the system. If the power of those in power is not kept in check then, like chemotherapy and radiation, the cure is sometimes worse than the disease.

The Biblical injunction that those who do not work should not eat is rendered absurd by the realities of how markets behave in global economies. Indeed, the whole argument over economic shares amounts to the ethnocentric residue of agrarian societies. In those ancient communities, where life depended upon the whims of climate and environmental suitability for agriculture, able-bodied citizens unwilling to help might have doomed a community. Today, the opposite is true. In America food is plentiful and inexpensive, yet people pursue jobs that endanger the environment in order to buy food. There are notable exceptions, but most communities make little effort to ensure that jobs are congruent with sustainable environments.

If human beings are really to be considered more important than our need to trade, then the word *welfare* can't continue to be a pejorative term. Welfare defined simply amounts to a state of well-being. The welfare of human beings is radically important in a world where capital moves about freely in cyberspace and many of the activities we call work actually poison our surroundings. In the past, all of the blame for being without employment has fallen on the individual, while the system or the market as means has always had a free ride. Or, as John Kenneth Galbraith likely would have explained it, capitalism gives functional anonymity to those who exploit people in the name of profit. Indeed, just as capitalism is a great force for dynamism, so has it also been a tool for laundering conscience and sleight of hand as the public unwittingly funds private enterprise through what ironically has become known as corporate welfare.

But today, public understanding about how the world works is beginning to deepen. The financial crisis in the fall of 2008 was a wake-up call of epic proportions. In an increasingly wired world, where everyone watches in real time as the tidal waves of global capitalism crash on the shores of both large and small economies, the absence of virtue in our means is self-evident. The exploitation is obvious. Capital moving freely at high velocity around the world makes the distinctions between means and ends crystal clear. As the whim-ridden waves of speculation leave one community after another in shambles, it becomes blatantly transparent that corporations have become the only true entities with the status of ends.

Corporations have rights far beyond those of any individual. And so it turns out there is more than one road to serfdom: Anyone who thinks a world run by international corporations capable of wielding power greater than that of any government is not a recipe for serfdom is either mad or a CEO. While the Internet is surely no panacea for today's economic problems, it may of necessity demonstrate the wisdom of rigging our system of economics to meet the *needs* of all of our citizens cooperatively while we compete enthusiastically at the *want* level.

Complexity theorists tell us that we have reached a point in time where our successes in both public and private life require the functioning equivalent of open systems. By this they mean systems that thrive on feedback and real-time learning, and that do not rely on antiquated rules and ancient prejudices. Open systems are radically aware and dynamic enough to understand fully, without partiality, that meeting basic human needs head-on is less of a burden than avoiding the subject. They acknowledge that it is cheaper to give drugs to addicts in a controlled medical environment than to produce an economy dependent upon and fed by crime and by the creation of a "criminal industrial complex." They recognize that inclusive health care is by far more efficient, humane, and cost-effective than a system which leaves millions without. Indeed, a civilization that can't meet the needs of its most vulnerable citizens without a lot of whining and finger pointing is neither advanced nor civilized. Inequality, in point of fact, depends upon a surplus of disrespect. Thom

Hartmann puts it this way: "If a nation wants a middle class, it must define it, desire it, and work to both create it and keep it."[212] But to achieve a state without glaring inequality, in my view, requires a dramatic reduction of contempt and hostility among all individuals and groups who perceive of themselves or others as disrespected outsiders. The clichéd "We are all in this together" is spoken often but seldom aspired to or realized en masse.

What I've been describing is only an exaggerated inference. But the reality of the world today is that inequality is growing at a faster rate than at any time since the Great Depression. In America, the voices of low-wage workers are marginalized, while the poorest of the poor throughout the world are treated for all practical purposes as if they do not exist.

In an open system based upon inclusive data, and increasingly dependent upon unrelenting communication, poverty becomes too expensive to be endured. Our technologies have never held more promise. We are on the threshold of discovery in multiple disciplines that will have the capacity for improving the quality of our lives to levels that are very nearly incomprehensible. Yet we still have silly arguments about food and health care, as if certain human beings should forgo them when those basic commodities appear to come at *our* expense.

Though still unarticulated in a social context, the great stock bubble of overvalued Internet stocks in the 1990s, the housing bubble of 2008, and the predatory lending that has been ubiquitous in recent years were driven by more than just investor greed. There was and still is an air of anticipation that a wired world has great potentialities, though we have not yet figured out what they are. At the same time, the tired old arguments by those who try to justify growing inequality by harping about failures in education and skill shortages are becoming transparent as platitudes. The early years of a new century are an appropriate time to still the infantile argument about meeting basic human needs without obsessing over whether the recipients actually deserve it. There will always be people who take unfair advantage of any attempt to help people help themselves, just as there will always be people whose sacrifice for this country is all out of proportion with what they've taken from it. If you have doubts about this, take a walk through Arlington Cemetery.

Economic equity is the path to economic justice. And economic justice is not just a remanufactured notion of New Deal liberalism. Instead it is a calculated, mature declaration that preserving planet earth as a sustainable, healthy place for human habitation requires the same kind of inclusion that gives rise to great expectations about the Internet and broadband.

It was during the Cold War that Americans became so adversely sensitized to socialism as a step toward the implied evil of Communism that still to this day millions of people cannot discuss the subject rationally. Decades of Cold War paranoia and the red-scare tactics that led to McCarthyism, combined with unrelenting political propaganda between America and the former Soviet Union, became an ideological war internalized as good versus evil on both sides.

But what does the word *socialism* really mean? There are many theoretic varieties of socialism, but most revolve around economic systems in which cooperation trumps competition, and collective ownership trumps private property rights. The most extreme example of socialistic behavior is military service, in which members of the group are actually called upon frequently to give up their lives to save others. If you point this out during political discourse, however, you will likely be regarded as completely mad by those who still recoil at the mere mention of anything that appears to be overly shared. Military service is not generally thought of as socialistic, but that's indeed what it is.

Economic socialism is simply an ethos that enlarges the group and increases the equity of ownership on the part of individuals in the group. It's neither good nor evil in and of itself any more than capitalism is good or evil without regard to the conditions in which it operates. Social security is somewhat of a mixture of socialism and capitalism because what one receives in benefits is dependent in part on the amount of one's contribution.

The shrill mantra of free markets took a big ideological hit in the fall of 2008. The bailout legislation begun at the time intended to stave off a global financial crisis has done more to make a philosophical case for greater equity in the lower echelons of society than decades of clamoring for economic justice by liberal politicians. Of course, privatizing profits and socializing losses is nothing new; it's just the scale and visibility of these actions that make them seem so. The collusion of government and big business has been successful for many years in maximizing profit and minimizing the losses of the politically well-connected, mostly under the radar of public scrutiny. But now that bubble has burst. And although we have not heard the last from those who shout about the virtue of free markets and deregulation, their argument has lost authority. Survival of the fittest has been overwritten by the ubiquity of corruption. Unfettered markets discourage reasonable restraint.

In spite of all that has happened to America's financial infrastructure, a more equitable future for our citizens is still little more than an aspiration. If we gain a fairer system for a more just distribution of wealth—one that rewards work over capital and acknowledges that anyone who works full time is due a living wage—it will be because thoughtful citizens demand it.

In a world where human beings are really important, nothing less than inclusion is acceptable. In a communication-driven world, feedback is critical. Exclusion creates a false reality. If experience has taught us anything about economic reality, it is that an inclusive world is more cost-effective than one driven by short-term profit. Genuine democracy cannot and will not exist in America until such time as everyone is truly represented. Achieving this will derive from a well-thought-out, evenhanded measure of economic justice. If those of us in September University can't figure this problem out, then I fear no one will.

The great question is, what will it take in terms of human learning to reach a point where people all over the world begin to see the people of other nations as ends in themselves and not simply as a means to an end? It is a question worthy of the wonder of existence on a grand scale. If the poor can be provided for in an equitable enough way to eliminate *poor* as a category, then that very well might be the key to environmental sustainability. No doubt it would require a measure of thoughtfulness the likes of which we have never witnessed in the history of humanity.

Not long ago I heard a businessman being interviewed on National Public Radio about the problem of immigration and low wages. He complained about the fact that no one wanted to work for the wages he paid and so he was forced to use illegal aliens from Mexico. Twenty or thirty years ago I might have sympathized with his predicament. But listening to this complaint now, when I'm in my sixties, I wonder how we ever got so far out of whack with Kant's notion of treating people as ends in themselves. How can we accept it as normal and right that an entrepreneur can exploit desperate people with slave wages? Why does the injustice of it not eclipse his misfortune in not finding enough employees who are willing to work for next to nothing?

I find myself convinced now more than ever that any job that does not pay a living wage is an activity that is best left undone. Economists frequently speak of nonliving wages as if they are the result of an inevitable divine force that can't be stopped. This utter nonsense stems from internalizing academic texts without regard for the subtleties of power. Nonliving wages are the result of political power, or the lack of it, nothing less and nothing more. Nonliving wages represent the personification of I-It relating and an in-your-face declaration of *better than*. The only thing absolutely necessary for nonliving wages is the decision on the part of employers to pay them.[213] Adam Smith would have approved no more of slave wages than of slavery itself.[214] But life has changed dramatically from the pre-technological days of Adam Smith, and we should pay very close attention to what these changes foretell. Technology is infamous for bringing changes we did not expect.

Marshall McLuhan said there are four questions that should be asked of every new tool of technology: What will it enhance? What will it obsolesce? What will it retrieve? And finally, what will it reverse? His aim was to make fish aware of water. He cautioned us that too much of anything would bring the opposite of what we thought we were getting. When there are too many cars, traffic slows to the earlier pace of horse and buggy. Too many books, and only bestsellers are read. The consequence of setting out to be consumers is that we will be consumed. He warned constantly that the only way we can escape being manipulated by the very tools we use is to be hyperaware of their effects.

McLuhan died in 1978. During the last few years of his life, he was unable to speak because of a stroke. His work has been treated mostly as a passing fad, but several pundits have remarked recently that it might be time for another look at the man who tried to tell us that the way we use technology is more significant than the information it contains. Reality television is evidence that our culture didn't get his message about the societal effects of media. Future generations who are unable to read media technologies in the way McLuhan suggested will be ill prepared to navigate their way through daily life.

One thing is for sure: our descendents will have a better chance of navigating their way through life if we live up to our civic responsibilities. Increased technological capability without an increase in the sense of responsibility that goes with it cannot bode well for the future. Recall that Thoreau wondered why we should have a conscience at all if we do not use it. Will you speak up and reach out to others for the sake of peace and posterity?

FIFTEEN

SPEAKING UP AND
REACHING OUT

*We may live to see wisdom become a
distinct political possibility, and compassion
the reigning social ethic. . . . Longevity, when it
embraces so many, cannot help but be
a great maker of history.*

THEODORE ROSZAK

The epigraph above is from *America the Wise*, published in 1998. Thirty years earlier, Theodore Roszak wrote *The Making of a Counter Culture*, a thoughtful book examining the disposition of the leading edge of baby boomers in the tumultuous 1960s. Those of us who lived through those years can easily recall the feeling that the world was coming apart. Civil rights advocates and war protestors filled the streets and dominated the news. It was a great reckoning. And now this same group that Roszak once considered a young revolutionary force of idealists is an old force that he hopes has the same predisposition. He expects to see them take up action again.

Roszak's first book was in part a critical examination of the trajectory of technology, a warning and a fervent hope that we would use our technological tools instead of being

191

used by them. He wrote about the "spirit of the times" and our desperate need to understand what was happening to us.[215] He feared that we were "machine-tooling" the young to meet the needs of a military-industrial complex.[216] Indeed, the fact that we wasted in this pursuit money enough to otherwise have made everyone on the planet financially solvent should not escape our attention.[217]

Being the astute observer that he was, Roszak brought our awareness in the late 1960s to the notion that there were lots of things in our popular culture that didn't represent reality. "Archie and Jughead never kissed Veronica and Betty. Superman never kissed Lois Lane."[218] We were prudish about human sexuality while becoming dangerously secretive about matters of national security that reached a pinnacle with the Nixon Administration. Come forward to the twenty-first century, and most anything goes for Veronica and Betty, even in primetime; during the Bush administration our politicians once again became so secretive that their actions posed a threat to democracy. In the 1960s, we were in denial about a lot of very important issues: racism, gender inequality, and a military-industrial complex that President Eisenhower had warned us was out of control. Back then, the same impediments to experiencing the wonder of existence existed as they do today, but they were even more obscure. Still, Roszak was and is an optimist. Although my optimism sometimes wavers, I couldn't agree more with his assertion that "the future belongs to maturity."[219] And it is this premise of promise that Barack Obama wrote about in *The Audacity of Hope,* when he said of ordinary citizens, "I imagine they are waiting for a politics with the maturity to balance idealism and realism, to distinguish between what can and cannot be compromised, to admit the possibility that the other side might sometimes have a point. They don't always understand the arguments between left and right, conservative and liberal, but they recognize the difference between dogma and common sense, responsibility and irresponsibility, between those things that last and those that are fleeting. . . . They are out there, waiting for Republicans and Democrats to catch up with them."[220]

CITIZEN CRITICS

Will and Ariel Durant were staunch advocates for participating in the creation of culture. They wrote, "Civilization is social order promoting cultural creation. Four elements constitute it: economic provision, political organization, moral traditions, and the pursuit of knowledge and the arts. It begins where chaos and insecurity end. For when fear is overcome, curiosity and constructiveness are free, and man passes by natural impulse towards the understanding and embellishment of life."[221] Such is the great challenge for Sept-U.

I have always had the utmost respect for universities, and I am a vigorous advocate for an existential education—not just for college students, but for everyone. I'm also in agreement with Edward O. Wilson when he says we need a theory for everything.[222] Even so, I don't think it's too bold a statement to suggest that many college professors would resent the idea of members of the general public joining in discussion about the creation and value of American culture. Yet this is precisely what I say we need to do to raise the level of intellectual discourse on every issue that matters to us.[223] All of the components of the culture that envelops us are important to each and every one of us, not just to a small cadre of academics who make a living by trying to discern what is really worthy of scholarship. Again, I don't want to paint with too large a brush here because I'm also certain that there are plenty of academics who would like nothing better than to begin a genuine public dialogue about what is and isn't worthy of our attention. Perhaps, then, a good place to start is with art and entertainment, since it's something we all share.

It should come as no surprise that we learn to appreciate the kind of art that supports the worldview we already hold. Art is power. Aesthetics is a social scheme and at times an enigma. But art is art because it has the capacity to startle us into thinking or seeing anew. Convention is replaced by the unconventional in a never-ending semblance of emotional fits and starts, in spite of people who try to hold on to the authority to define the quality embedded in art. And, just as perfectionism is an enemy to democracy, so is it detrimental in the making of culture and in making sense of culture.

Cultural criticism plays an important role in society, and indeed it is a role that all of us should aspire to, at least to some extent. I'm in agreement with Herbert Gans, who suggests in his book *Popular Culture and High Culture* that we all have aesthetic urges that need to be satisfied. And he provides a thoughtful approach: "A comparative analysis of high and popular culture must begin not with personal judgments about their quality but with a perspective that sees each of them as existing because they satisfy the needs and wishes of some people, even if they dissatisfy those of other people."[224] In this regard I'm often reminded of Walter Truett Anderson's admonition, "You can only become truly tolerant of other people's realities by having found some new way to inhabit your own. . . . To develop tolerance is to develop a story about stories, a perspective on all of our values and beliefs. We need such a story desperately now, as much as we need sound environmental management and respect for human rights."[225]

So, are we simply creatures of culture, or are we to be the creators of culture? Should we be driven by culture, or is it time to get behind the wheel? Yes, on all counts, is my answer, and everyone should participate to the degree that we are able. Unfortunately one of the major hurdles in bringing about a meaningful dialogue between academia and Sept-U participants in the manner that I am proposing is the long-standing threat from misanthropes. H. L.

Mencken said the motive of critics who are really worth reading is "the motive of the artist."[226] But in every culture there are those critics who live by no other means than by tearing down any and all comers who venture forth with a message about hope for the future. These individuals may be brilliant—geniuses, even—but they live to destroy, to rip and tear down rather than to build up or support worthwhile efforts. These people seldom write books for fear of rendering themselves vulnerable to the scrutiny of their own kind. Misanthropic critics emulate the class bully, who gains attention by picking on the less able, and yet they very often attack those who have something of real value to offer. Their voice is shrill, and they would decry perfection, if it were to exist, because it would threaten their legitimacy.

The unfortunate result is that these people inhibit others from speaking up, especially in a culture such as ours that is so dependent on academic credentials. Speaking out and yet being unprepared to defend one's argument against such a vitriolic attack seems too great a risk. Do not fear these self-righteous puritans and their hypercritical rages about the art and letters of everyday life. Infantile fits and temper tantrums are often all these individuals have going for them. It is only through destruction that they can draw attention to themselves, for it is only in the moments when they seek obliteration of anything short of perfection that there is room for them to exist. They spend their lives chasing peanuts with sledgehammers. The pragmatists are correct in observing that some of the minutiae these individuals focus on obsessively do not amount to a flyswat's worth of consideration.

With this aside, it's time to turn our attention to setting an agenda for those who are stuck in the quick of popular culture and the reality of its mundane practical requirements—like nonmeaningful work and all that goes with it, especially a shortage of time—because that's where September University changes the rules. Millions of senior citizens who have clear ideas about the creation of culture, and who have more time on their hands than they used to, have the potential for conducting a spirited and meaningful dialogue about the future. Eduard Lindeman, a pioneer in adult education and an early advocate of lifelong learning, thought that adult group education and social activism are one and the same and that the former should result in the latter.[227] I think he would have been very supportive of the idea of Sept-U.

Choosing the subjects for public discourse will set the agenda. Tom Fenton reminds us that there "is no Victorian recipe for virtuous seriousness—that anything that hurts, tastes bad, or bores you must be good for the soul. But who says the alternative to gloom and doom has to be news that competes with Celebrity Blackjack or elima-Date or reality TV?"[228]

In *Visual Shock: A History of Art Controversies in American Culture,* Michael Kammen explains that visionary exploration in the arts will always stir controversy and provoke resistance, but whether we resolve these issues civilly and educationally or through sensationalism depends upon the role the media wish to play.[229] I would argue, however, that it could just as well depend upon the role that you and I wish to play. At the close of 2006, *Time* magazine's "Person of the Year" issue featured a mirror on the cover to reflect the idea that you the reader have achieved the status of being in control of media in the information age.[230] Of course, this promotion belies the makeup of gimmick marketing, but it may well reveal a bit of a willingness to acknowledge a newly emerging reality: the critical mass of communication technologies is changing the way people relate and respond to media.

As a group we have the power to snap pundits obsessed with celebrity and superficial drivel back to reality—back to subjects that need to be discussed. We don't have to put up with what Neil Postman described as "a sea of amusements" without protest.[231] What could be more appropriate for the group with the wisdom of experience than to keep pointing out what should be pointed out? Nothing rings truer than an idea whose time has come. Now is the time for the group with a mushrooming demographic force to challenge those who would dare to insult us with the nonsense of celebrity and sensational gossip. Twenty-four hour news organizations routinely fixate on nonissues, with cameras focused on nonevents, spending hour after hour explaining that they know nothing new about incidents that shouldn't have been brought to our attention in the first place. All the while, truly important matters go unnoticed, matters of life and death, but we hear not a word, not a whisper from those who tell the camera where to point.

A CAMPUS OF CARING AND CONCERN

Within Sept-U, liberals, conservatives, and libertarians of all political persuasion and points of view are welcome. Sept-U is a call for a culture of freedom, in which freedom of expression is an unwavering acknowledgment that all points of view must be considered, if there is to be any hope of determining the better argument and putting its reasoning into practice. The only prerequisite for participation is caring enough about posterity to engage in a civil dialogue. Sept-U participants on all sides of the political divide have the opportunity to change the world by insisting that media spotlights shine on issues that really need attention. Indeed, this may prove to be a shortcut toward real democratic reform.

Traditionally we have placed vital emphasis on letting our politicians know where we stand as citizens. Now, by aiming our concerns directly at media, we can, in effect, turn the carrier into the wind, knowing that, when we do, the politicians will follow. Politicians fear intensive media scrutiny even more than they fear annoyed citizens, and the media have the power to awaken still more citizens who are not yet motivated to speak out.

Communication technologies have given rise to a metaphorical identification with the biological world such that it is customary to speak of swarms, not of birds or bees, but of independent individuals acting in concert so as to imitate the actions of a single organism. In his book *Emergence*, Steven Johnson wrote about a slime mold that "oscillates between being a single creature and a swarm."[232] In similar fashion, thousands of Sept-U participants expressing similar concerns at the same time all over the country could create a swarm of protest or concern about a particular issue. Imagine the result if thousands of seniors entered into a dialogue, posing questions about shared concerns and refining their answers until they reached conclusions that were profoundly wise because of the vast amount of expertise and experience applied.

One place to begin might be the subjects that are on most everyone's minds but are frequently absent from media attention unless something sensational has gained notice. For instance, at some point as we age, unless we are hopelessly self-absorbed, our concerns begin to drift toward the times we will not live to see. Thoughts such as these bring the character and nature of succeeding generations into sharp comparison with our own. Observing children and comparing their behavior with our life experience can lend valuable insight.

As a case in point, my granddaughter seems to have been born talking and with exceptional syntax. One morning, having awakened from sleep in bed with my wife and myself, well before she was two years old and still unable to distinguish between herself and others, my granddaughter opened her eyes and said, "That was a good dream, wasn't it, Grandpa?" I was studying child development at the time and had just about convinced myself that, in terms of personality development, my granddaughter was already who she was. In other words, although she still had many stages of childhood to experience, the template of her personality was already in place. Thus, I was again reminded that perhaps our worldview and how we relate to existential change and uncertainty is intricately bound up in our personality, our temperament, and our interaction with others. Shortly thereafter I read Judith Harris' book *The Nurture Assumption*, which supported my observation.

I'm going to pause here and call your attention to a clear case of the power of the better argument. Having no university affiliation and having once been rejected from a doctorial track in academia, Harris wrote a magazine article about how peers matter more than parents in childhood development and how our genes predispose our personalities. The article was so compelling that it prompted renowned psychology professor Steven Pinker to contact her and suggest that she write a book. That book became *The Nurture Assumption*. In the foreword, Pinker writes that reading the finished book was a high point in his experience as a psychologist and that the book would mark a turning in the field of psychology.

My purpose in introducing this example is threefold: First, this is a clear demonstration of regard for the superiority of the better argument (read the book and you will see what I mean).[233] Second, with credentialing requirements and the world of academia being what they are, it takes an academician extraordinarily comfortable with himself and secure in his own knowledge and standing to make the kind of claim Pinker made—a very courageous and noble thing to do, in my view. Finally, Harris shows us in articulate, well-researched detail that too often parents and grandparents blame themselves for the way their children turned out, when they actually had far less influence than they thought. This is not to suggest that childrearing doesn't matter, only that it matters less than is naturally assumed.[234]

The whole issue of blame wreaks havoc with our ability to think responsibly. In his book *Too Soon Old, Too Late Smart*, Gordon Livingston puts the dilemma in perspective in a chapter titled, "The Statute of Limitations Has Expired

on Most of Our Childhood Traumas." He writes, "Every
adult American has been sufficiently exposed to pop psychology that he or she is inclined to connect past difficulties to present symptoms. Because acceptance of
responsibility for what we do and how we feel requires an
act of will, it is natural to blame people in our pasts, especially our parents, for not doing a better job."[235]

To me, this means that our concerns about the generation to follow can and should shift away from the usual
guilt and recriminations of *Long Day's Journey into Night*.
We should concern ourselves instead with ensuring that we
convey to our descendents the kind of knowledge that will
help them on their own journeys in life. My granddaughter's generation appears so much smarter than my generation that I take it as a very hopeful sign for the future. All
the more reason for us to move ahead and confront one of
the most serious issues we face—finding common ground
for people with dramatically different worldviews.

RELIGION VS. SECULAR: CREATING COMMONS

More than a half-century ago, Freud said it would take
everything we could muster to keep our fears and anxiety
about otherness from destroying ourselves.[236] Today the
global friction between Christianity and Islam has people
all over the world becoming suspicious of their neighbors.
If we are honest with ourselves, our perspective over time
has a way of slowly making us aware of things we have
been reluctant to acknowledge. Such dissonance doesn't
always overwhelm us but instead gnaws at us little by little until, with a measure of intellectual courage, we can see
anew without our readymade lens of cultural bias.

Nearly all of my adult life, I have felt uncomfortable
toward religious dogma. I recall as a small child listening
to a Sunday morning sermon, the subject of which I have
long forgotten. The impression that stayed with me was of
the minister referring to other people as being inferior in

some way. It was clear in my mind at the time that this gentleman, though many years my senior, didn't know what he was talking about. This was long before I understood the nature of adult dialogue, but, if a child can discern disingenuous rhetoric in religion, perhaps both the destructive and constructive qualities of religion can be readily detected by most adults.

At times during the presidency of George W. Bush and the ascension of the Christian Right, I viewed the rising popularity of books critical of religious fundamentalism as a sign of hope. Works by the likes of Sam Harris, Daniel Dennett, Richard Dawkins, Christopher Hitchens, and Chris Hedges, among others, achieved best-selling status. In part, I perceived the success of these books as a backlash against the social divisiveness fomented by the Christian Right.[237]

Now, after years of study and a constant preoccupation with the existential angst that comes with the human condition, I've reached the inescapable conclusion that the only practical way to bridge the spiritual gulf between believers and nonbelievers is to focus on the affirmative aspects of religion and the reasoned goodwill of nonbelievers. There are clearly positive social aspirations that come embedded in most religious creeds, and the same can be said for the good intentions of people who profess no religion. While admitting a sense of satisfaction from the popularity of books that criticize the poisonous aspects of religion, I'm simultaneously drawn to the sincerity and resourcefulness in Karen Armstrong's unrelenting scholarly efforts to reveal the positive nature of religious compassion.[238] Consider my previous commentary about relating, misrelating, us and them, truth by association, the fear of death, social conflict, and a lack of curiosity. When I think about these conditions in sum, an assertion by William Barrett comes to mind: "The freedom of any individual life is thus inseparably bound with the presence or absence of some sense of meaning in that life. The question of human freedom, therefore, turns ultimately on the question of what makes life meaningful or not."[239]

I can appreciate that, on some level, existential meaning is bound up in a primeval sense of belonging, a deep craving for significance, and an emotional grasping for some appearance of permanence and stability, even if the experience is steeped in illusion. Our penchant for superstition appears to stem in no small part from a desire for some measure of control over situations that appear uncontrollable. I'm reminded of John F. Schumaker's "paranormal belief imperative." In *Wings of Illusion*, Schumaker observes that there seems to be something innate, even in those of us who claim to be skeptics, that makes us feel that human powers can stretch beyond the possible, as when, for example, we twist our body after sending a bowling ball down a lane. At some visceral level we believe that our detached physical action can, even after the ball is already in motion, somehow cause more pins to fall.[240] In other words, we seem to have a predisposition toward the ability, if not to actually believe the unbelievable, at least to entertain it. Think about it this way: If this were not true, and if we were not predisposed to believe our eyes when our good sense whispers otherwise, then magicians would not be able make a living by amusing us with magic tricks.

Anthropologist Barbara J. King makes the point I'm striving for in *Evolving God*: "The religious imagination thrives on the human yearning to enter into emotional experience with some force vaster than ourselves. This pattern, then—in its essence rather than in its details—stretches back far into our prehistory. For millions of years, human ancestors sought belongingness within their social groups; as they continued to evolve physically, behaviorally, culturally, and spiritually, humans began to seek an emotional connection with God, gods, or spirits. What happened was gradual rather than a spiritual 'big bang.' The human religious imagination developed in ever wider circles of engagement from immediate social companions, to members of a larger group, then across groups, and, eventually, to a wholly other dimension, the realm of sacred beings."[241]

I have little doubt that a serious desire for belonging and meaningful human relations is bound up in the impulse to practice religion. And I do not doubt that the large groups of worshipers frequently featured in TV news clips, standing with arms raised, eyes closed, and swaying back and forth as if in a hypnotic trance, are sincere in their efforts to reinforce their sense of communal belonging. If they happen to put themselves in the company of misanthropic clergy, as many clearly have, their efforts may ultimately result in misrelating, but I can accept that most of these people are drawn to organized religion for positive reasons. King reminds us that religious ritual can be deeply moving at an emotional level and that uplifting feelings of connectedness can be enthralling. William Barrett said, "[A] culture is the sum of its rituals."[242] In effect, religious ritual is an effort to simulate and experience religious meaning in the same manner that repeating a mantra might summon a state in which the self is dissolved and one experiences becoming part of something larger than oneself. I suspect that ritual replenishes religious resolve in the same way that dreaming refurbishes our mental apparatus to face yet another day.

It's easy to imagine how, throughout history, the deaths of loved ones have encouraged religious thoughts about how to compensate for the loss and in some fashion deny death's inevitability and its eternalness. You only have to recall your own experience at funerals to validate this awareness. Barbara King writes, "Attending the funeral of an acquaintance, we may find ourselves in tears. We grieve not only for the dead person's friends and family but also for our own remembered losses as well. The intensity at the core of our deepest relating is familiar to us all."[243] Religion is coping. Ritual may seem mindless, but it may provide an impetus for communal connections in the lives of those who participate. It has the capacity to induce feelings of transcendence.

Recognizing the social dynamics of religion as a reaching out to others, a means of belonging, and a path toward symbolic transcendence gives nonbelievers a way to establish common ground with those whose beliefs otherwise seem untenable. The foundation of King's argument for the social belongingness aspects of religion stems in large part from her study of the interaction of primates. Her examples of their behavior make it convincingly clear that our distantly related primates derive meaning from their actions with others of their own kind.[244] That we have evolved with levels of sophistication for relating and misrelating on many orders of magnitude above those of our primate relatives is not surprising. The puzzle is why we've taken so long to think objectively about how we relate en masse such that we can reach a point of settling our differences peaceably.

What I've learned from studying anthropology and religion is that, however essential they may seem, the actual beliefs of a particular religion are secondary to the experience of *living* that religion. In many cases "secondary" may still be too strong a term to use for the importance of belief.[245] In *The Great Transformation,* Karen Armstrong makes this point with regard to the Axial Age, the time in history when the great religions came into being.[246] She puts it this way, "The Axial sages have an important message for our time, but their insights will be surprising—even shocking—to many who consider themselves religious today. It is frequently assumed, for example, that faith is a matter of believing certain creedal propositions. Indeed, it is common to call religious people 'believers,' as though assenting to the articles of faith were their chief activity. But most of the Axial philosophers had no interest whatever in doctrine or metaphysics. A person's theological beliefs were a matter of total indifference to somebody like the Buddha. Some sages steadfastly refused even to discuss theology, claiming that it was distracting and damaging. Others argued that it was immature, unrealistic, and perverse to look for the kind of absolute certainty that many people expect religion to provide."[247]

The benefit of religiousness is tilted more in favor of the *doing* than in the believing. Religious beliefs are all over the map, but the sense of belonging is ubiquitous, regardless of the religious creed. People leave one church and join another without nearly as much dissonance over conflicting beliefs as we might expect. This doesn't mean that beliefs aren't still serious points of contention. They clearly are, but I trust that the value to be derived from these observations is profound: People who are drawn to religion for benevolent reasons can be reasoned with by appealing to their sense of compassion and justice; if they can't be reasoned with, then they are not compassionate and cannot in the most beneficent human sense be considered spiritual. Religion matters because people matter. Reasonable people can appreciate this fact, regardless of how their particular religious beliefs clash with those of others. This reality can be explained in part because our tribal instincts and our Stone Age minds are still relevant, even if their significance is unappreciated.

Recall the earlier discussion about how useless it is to argue over claims that can neither be proved nor disproved, and then try to imagine how many thousands of years our ancestors spent engaging in ritual—interacting with one another in feast and famine, peering into one another's eyes in times of terror and loving calm, embracing each other in matters of life and death—long before they were articulate enough in their use of language to even begin to discuss their particular beliefs, not to mention whether or not they were in agreement about them. Our judgments about one another did not then, and do not now, need to lead to violence. We need to take a step back and resolve that getting along can be based upon the *doing* required of us in life and not the thinking that divides us.

As a function of ideological amplification, people who share the same views can, when getting together, work themselves into a frenzy of agreement right up to the point of hanging someone. Apply this to the entranced church members swaying back and forth with hands raised, and imagine what can happen when their clergy asks them to focus on the negative aspects and the seemingly adversarial beliefs of outsiders. Here is where understanding the concept of ideological amplification becomes critical to peaceful coexistence.

There are many people who feel compelled to act as apologists for religion, and they frequently make the point that humans cannot live by intellect alone, that in some very important matters, intellect cannot be trusted at all. Fair enough. Let's apply this thinking to the problem of divisiveness over conflicting beliefs. When groups of like-minded people come together and try to reason about the superiority of their worldview over those of others, especially in matters of religious beliefs, there is nowhere to go except down a slippery slope into the abyss.

In ancient times our ancestors didn't need to rely upon a variation of beliefs in order to wage war; they fought for very superficial reasons having to do with identity. In other words, they looked for any discernable difference that might be used as an excuse to exclude others as not being one of us. We should be long past this infantile disposition. More importantly we should not spend our time trying to use our intellect to justify the righteousness of our own identity as opposed to those whose worldview clashes with ours. We do not need to replace superficial reasons with intellectual efforts to justify hatred by coming up with better reasons to hate. It's not okay to say that happiness cannot be found through the intellect alone and then claim that the intellect is useful for figuring out whom to hate and why. Karen Armstrong says, "The test is simple: if people's beliefs—secular or religious—make them belligerent, intolerant, and unkind about other people's faith, they are not 'skillful.' If, however, their convictions impel them to act compassionately and to honor the stranger, then they are good, helpful, and sound. This is the test of true religiosity in every single one of the major traditions."[248] I would add that it applies to skeptics and nonbelievers as well. Barbara King puts it thus, "Doing and relating are the bedrock of spirituality, and they *create* spirituality."[249]

For centuries secularists have argued that religion is the bane of human existence, and religious believers have made the same claim about secularists. But each and every person from every point of contention in this millennial dispute could honor themselves and their detractors, concede none of their beliefs, and still serve humanity by simply agreeing to be intolerant of intolerance. Religion and doubt will be with us always. The real test for proponents on either side of the divide is to treat the *others* as if they matter as human beings. This is much more than a simple matter of etiquette; it's an urgent appeal that we seek to uncover the very essence of spirituality, regardless of whether you're a pious minister or a skeptical scientist. The underlying impediment to achieving this kind of mutual concern is that it is so hard to do that most of us do not even try.

I believe that the life-affirming component of religion is not its doctrine or dogma but the degree to which its practice brings people together for reasons that have nothing to do, whatsoever, with being against others. As such, religion takes our Stone Age minds only so far. It's up to philosophy and public discourse to do the rest. The faster we advance technologically, the more uncertainty we will encounter and the more we will feel the primeval need to maximize our differences and segregate ourselves from those we regard as different. We do this still because we find comfort in small groups where everything we know and do makes sense within our own group. But the world is changing at remarkable speed, and our predisposition for ethnocentric behavior is both obsolete and dangerous.

What we do during the last chapters of our lives weighs heavily on the future in direct proportion to the level of our efforts. What we do in our later years may not echo for eternity, but it can make a difference in the foreseeable future.

Perhaps we can say it is our capacity for appreciating art, beauty, knowledge, and religion and not our possession of these things that makes us human. Art and literature represent investments in humanity. Minus ethnocentrism and intolerance, maybe the same can be said of religion, especially since art was born of religion. My hope for Sept-U is to emphasize the positive aspects of religion that bring people together and eradicate those that foster hostility toward *others*. Many religions share the conviction that the very idea of God is something that transcends any and every attempt to describe God. So I wonder, then, why this premise cannot represent a foundation for peaceful coexistence. After all, if no description is good enough, shouldn't everyone be free to give it their best effort?

In *Losing Moses on the Freeway*, Chris Hedges, a Christian who speaks out against evangelical extremism, reminds us that compassion and affection can overcome estrangement. In my view, he puts the idea of God into the kind of perspective that makes room for everyone when he writes, "Love is the mysterious life force that comes closest to putting us in touch with the power and majesty of God. It is the spark of divinity we carry within us. It is what we pass on to others. It is life. The more we reach out to sustain life, as individuals, as communities and as a nation, the more we affirm that which we know we must affirm."[250] He goes on to explain that if we continue to live without sufficient regard for others we will do so at our peril. My response is to say amen.

SIXTEEN

AMERICA'S
UNACCEPTABLE
STATUS QUO

We cannot solve our problems with the same
thinking we used when we created them.

ALBERT EINSTEIN

W hen I think about the future, especially about a
time I will not live to see, I'm aware that my
assessment of what might be cannot be realistic
without a more purposeful examination of the present. For
more than twenty years, I've studied myriad subjects in no
special order and not as a part of any curriculum other
than my own obsessive need to figure out what's going on
in the world and why. All of my life I've been observing
politicians and media pundits who I suspect are not really
leveling with us about what they think and why. If we do
not use the remaining years of our lives to break down the
facades that hide the in-our-face injustices that confront
us daily, then what good can come from our experience?

Psychiatrist and geriatrician Gene D. Cohen, author of
The Creative Age: Awakening Human Potential in the Second
Half of Life, reminds us that the baby-boom generation is

the first generation raised to expect great things from the fall and winter of life. Cohen suggests that aging can and should be a creative experience. In a later book, *The Mature Mind*, he tells us that "Social intelligence, memory, and wisdom are closely related fruits that age alone can ripen."[251] This resonates with my own experience. With each advancing year, I have felt as if I am getting closer than ever to comprehending the wonder of existence. Of course, there is no shortage of people who look to the future and see little more than doom on the horizon.[252]

There is indeed much to be concerned about, and the global economy is at the top of the list. But despair brings us nothing but more of itself. Born in 1961, Barack Obama represents the rear guard of the baby-boom generation. His election as U.S. president has reinforced the sense of optimism I felt reading a *Time* magazine prediction that there will soon be seventy-five million people in America working as volunteers.[253] As Thoreau said, "To enhance the quality of the day . . . that is the highest of the arts."[254] Still, in light of the self-interested economic ethos so often ascribed to us, the prospect of this many volunteers requires further exploration.

CRITIQUING THE PRESENT

In an essay long ago in *Harpers,* titled "Army of Altruists," anthropologist David Graeber offered some perceptive and insightful observations about how our market economy and our educational system may be the cause of systemic psychological confusion. These forces have obscured the reality that the greatest satisfaction from life comes not from piling up wealth, but from helping others—a fact that's not readily apparent unless one is super rich or poor.[255] Graeber asks whether we might not be a nation of frustrated altruists. His essay brings to mind insights into the contradictions that bedevil our us-and-them social conundrum.

Graeber explains that we use rational theories to describe the motivations for our actions, but that these theories sometimes do not line up with the realities of what we really care about and what we actually do when we are able to do as we please. For example, poor people are notoriously generous, and so are many people whose wealth is so great that it loses its ability to motivate because gaining more would be meaningless. It's clear to me that a few millionaires and billionaires have figured this out, just as have our poorly paid soldiers and Marines who are helping people get on with their daily lives in the war-torn Middle East.

One of the most bewildering aspects of life as a human being is trying to convert the value that one feels deep inside into the value equivalency of money. It's kind of like making sausage: what we put in at one end looks very different when it comes out the other, and the final result seldom matches our expectation. Trying, for example, to buy love with money almost always produces a negative result. So, when we put the thrall of money aside altogether and simply follow our instincts, our actions often surprise us.

The very task of trying to envision how differently we would likely relate to others if we were able to treat people the way we really feel about them, without regard for their economic status and the authority they derive from it, is enough to stagger the imagination. Think about how many people in your workplace have more authority than you do. How often do you go out of your way to please these people? If money were not an incentive, would you still defer to them? Would you even speak to some of these people if not for their elevated place in the hierarchy? The point here that Graeber raises is simple but profound. We live in day-to-day circumstances that are subtly coerced, not by the forces of morality or justice, but by an economic supremacy which begs our constant attention.

As discussed earlier, it's only through a heightened sense of awareness that we are able to compensate for the default I-It ethos of relating that seems to come to us so effortlessly. This is not to suggest, however, that choosing not to associate with people of higher status over us is an example of virtuous relating. It's simply to make the point that our relationships too often are arbitrarily contrived by extrinsic forces. To be authentic, we must make ethical choices, especially when those in authority ask us to do things that our conscience tells us we shouldn't.

To have any hope of positively affecting the future, we have to be completely honest with ourselves about today's realities. And although I've already discussed the subject of social justice, we'd best not tackle the future without taking a deeper look at our economic and educational system of advancement and the so-called meritocracy that many of us perceive as actually existing.

WORK AND REWARD

I began this book with hopeful observations about the altruistic behavior of some noted American capitalists. But relying on the goodwill of philanthropists alone will get us nowhere in the quest for economic justice. It was only a few years ago that social pundits were predicting the end of work. What we are seeing instead is the end of jobs that pay enough to support a family.

In our social arrangement of work and reward, corporate interests, with the aid of our elected representatives, have created a grand scheme in which the bulk of the rewards for our labor goes to those who maintain control of the system. For a half-century the tax burden has been steadily shifting away from corporations and onto the backs of poorly paid individuals. Many employees in lower corporate echelons experience a treadmill existence—a frenzy to get ahead, to stay employed, and to keep from losing ground in a work environment that is perpetually downsizing. Too much external carrot-and-stick motivation overrides our ability to perceive and experience intrinsic satisfaction, so much so that people are befuddled by the very prospect of figuring out what they would really like to do if money were not a concern. For millions of low-wage service sector workers the downward pressure on wages and benefits is letting the air out of the American dream with a vengeance.

Succeeding in the corporate world often takes on a suck-up-kick-down ethos that in time becomes a self-sustaining pathology, oozing cynicism throughout the workplace. For decades, cadres of corporate elites have been, in effect, looting the wealth of the nation (they do this whether their company is making money or losing it) while touting the ethos of independence, entrepreneurship, and free markets. Moreover, the corporate spin justifying this outrageous behavior has been so effective that the essential requirement for excessively low wages is taught in classrooms of universities as a necessity. I bought into this ridiculous notion in my youth, but now, in my seventh decade, I would like to see the folks who spout this nonsense dipped in ice-water until they wake up. Living wages signal a civilized society; absurdly low wages at the bottom of an organization are no more necessary than absurdly high salaries and bonuses at the top.

Abraham Maslow's hierarchy of needs theory has long been criticized as being a gross oversimplification, and yet a hard look at military personnel can illuminate something worth further study about our needs-based behavior.[256] The basic needs of service personnel are a given. Immediately upon enlistment, recruits' identity problems are solved by way of membership in a long-standing honorable organization. Respect is abundantly forthcoming from those whose opinions matter to them, and their meager pay reinforces their sense of making a voluntary and sacrificial contribution. Thus, soldiers, Marines, and sailors achieve a meritorious feeling of exemption from the rat race—they are free to fight or lend a helping hand, and in most cases, the evidence shows that they prefer the latter.[257] You see, the real battle, Graeber argues, may be for the right to behave altruistically. He speculates that altruism may not be the strategy but may indeed be the prize.

Perspective gained near the end of life reveals that much of our human energy is wasted by simply failing to understand what it would take to make us happy to begin with. Capitalism is a tremendously powerful system; it has made the lives of millions of people worthy of envy, but, like any great force, it needs restraints. It's not capitalism in and of itself that presents our greatest problem. It's the special interest collusion among politicians and corporate entities that requires a mighty intervention and, in my view, a legal makeover. This point became tragically clear during the financial credit crisis in October of 2008. To be equitable, our system of work and compensation requires safeguards that reward work over capital and recognize that some of the most meaningful aspects of our lives, like caring for our young and old and respecting the environment, have to be factored into our economic equation so that they cannot be excluded from economic compensation.

For more than two centuries Adam Smith's metaphor of an invisible hand has been used as self-evident proof of the virtuous effects of unfettered capitalism. But what has long been forgotten is that Adam Smith assumed the persons attached to these virtuous hands were subject to a conscience that included empathy and compassion and that took seriously a moral edict for I-You relating and fairness at a far greater depth of thoughtfulness than is likely to occur today.[258]

Our brand of capitalism is fettered by corporations powerful enough to get special tax treatment and bailouts from politicians. Responsible capitalism needs government not as a co-conspirator on the part of business interests but as a mediator for justice and equal opportunity to ensure that an ethos of greed does not run roughshod over the most vulnerable members of society. In our current system special tax subsidies that favor business interests dwarf those afforded the poor, and yet the former have frequently been treated as if they are nonexistent while the latter have been blamed for destroying the moral fiber of society. Moreover, there is such a feeling of entitlement among the upper-earning echelons that Wall Street executives assumed that the financial bailout money authorized by Congress in 2008 would be available for their traditional bonuses. Our economic system needs to be drawn into closer alignment with an I-You manner of relating and away from the surplus of contempt that comes with relating to others as means and objects in I-It fashion. The only practical way to achieve a significant measure of economic justice, it seems to me, is to emulate the Rawlsian notion of cutting the pie without knowing which piece the cutters will get. Although this sounds difficult, it is not as problematic as the effects of doing nothing. The kind of economy that requires a higher level of citizen equity was recognized as being a feasible reality long ago by Nobel laureate Milton Friedman, although this part of his philosophy is seldom acknowledged by the so-called champions of free markets.[259]

RETHINKING EDUCATION, ECONOMICS, AND OPPORTUNITY

The lesson, as Graeber points out, is that every time in our history when the believability of the promise of a better future has seemed to be in jeopardy, unrest has followed and our democracy has been threatened. The closing of the frontier, the labor movement, and the Great Depression are clear examples. Today, the soaring cost of higher education and scarcity of student loans are leaving more and more people behind. Those who do attend college increasingly enter into a kind of indentured servitude to debt, and in many cases the employment for which they ultimately become qualified will never pay enough to have made their education a wise financial investment. Simply put, the social mobility afforded by one's education that has long been taken for granted is now in serious trouble. Moreover, as Graeber observes, educated elites have long had the means to get their own progeny into the mainstream of the intellectual professions and have, in effect, stacked the deck with unpaid entry-level liberal arts positions that only people with connections to social and cultural capital can gain entry into.[260] Thus, for generations, our society has slowly but surely been fracturing into two distinctly different worlds of expectation. It's perhaps the clearest us-and-them category of distinction, based mainly on formal education, and it is becoming increasingly castelike and rigid.[261]

Working people can imagine themselves becoming rich, but they have great difficulty, Graeber notes, seeing themselves as ever belonging to the group they regard as "educated elites." Moreover, working people know they are looked down upon by this so-called intelligentsia, and they resent it with justifiable irritation. Graeber argues that we should not be surprised that blue-collar workers reject the values from which they feel excluded. Thus, anti-intellectualism is in many cases a reaction or a grievance based upon a perception of being disrespected. It's not that the people who feel slighted in this manner are against learning and ideas per se. Rather, they are put off from intellectual exploration by a social chauvinism that has nothing, whatsoever, to do with their ability to derive satisfaction from learning. This is tragic. To fail to pursue something that adds so much value to life for reasons so facile is a human catastrophe, and no politically ideological stance, left, right, or center, is without blame for not working toward a remedy. There is no difference between blue- and white-collar employees in terms of their worth as human beings. The only difference is in the color of their shirts.

Graeber suggests that the political right is in large part responsible for the excesses of corporate America and charges that the political left is responsible for the cultural divide in higher education. It's an unsettling irony, but nevertheless I believe this view contains some important truths.

Education is not a zero-sum game, although the system is rigged as if there's only so much knowledge to go around.[262] In fact, the more learning takes place, the more knowledge is available; it increases exponentially. The ubiquitous claim is that education is the answer to nearly every kind of problem we have, and yet access to it is increasingly scarce. That education is more and more expensive and further out of reach of most people makes no sense.

At the very time when our technologies are capable of incredibly sophisticated intercommunication on a global scale, why should anyone have to pay a fortune to obtain knowledge or be forced to get it in no other way than the way it traditionally has been parceled out? Age-old colleges and universities have legacy funding into the stratosphere—in some cases holding on to billions of dollars in wealth—while tuition escalates to heights out of sight for people of average income.

Not surprisingly, with wages under constant downward pressure globally and unemployment on the rise, it's getting harder and harder for millions of average Americans to have hope in prosperity. The growing gap of economic inequality has become a threat to democracy, and even though rich and poor alike have incurred losses in recent downturns, the middle class doesn't have that much to lose before it ceases to exist. Pensions are being dropped, medical insurance cut, wages slashed, jobs relocated out of the country, and until the credit crisis of 2008, the credit card industry had taken on a loan-shark persona with congressional approval. The assumption that corporate profits can skyrocket concurrently with layoffs has suddenly become worthy of serious attention.

Now let's look at the realities of educational opportunities in a deck stacked by the dealers and frequently dealt from the bottom. Graeber's article suggests that we misunderstand our motivation about what is really important to us at a fundamental level and that we are much less

selfish than we are made out to be. I believe we make precisely the same kind of error in our pretensions about
learning. It is a myth, for example, that any job cannot be
learned on the job, and that includes brain surgery.[263]

More than a decade ago, educator Lewis J. Perelman, a
senior fellow of the Discovery Institute and a Harvard graduate, likened our growing credentialing system to that of a
criminal protection racket. He argued that academic credentialism is "eating the marrow" out of our economy. He
wrote, "A central part of the mythic American Dream is the
illusion that education is an effective conveyor of career
opportunity and economic advancement."[264] About classroom preparation for work he said, "Let's get clear about
this: There is no job in this economy that requires an academic diploma for its successful performance. None. Nada.
Zippo."[265] Perelman argued further that it's "a mistake to
assume that school simply deprives learning of *any* context. Rather, schooling replaces the contexts of real life with
the context of school life."[266] He says, "Ask your own physician or attorney whether the courses they took in medical
or law school have much use in the work they do every day
and the chances are very high they will tell you: not
much."[267]

In *The Trouble with Diversity*, Walter Benn Michaels
writes, "The entire U.S. school system, from pre-K up, is
structured from the very start to enable the rich to out-
compete the poor, which is to say, the race is fixed."[268]
Michaels says "rich people's mall" is another useful term
for universities, and he argues that the trouble with affirmative action is not that "it violates the principles of meritocracy; the problem is that it produces the illusion that we
actually *have* a meritocracy."[269]

The high hurdles of credentialing do more to protect
professional standing and institutional bureaucracy than
they do to improve the standards of skill. Otherwise, fewer
hospital patients would be dying year in and year out
because of medical error. Sociologist Randall Collins wrote

about this matter more than a quarter century ago, and he advocated abolishing credentialism as we have come to know it. He said, "As it stands, American medical training is attached at the end of a very long and expensive education that keeps the supply of physicians low and their incomes and social backgrounds very high. This formal education appears to have little real practical relevance; most actual training is done on the job in the most informal circumstances, through the few years of intern and residency. The existing medical structure is not only highly expensive, inefficient, and inegalitarian in terms of career access; but it is also tied to a system of job segregation in which the menial tasks are shunted off into a separate medical hierarchy of women with the assistance of low-paid ethnic minorities in service jobs with no career possibilities."[270] Progress has been made in opening up opportunities in some kinds of work, but in many areas credentialism is as bad, or worse, than it has ever been.

In *Disciplined Minds*, Jeff Schmidt tells us, "The fact that professionals are usually more well-informed than nonprofessionals contributes to the illusion that they are critical thinkers."[271] Professionals, Schmidt reminds us, have no more control over the ideology of their profession than nonprofessionals have over the design of the products they make.[272] This might not sound like much of a distinction, but, in point of fact, it means that compensation for professionals is not worth dramatically more than the work of nonprofessionals and in many areas a pay differential may not be necessary at all. Schmidt argues that "the pursuit of opportunity has been rationalized and institutionalized," which, in his view, makes it a "life and death issue" for the working class because of the disparities in compensation and medical benefits.[273]

There are millions of men, young and old alike, who view themselves as patriots, who voted for George W. Bush twice and would do it again if they got the chance. Many of these individuals would give you the shirts off their backs, risk their lives for yours, or walk into a hail of bullets if asked to do it in service to their country. They are not stupid or weak-minded; they are instead like the rest of us, confused by a saddle-horse education and the carrots and sticks that have been poked at us all of our lives. They are, as we are, addled by the multibillion-dollar efforts of Madison Avenue psychologists and semiotic specialists, who contrive 24/7 to craft messages that will make us ill at ease if we fail to buy the right products or use the right charge cards. Moreover, they have been tricked by circumstance into not realizing that learning more and more about the world and our place in it is one of the most powerful elixirs of life; that while knowledge does not make one person better than another, its acquisition dramatically improves our ability to experience aesthetic quality in life. They have yet to enjoy the thrall of serious learning to the point where it becomes a reward in its own right.

I offer my own life experience as evidence that blue-collar folks can break the intellectual barrier and appreciate a life of the mind as deeply as anyone who ever tread among the halls of our Ivy League universities. The buried truth of the matter is that all of us are more altruistic than corporate elites would have us believe, and we are also starved for learning without pretension. In my experience, the education that makes our lives worthwhile is free but for the effort required to attain it. And it matters not a whit where and how the knowledge is obtained. I envision a Self-University faction for young people that in time matures into a September University movement as we age: a self-educational, I-You alliance dedicated to becoming self-aware, culturally aware, tolerant, media literate, ideologically savvy, politically astute, and primed for a life's journey that leads to emotional and intellectual maturity.

Institutions of higher learning are under threat for very practical reasons. The educational monolith founded for noble purposes has become a monster, increasingly devoted to accepting exorbitant fees for sorting people into class distinctions that have nothing, whatsoever, to do with their abilities. Now this increasingly castelike system is in deep trouble because of its own excess: if students can't recoup their huge investments, especially when so much of their classroom endeavors are not necessary to begin with, then these institutions will not be able to justify their continued existence. But will this necessarily be a bad thing? Might we not be able to create something more useful in their place? When we go back to examine Neil Postman's fondness for the eighteenth century, we discover a time when formal education was considered of little importance in preparation for work, a period of very weak educational institutions compared to today. We also find a cadre of intellectuals sound enough of mind to have drafted our U.S. Constitution.

If twenty-first century institutions of higher learning are to walk their talk about the value of education, they will have to change dramatically. Instead of behaving as if their knowledge is precious and scarce, they ought to dispense it as if it is too hot to hold on to. Then maybe we will believe them when they speak about the value and necessity of education. In a truly dynamic world, both for individuals and for institutions, the power of knowledge can be increased far beyond expectation, not by holding on to it, but by giving it away. We are on the threshold of the kind of technological open-access systemization that can make knowledge-sharing possible in ways we've never dreamed.

Someday, in the not too distant future, I would bet that intelligent employees who need specific knowledge for a particular task will learn it, not in advance and not in a classroom, but in their workplace, in real time—they will access or download state-of-the-art knowledge, absorb it, discuss it, and apply it as a routine part of their jobs.[274] Perhaps individuals, businesses, and entrepreneurs will someday use learning institutions in the same way we now subscribe to magazines or pay for special services like insurance. Think of it as access to virtual knowledge. The big difference between this kind of experience and the traditional classroom is that the competitive nature of the enterprise would likely prorate the expense across the breadth of society so effectively that it would be a bargain for all parties. Last but not least, the users of these future educational services are likely to never, ever forget what they have learned.

My aspiration for September University is that we relight the flame of curiosity in our own lives and that we read as if the future depends upon what we learn. That we apply our learning, our philosophy, our wisdom, and our values to and throughout the whole breadth of popular culture and media culture. That we contribute our opinions, based on our experience and our self-education, to the conversations that need to take place about subjects that need to be discussed. That we use the wisdom of detachment to break the codes of culture, and that we emulate the care and forcefulness of Emerson and Thoreau in applying our sense of social conscience.

It is no longer possible to have a positive vision for the future unless we understand our predicament at a much deeper level than we ever have before. We have to pay attention to what's going on around us. Above all, we have to speak up while we still can. How we see ourselves today is visccrally bound to the way we imagine the future.

What kind of a future will you help create? What are your aspirations? Do you have a plan? Are you willing to critique popular culture with the aim of establishing a sustainable civilization? Do you see yourself as a consumer or a citizen? Will you help in the quest for achieving generativity?

SEVENTEEN

A VISION FOR POSTERITY

*If you have built castles in the air, your work
need not be lost. There is where they should be.
Now put foundations under them.*

HENRY DAVID THOREAU

The gauntlet for the boomer generation is down. In his book *50 + Igniting a Revolution to Reinvent America*, Bill Novelli calls on boomers to transform healthcare, to make social security solvent, to bring radical change to the workplace, to overhaul the marketplace, build livable com munities, and leave a lasting legacy. A tall order, no doubt, but one that is achievable if we really believe Thomas Paine's declaration that "we have it in our power to begin the world over again." The vital task for each of us is to develop our own plan. Change was the agenda that drove the presidential election in 2008. The fact that it was a winning ticket is evidence that we can accomplish the makeover we believe is necessary, so long as we believe it with enough conviction to act.

MY PLAN

My plan for affecting the future in a positive way includes these activities: I'm going to continue to study

223

psychology, philosophy, political science, sociology, the natural sciences, the humanities, and any and all subjects that might be fruitful in developing insights in meeting my objectives for posterity. I'm going to press for public discourse in all subjects that need attention. I'm going to start a group for discussing all relevant subjects and for posting and continually refining the better argument, and I'm going to join like-minded groups that are already in place. I'm going to participate in the blogosphere with the goal of making people aware of Sept-U.

I'm going to further develop e-mail lists of media pundits, politicians, product sponsors, television producers, and anyone else that I might have a chance of influencing about legislative matters and all facets of art and discourse intended for public consumption. I'm going to send all of these people e-mail messages about matters that I consider important every time I have the opportunity to do so. I'm going to continue to read books, newspapers, magazines, and web material with the intention of sending my feedback and comments to the authors. I plan to study cinema and offer my critique to everyone who might find it worthy of discussion.

Challenging though it may be, I'm going to spend time studying the popular culture of youth, to ascertain the appeal of reality television and to explain its value or lack of it. I'm going to try as best I can to engage younger people in a dialogue about art and culture, and I'm going to write essays and letters to the editors of newspapers and magazines about the issues that I care most about. I am going to urge young people to see the absurdity of the culture of celebrity and the ridiculousness of confusing their own personal identity with brand names. Above all, I'm going to continuously make a case for laying aside ethnocentric contempt in favor of Kant's argument for treating people as ends and not means.

POSTERITY

Sept-U is an ambitious exercise in idealism. Better still, if you and I can reason the kind of society we would like to see when our grandchildren have grandchildren of their own, then we have a criterion against which to examine each and every idea we have. How might it play out to a time we will not live to see? The closing chapters of our lives present an opportunity to write a final estimation about what matters, an ethical will, or simply a statement addressed "To Whom It May Concern" as aspirations for posterity.

What follows is my vision of the country I would like for my great-grandchildren to see. If I could have things my way and write my graduate thesis for Sept-U, here is how I would like America to be in another fifty years:

A country
- free of domination by special interests
- free of bought-and-paid-for politicians
- free of racial discrimination
- free of mismanaged toxic chemicals
- free of frivolous lawsuits, and protective against injustice

A land where
- "of the people, by the people, for the people" is more than a slogan
- the Bill of Rights is respected and enforced
- hard work is respected and rewarded more than capital
- people who work harder have more, but everyone has enough
- any job worth doing provides a living wage
- taxes are considered fair by the majority
- environmental ruin is acknowledged and redeemed through realistic product costs
- courtroom justice does not depend upon the size of one's wallet

- military obligation or public service is shared at all economic levels
- education is free
- credentials are based on demonstrated competence
- ethnocentrism is overridden by a concern for people all over the world
- a free press respects the idea of a fairness doctrine
- media monopoly is not possible
- government checks the power of corporations
- the people check the power of government
- the FDA protects people rather than business interests
- the majority cannot violate the rights of minorities
- financial institutions cannot engage in predatory lending
- the right to bear arms is upheld, but assault weapons are outlawed
- global trade policy respects the environment and worker rights
- the cry for free markets will be eclipsed by cries for a just society
- the military industrial complex is not the tail that wags the dog
- most people are concerned that our economic activities be sustainable
- the war on drugs is finally recognized as a war on poor people
- drug abuse is considered a medical and not a criminal problem
- racial profiling does not exist
- clean air and water are matters of high priority
- fish can be eaten safely regardless of their water source
- animals raised for food are treated humanely
- environmental sustainability is considered more important than jobs
- people are considered more important than jobs
- it is commonly understood that, in terms of economics, better off does not mean better than
- quality of life is considered more important than the GNP

- most people know the difference between busyness and meaningful work
- people are smart enough not to confuse their identity with name-brand products
- universal health care, free of the requirement for employment, is a right
- abortion is rare, but every woman has a choice over the sanctity of her own body
- separation of church and state is guaranteed
- history that excludes multiple points of view is widely regarded as false
- having an education is more important than where or how it was acquired
- most people understand that the pursuit of wisdom is more fruitful than the pursuit of happiness
- developing strong interests is considered more important than getting good grades
- excellent teaching takes precedence over tenure
- equal opportunity for education means equal resources
- anti-intellectualism is considered an absurd mindset
- institutions that forbid questions are rare
- most people aspire to be citizens instead of consumers
- the pursuit of awe and wonder is common
- more people view themselves as citizens of the world than don't
- everyone past middle age is assumed to be a student of September University

I hope you will see fit to record your own views about possibilities for the future. In my experience a list comes to us only after we have asked and answered our own questions about what is really important and why. Because of our large numbers, the Sept-U generation has tremendous potential for bringing about positive change to a time beyond our years. This is where our idealism meets reality. In *The Spirit of Disobedience*, Curtis White says, "Reclaiming the right to ask serious questions is no doubt an invitation to utopian thinking, with all the good and bad that form of thought has always implied. But what utopian thinkers have understood best is that if utopia is 'nowhere,' *so is everywhere else.*"[275]

Our agenda is straightforward: We must reclaim the character of and expectation for the kind of self-education that arose during the Enlightenment, and we must use our time and resources in such a way that our legacy issues will take care of themselves. In other words, we make our case for posterity, each in our own way and to the best of our ability. We learn to examine our life experiences in contrast with those of people in other cultures while we strive to develop affection for the better argument. We set aside the fear of our own death, along with any superiority we might feel over those whose worldviews clash with our own. We use our growing communication technologies to engage in a human dialogue that searches for points of common ground. We grant everyone on the planet enough equity to live a life of quality.

While I am a strong advocate for renouncing contempt in all of its illicit manifestations, I'm also for raising to culturally audible levels our indignation over ignorance and bigotry. There are many good reasons for being indignant, and it's up to us to point them out. When millions of parents are so busy earning a living that the raising of their children gets short shrift, a coarsening of public behavior develops to such a degree that rudeness in the extreme is evident nearly everywhere. Perhaps Sept-U participants can help turn the tide here as well.

One further contribution that I believe the Sept-U generation is best suited to make is to keep our sense about us in times of great stress. When it's most needed we can bring a big-picture perspective to bear on the world. Such an outlook can enable people everywhere to radically enlarge the group they identify with, making clear to everyone that we really are all in this together.

OBJECTIVES

When I speak about my objectives for Sept-U, people sometimes misunderstand my goals. While my aim is definitely to persuade others to perceive the value of my arguments, I do not want to repress the views of those who disagree with me. I am not interested in starting a moral crusade, pursuing witch-hunts, or establishing a new era of Puritanism. I'm not out to stifle dissent but rather to increase it. Although I do care about decency, I'm not planning to join in on what Frederick S. Lane has described as the decency wars.[276] The whole thrust of my work is to up the ante of discourse: to strive to get my peers to think above and beyond mediocrity and to enter into a dialogue that will ultimately arrive at the better argument.

My intention is to be vigilant about citizenship, civil rights, voting rights, public safety, protecting science from superstition, and striving to shed the light of reason on the misguided perpetuation of ignorance for political purposes. I am for broadening the definition of decency as Frederick Lane advocates: "Campaigns in this country should be about decency, but the critical issue is not, ultimately, who is sleeping with whom or what body parts might be visible; the central question should always be whether this nation is treating its own citizens with basic human compassion and is a moral participant in the world community."[277]

In the arts, I am a proponent for good taste but not an advocate for censorship. I do, however, want to expose the exploitation of ignorance, whether it is done for sinister reasons or simply because it amounts to cheap entertainment. I also want to contribute toward discouraging indifference and eliminating bigotry and the malignancy of ethnocentrism by exposing racism for what it is, whenever and wherever it occurs.

When I write to advertisers to complain about their sponsorship of programming that depends upon the humiliation of ignorant people (as is the case with some so-called reality shows), I'm not proposing legislative action to make them stop; I'm asking them to examine the cultural implications of what they are doing and to ask themselves if the results of their actions will support the kind of society that will best serve the future. When I write to politicians about matters that I believe are important, I want them to consider as many viewpoints as possible because I want them to be capable of making the best decisions possible.

I believe in the First Amendment. I believe in freedom of expression. I don't want to enact laws to prevent the horror of war from affecting the sensibility of television viewers. I'm with Emerson when he says that "no picture of life can have any veracity that does not admit the odious facts."[278] Still, I want television producers and executives to know that, if they stoop too low to collect their paychecks, by delivering programming on the cheap that plays to our worst instincts, many people like me will express their distaste and disapproval to their sponsors.

I don't want to tell people what to think. But, when people in positions of power act irresponsibly, I want to bring it to their attention. For example, I recently wrote a letter to the chairman of the board of a major communications firm because of his company's television commercial for their cell phone service. The commercial featured a young woman in driver's training answering her cell phone while driving. She continues talking while driving erratically and running over traffic cones as the instructor grades her performance. The commercial, according to the company, is a public service announcement because the driving instructor mumbles about deducting points from the young woman's driving test. But the production is pretentious and disingenuous to the extreme as a public service; its aim is to be amusing. The message teenagers are likely to take away from the commercial has nothing, whatsoever, to do with safety. Making light of driving while talking on a cell phone is not funny—it's dangerous. Putting other people's lives at risk is not cute.

Writing the letter took ten minutes. Handwritten or typewritten, letters can be very effective. My letter alone may or may not influence the company to reconsider its advertising policy, but if enough people were to complain, I think it might help. With Internet technology it is now possible to send messages to hundreds of people in a very short time. An hour a day devoted to speaking up and speaking out begins to add up quickly; when many people participate, the effects are audible.

Passivity is cancerous to democracy. Indifference at best is a license for oligarchy; at worst, fascism. And, while entertainment is a necessary ingredient for quality of life, there is a real danger of our minds being distracted and largely overwritten by worthless entertainment, as Neil Postman warned. My aspiration is to personify active citizenship as an example for others to follow.

Sometimes, despite our best efforts, what we do does not bring the expected result but rather its opposite. Even so, we are much more likely to succeed when we are striving toward an objective than by remaining apathetic. When we have gone to the trouble to think and reflect on the kind of future we would like to imagine for the generations to follow, then we are more likely to recognize ways in which we might be able to help when opportunities arise.

A rigorous public forum has the potential to add quality to our lives as individuals and as a society. By its very nature, a continuous dialogue about how to achieve a better world raises our awareness to a level sufficient to deal with our predicaments. We can take any subject and up the level of discourse to the best of our ability, and then we can make better decisions because of our enhanced understanding. If we really care about our children's and our grandchildren's future, then we will rise above petty politics and sincerely try to understand why those opposed to our worldview feel and believe as they do. If we do this with enthusiasm, we have the possibility of achieving a threshold of thoughtfulness that enables us to find common ground.

WHAT OTHERS ARE DOING

Marc Freedman founded Civic Ventures with the notion of helping others to find new meaning in the second half of life, based on the realization that the vast experience of an aging generation should allow for paying a dividend forward. Frances Moore Lappé embraces the Sept-U future with *Getting a Grip: Creativity and Courage in a World Gone Mad.* Lappé believes a better future depends upon a spiral of empowerment. Sara Lawrence-Lightfoot explores the possibilities of our aging demographic in *The Third Chapter: Passion, Risk, and Adventure in the 25 Years After 50,* with living examples of seniors enthusiastically engaged in the fall and winter of life. AARP and Elderhostel are increasingly cognizant of the fact that there is more to retirement than relaxation, and they are providing new ways for individuals to get involved in projects worthy of pursuit.

Environmentalist and social activist Paul Hawken has turned his own brand of Sept-U enthusiasm into what he calls *Blessed Unrest,* the title of his book on the subject. His subtitle is bold and daring: *How the Largest Social Movement in History Is Restoring Grace, Justice, and Beauty to the World.* Hawken describes his own initial efforts to discover what others are doing to help change the world and how astonished he was to find that the number of organizations devoted to posterity dwarfed his most imaginative predictions. Initially he thought there might be 100,000 such organizations, but then discovered he was off by at least a factor of ten. Hawken estimates there might be as many as two million organizations working for the betterment of mankind. The appendix of his book lists nongovernmental organizations devoted to a vast range of critical subjects that one can become interested in and involved with to take positive steps toward achieving a better world. At **www.wiserearth.org** Hawken and others have created the largest database of its kind listing organizations from 243 countries involved in trying to bring about a more positive and equitable future. I am also awestruck at the number of books being published that strive to call attention to matters that can positively affect the future. There are links to many of these books and organizations at: **www.septemberuniversity.org.**

THINGS YOU CAN DO

If you still need inspiration at this point, read Thomas Paine's *Common Sense*, the Declaration of Independence, the United States Constitution, and the Bill of Rights. Then read *Moyers on Democracy*. A stalwart defender of democracy and one of the most honorable journalists in our lifetime, Bill Moyers says, "The egalitarian roots of this country run deep. The time has come to reclaim those roots—to resurrect the revolution that held out 'life, liberty, and the pursuit of happiness' for all. The time has come to raise hell until America squares its performance with its promise."[279]

Or heed this bit of advice from David and Amy Goodman, who are both tireless activists in the manner of Thomas Paine. In their book *Standing Up to the Madness*, they declare that "We are the leaders we have been waiting for."[280] And then there is political organizer David Sirota who offers his own assessment of where we are politically with *The Uprising*. Sirota says that Americans both left and right are beginning to see through the old ruse of class warfare and we are nearing a tipping point. He writes, "An insurrection is on—a fist-pounding, primal screaming revolt from a mob wielding protest signs, ballots, computer keyboards, shareholder proxies, and even, in some cases guns."[281] A bit over the top, perhaps, but maybe not. You decide. If you plan to write, read Mary Pipher's inspiring book, *Writing to Change the World*.

Begin your own list of things to do.

- Decide what you really care about. Discern the genealogy of your own values, and try to comprehend why you value those things.
- Perform an exhaustive Internet search following your own interests to find organizations dedicated to shaping the future.
- Let your strengths and personal interests be your guide.
- Start your own September University chapter.
- Seek out discussion groups that share your interests.
- Look for opportunities to engage in civil dialogue.
- Invite members of other groups to join yours.
- Learn about the requirements for a sustainable future.
- Familiarize yourself with the arguments of those who appear to oppose your views.
- Join or visit groups who don't seem to share your values.
- Read the books you've always wanted to read.
- Study as if what you learn really matters.
- Study anthropology, psychology, and philosophy with the notion that these shouldn't be considered electives, if one is, indeed, a human being who feels and thinks as one.
- Join a book club or start your own.
- Audit classes at your local college.
- Create an e-mail list of legislators to contact.
- Make your own list of your hopes for future. How would you like for the world to be in fifty years?
- Decide why you think so many people stop learning. And if something has been holding back your own learning, discern what it is, and resolve to apply a remedy.
- Learn as much as you can about the virtual Internet world of teenagers. What are the perils they face? What are their opportunities?
- Help a youngster to become inspired about reading.
- What do you think are the three most important issues facing society? Can you make a difference?

- Visit a senior center and befriend people without family.
- Visit an orphanage and spend time with children without parents.
- Become a critic. Review books, art, and/or movies.
- Write frequent letters to the editors of magazines and newspapers.
- Write a letter to your great-great-grandchildren.
- Connect with younger generations and learn from them.
- Write your own autobiography and epitaph.
- Write about how you would like to be remembered.

In spite of our best efforts, what we do individually may not make great waves, but to live without having contributed even a ripple in the pond is a sad legacy. And who among us would want to be remembered for having done little more in retirement than having played a lot of card games or golf? The most important thing about our input as individuals in matters we think are important is not whether our position prevails, but whether it brings us closer to the better argument, regardless of the originating source.

In my view, shared aesthetics at all levels of society is the road to the kind of civilization we would wish for our descendants. Sharing art, beauty, music, literature, knowledge, and a quest for the better argument—this is the agenda and the curriculum I envision for Sept-U. I urge you to enroll and bring others.

Advanced in years though we may be, I believe the same curiosity and enthusiasm for learning we once had as toddlers still resides somewhere deep within. Once we are able to put aside our cultural distractions and become fully aware of the limited time we have yet to live, we can renew our wonder at having had the chance to live, and we can help shape the future in the process. Thornton Wilder ended *The Bridge of San Luis Rey* with these words, "There is a land of the living and a land of the dead and the bridge is love, the only survival, the only meaning."[282]

Meaning, in a human context, is graciously expressed through a notion of ethics in which morality trumps status and empathy prevails over arrogance. I find it deeply disappointing that during periods of soaring economic affluence, we become less and less charitable as we compete for status, and then, during hard economic times, our generosity resurfaces as if awakened from slumber. In spite of everything said up to now, if it still seems that you are powerless to have a positive effect upon the world, try an approach suggested by philosopher Peter Singer in *The Life You Can Save*: As long as we are in a position to find ourselves buying bottled water that we can get free from the tap or gourmet coffee that we can make for pennies at home, we still have enough economic power to make the difference of life over death for a fellow human being. If this is not meaningful, what is?

In the spring of 2009 gerontologist Ken Dychtwald published a piece on *Huffington Post* titled "Where Have All the Grownups Gone?" He said it's time to "gather our wits," "get off the bench," and act by envisioning "new solutions." In other words, it's time for the adults to help shape the future. Moving forward, keep in mind the simple equation at the foundation of September University: age + experience + curiosity x attitude = a greater quality of life and hope for humanity. How you make use of this formula will be yours to decide.

What will be your legacy? Where will your bridges lead and for whom will you build them? How will you be remembered? Thoreau was troubled by the possibility that a person might reach the end of life only to realize that one had not really lived.[283] Let it be said of us that we rediscovered the wonder of existence, that we did live deliberately, and the world is a better place for it.

EPILOGUE

*A hundred times a day I remind myself that my inner and
outer life depend on the labors of other people, living and
dead, and that I must exert myself in order to give in the
full measure I have received and am still receiving.*

ALBERT EINSTEIN

During the 1960s, when I was a police officer in
Dallas, I was called to a scene that was so horrific
I've never been able to forget it. Arriving on the
porch of a dilapidated house in bad need of paint, I was at
first struck by a knee-buckling odor. It was all I could do to
enter the residence, but then the visual effects inside over-
rode the stench. All about the house were old people in
varying stages of incapacity—all were bedridden, all were
lying in their own filth. They were white, black, and brown,
but too poor and sick to notice racial differences. I can't
remember who had called the police or even why, but I
must have put the problem quickly to rest, because I
became so outraged by the conditions these people were
living in that I was determined to do something about it.

I learned that the house was owned by an old woman,
who was herself physically impaired, and that she ran the
place with the proceeds of the residents' social security
checks. My first impression was that these people were
being exploited. So, even though it was outside of my
authority as a police officer, I made calls to social service

237

agencies and interviewed neighbors as well as people in the home. What I ultimately discovered was worse than I'd imagined. As it turned out, these elders were doing the best they could under the circumstances. After purchasing their medications, they had barely enough money left to buy food and pay for nurses or caretakers. It was a poor neighborhood, the poorest of the poor at the time. No one seemed to care. No one helped. Ever since then, I have been appreciative of the moral edict that the evidence of a virtuous society is to be found in the way it treats those least able to care for themselves.

It's been more than forty years since I answered that call, but I expect that today, with a little exploring, similar situations could be found in facilities all over America. If there can be any excuse for this state of affairs, the only one that seems plausible is ignorance. But even that is a stretch, since our news sources keep us aware that nursing home scandals are ubiquitous and incidents of elder abuse are growing.

If you and I live long enough and don't die suddenly, then we are very likely, at some point, to require some kind of assisted living. My hope is that a September University movement will amount to a war on ignorance without a lot of collateral damage and casualties along the way, especially with regard to end-of-life issues. Many social critics other than myself have made encouraging predictions about the possibilities of the baby-boom generation's contribution to posterity. I suspect this kind of optimism is contagious, and my hope is that it will generate enough passion to deal with our most pressing problems.

Marc Freedman points out that many people view the demographics of aging as a kind of malignancy that will likely kill us if we don't take action.[284] One of the problems most frequently discussed is a financial train wreck for social security. Yet no amount of reasoning that our social security system can be fixed with minor or even major adjustments seems to convince the people who want to do away with it.

Well-laid plans can go awry. I'm very much aware that my state of physical health, or any number of life's problems, may interfere with my ability to make even a small difference when it comes to the formidable subject of posterity. My goals are idealistic and my plan is admittedly ambitious. But I aim to do what I can, for as long as I can, and I trust others will do likewise. If a massive segment of our population changes its mental orientation from time being money to time being precious for its own sake, then there cannot help but be a shift in our moral codes.

A key to success in positively affecting the future is to know our strengths and when and how to use them. But, even as we expect a tidal wave of good intentions by people whose values have changed, there is also going to be a tsunami that may contain the power to eclipse the positive energy of the baby-boom generation, if it is not confronted in the near future. Earlier I asked if there could be any subject more pressing than getting beyond us and them. Clearly, end-of-life issues for an aging population may be a close second. Indeed we should not overlook the fact that the two matters are related through the dynamics of cultural conflict, the angst of indifference, and the fear of nonexistence.

Death awaits us all. Regardless of whether we believe in heaven, hell, or a vacuum of nothingness, in the final analysis, what we accept as true, matters only to ourselves. Death is the ultimate mystery—so estranged from the act of living that comprehending it is as impossible as the chance of light escaping from a black hole. We can relate to death only as something that happens to other people. We can imagine death as being analogous to sleep, and yet, in sleep, we dream. Understanding the concept of never waking up seems easy, but actually it's beyond our comprehension because understanding requires consciousness. Thus the task hits a metaphysical brick wall, impossible to breach, because the act of formulating a concept violates the assignment. Nevertheless, we are all bound for this inexplicable abyss, this unfathomable void, where we return to what we weren't before we were, so to speak.

The only real certainty in the world is that, unless we die suddenly, the existential question of nonexistence will be the final exam question of Sept-U, albeit one that can neither be avoided nor answered, only asked. Recalling the reek of hopelessness and utter despair of that poverty-stricken attempt at providing nursing home services, I'm convinced there are indeed fates worse than death. Working through this challenge could be the ultimate legacy of Sept-U.

Especially considering the demographics of the baby-boom generation, serious end-of-life issues need to be addressed now: Alzheimer's disease, euthanasia (physician assisted suicide), DNR (do not resuscitate) directives, and life-support decisions. How do we feel about spending most of our financial resources for a few more months of life, sometimes in little more than a persistent vegetative state? These are not just questions for the medical profession; they are everyone's business. Theodore Roszak acknowledges that, because of our growing numbers, death is becoming "a new kind of problem." In *America the Wise,* he wrote, "More people are going to have to choose when and how and at whose hands they or those they love are going to die. Or they will have to choose someone to make that decision for them if they cannot. For the first time in human history, ordinary people—not existential philosophers—will have to decide whether life is worth living."[285]

My maternal grandparents both lived to the age of ninety-two. They were wonderful people, and both of them endured years of excruciating but avoidable misery because of our culture's inability to come to terms with the reality that quality of life matters more than a pulse. I knew my grandparents well enough to know without a doubt that they would not have chosen to live beyond their ability to be independent and clear-minded. And I know myself well enough to know that I will not go quietly into a state of nursing-home helplessness if I have any volitional powers left at all: assisted living may or may not be tolerable, but being overly-medicated and warehoused is certainly not. In *Final Exam,* surgeon Pauline Chen says, "Preparing for death may be the most difficult exam of all, but it is one that will, finally, free us to live."[286]

I'm not going to propose a solution for others but will instead suggest that, if we do nothing else between now and the death of the last of our generation, we should come to terms about end-of-life issues without resorting to ideological wars based upon skyhook arguments. I am incensed that others would attempt to have control over how, when, and where, I am to die, and I will make no effort to tell others how to as well. Nevertheless, if we do not decide these things in advance, we may severely diminish our legacy for posterity in the process.

A positive future requires both maturity and creativity. As Mary Pipher reminds us, "The saddest thing about old age isn't loss but the failure to grow from experiences."[287] It would be a loss, however, if we cannot create the kind of political environment that enables a generation to take its leave by facing death maturely. Our society is growing old; the Sept-U generation needs to make sure that wisdom keeps pace with our age.

Imagine for a moment that we were to learn that a huge comet is on a cataclysmic collision course with the earth, that it will happen in a few short years, and there is absolutely nothing that can be done to save the planet. I would wager that all of the labels we use to describe our differences with other peoples of the world would dissolve instantly. From all over the planet, people would come together simultaneously, hand-in-hand, to lament our demise. We would celebrate each other's uniqueness and commiserate about our very unfortunate but common fate. Fighting over matters of religious belief would suddenly seem absurd. Why then, granted our short lives, do we not appreciate the same effect when faced with our own inevitable death? The result will be the same, regardless of whether we die because of an aberrant comet or from natural causes.

One reason, I suspect, is that our culture both supports and promotes a false impression that obscures the inevitability of death. On the one hand, this deception appears to soothe our psyches from excessive worry. But, on the other hand, this appeasement blinds us to the price we pay for the illusion. For example, imagine two people of advanced age in a situation where one of them has been given a medical prognosis of only few days left to live. The other person, though intellectually aware that his or her own time is short, is still likely to regard the future as a never-ending possibility. This psychological blind spot is part of what Edward O. Wilson captures in his book *The Creation*, where he describes our species as "a mix of Stone Age emotion, medieval self-image, and godlike technology."[288] This characterization, Wilson says, makes us indifferent to our long-term interests. I would add that, on the face of it, the bliss of escaping the harshness of reality is more apparent than real. The price we are paying for a worry-free present is too high.

My objective for Sept-U, in an age when terrorism is a part of daily discourse, is to acknowledge Wilson's observation and also press us to heed Socrates' advice that philosophy is preparation for death. We must use this knowledge to convince the world that what we can imagine for human relations in the case of certain destruction by a comet can be achieved without such a threat. It could be possible simply by thinking the matter through and by caring more about our progeny's future than the petty differences that distract us from the wonder of living.

NOTES

1. This is true even if some are still bound to money because of economic necessity.
2. John Wood, *Leaving Microsoft to Change the World* (New York: HarperCollins, 2006). It's worth noting that Wood was born in 1964, which means he represents the final wave of the baby-boom generation.
3. There are two additional demographic waves coming ashore that need to be acknowledged, although I do not deal with these subjects in this book. The first issue is the impact on society and the nation's health care system when millions of seniors in failing health require more and more major medical intervention at the end of their lives. The second is the many millions of aging citizens who are financially ill prepared for retirement. These topics deserve our undivided attention and may test our ideas about equity and social justice.
4. Robert Winston, *Human Instinct: How Our Primeval Impulses Shape Our Modern Lives* (New York: Bantam Press, 2002), p. 5. Critics of the Stone Age mind theory argue with some merit that our potential for adaptability trumps our predispositions. While I'm sympathetic with this view, I believe the tragic consequences of human conflict throughout the world are evidence enough that we still suffer the overinfluence of a primeval disposition.
5. David Berreby, *Us and Them* (New York: Little, Brown, 2005), p. 327.
6. David Graeber, *Fragments of an Anarchist Anthropology* (Chicago, IL: Prickly Pear Press, 2004), p. 41. Graeber points out that anthropologists have been trying for decades to impress on the public that the words *tribal* and *primitive* do not by necessity reflect societies of simpletons. I agree. My perspective is that our present social circumstance is so complicated because of our population and intricate relationships that we have to use more knowledge and care than ever in the way we relate to others.
7. William H. Thomas, *What Are Old People For?* (Acton, MA: VanderWyk & Burnham, 2004), pp. 93-94.

8. Ibid., p. 62.

9. Ibid., p. 52.

10. Will Durant and Ariel Durant, *The Story of Civilization*, vol. 1, *Our Oriental Heritage* (New York: Simon & Schuster, 1935), p. 4.

11. Ralph Waldo Emerson, *The Collected Works of Ralph Waldo Emerson*, vol. 2. (Cambridge, MA: Harvard University Press, 1971), p. 43.

12. I have always had the utmost respect for Carl Sagan. So I don't intend that much be read into the notion of what he found intriguing, because without his input we have no way of knowing for sure what he meant. One thing I'm sure of, though, is that through his work Carl Sagan proved himself to be a champion of self-education.

13. Joseph F. Kett, *The Pursuit of Knowledge Under Difficulties* (Stanford, CA: Stanford Univ. Press, 1994), p. 15.

14. Neil Postman, *Building a Bridge to the Eighteenth Century* (New York: Alfred A. Knopf, 1999), p. 65. Postman makes this point with reference to Thomas Paine.

15. Daniel S. Janik, *Unlock the Genius Within* (Lanham, MD: Rowman & Littlefield, 2005). This book provides evidence of the trauma of traditional education. Using the word trauma in this context seems a stretch until one tries to explain the ubiquity of arrested intellectual development among adults in this country and throughout the world.

16. Leon Botstein, *Jefferson's Children: Education and the Promise of American Culture* (New York: Doubleday, 1997), p. 39.

17. Postman, *Building a Bridge*.

18. Edward O. Wilson, *Consilience* (New York: Alfred A. Knopf, 1998).

19. David Solie, *How to Say It to Seniors* (New York: Prentice Hall, 2004), p. 39.

20. Ibid., p. 45.

21. At times I think my penchant for skepticism and existentialist philosophy is hard-wired into my biological makeup and has little to do with my real life experience.

22. Walter Kaufmann, *Existentialism from Dostoevsky to Sartre* (Cleveland, OH: Meridian Books, 1956), p.12.

23. Søren Kierkegaard, *The Sickness Unto Death*, ed. and trans. Howard V. Hong and Edna H. Hong (Princeton, NJ: Princeton Univ. Press, 1980), p. 13.

24. Florette Cohen and others, "Fatal Attraction: The Effects of Mortality Salience on Evaluations of Charismatic, Task-Oriented, and Relationship-Oriented Leaders," *Psychological Science* 15, no. 12 (2004): 846-51.

25. Friedrich Nietzsche, *Beyond Good and Evil*, trans. Walter Kaufmann (New York: Penguin, 1973), p. 102.

26. Arthur Schopenhauer, *Essays and Aphorisms,* trans. R. J. Hollindale (New York: Penguin, 1970), p. 72.

27. Carl Sagan, *Billions and Billions: Thoughts on Life and Death at the Brink of the Millennium* (New York: Random House, 1997), p. 215.

28. Richard Dawkins, *Unweaving the Rainbow: Science, Delusion and the Appetite for Wonder* (New York: Houghton Mifflin, 1998), p. x.

29. Albert Camus, *The Myth of Sisyphus,* trans. Justin O'Brien (New York: Vintage International, 1955), p. 122.

30. Ibid., p. 8.

31. Daniel Dennett, *Breaking the Spell: Religion as a Natural Phenomenon* (New York: Viking), p. 45.

32. Alain de Botton, *Status Anxiety* (New York: Pantheon Books, 2004), p. 118. De Botton characterizes Schopenhauer as "a leading model of philosophical misanthropy."

33. Arthur Schopenhauer, *Essays of Arthur Schopenhauer,* trans. T. Bailey Saunders (New York: A. L. Bert, 1949), p. 381.

34. Robert Wright, *The Moral Animal* (New York: Pantheon Books, 1994), p. 337.

35. Nietzsche thought the Buddhist aspiration to achieving a state of nonexistence where one is free of all desire is something akin to sleep. He also thought, and I agree, that there is much more to be had from life than striving for oblivion.

36. Rollo May, *Freedom and Destiny* (New York: W. W. Norton, 1981), p. 237.

37. Friedrich Nietzsche, *The Portable Nietzsche,* ed. and trans. Walter Kaufmann (New York: Penguin Books, 1982), p. 618.

38. I have read similar and more eloquent assertions expressed in Buddhism.

39. Walter Truett Anderson, *Reality Isn't What It Used to Be* (San Francisco, CA: Harper & Row, 1990), p. 156.

40. Michael Lerner, *The Left Hand of God: Taking Back Our Country from the Religious Right* (New York: HarperCollins, 2006), p. 18.

41. I've given this subject a lot of thought, and I think I know why there is so much confusion. While it is correct to say that scientists do not perceive of science as a religion, I believe the existential benefit they derive from serious inquiry serves as a viable substitute for the comforting aspects some people gain from religion. It doesn't make science a religion, but it explains why it is often mistaken for one.

42. Carl Sagan and Ann Druyan, *Shadows of Forgotten Ancestors* (New York: Random House, 1992), p. 413.

43. Carl Sagan, *The Varieties of Scientific Experience* (New York: Penguin Books, 2006), p. 31.

44. Friedrich Nietzsche, *Beyond Good and Evil*, ed. and trans. R. J. Hollindale (New York: Penguin Books, 1973), p. 90.

45. Daniel S. Janik, *Unlock the Genius Within* (Lanham, MD: Rowman & Littlefield, 2005) p. xviii.

46. Of course, this doesn't apply to everyone. Some people love schooling as is and continue to learn for the rest of their lives. My experience, however, leads me to believe that the toxic effects of traditional education are far greater than we can imagine and that someday in the distant future our experience will seem unbelievably quaint.

47. This notion first occurred to me while reading Judith Harris's book *The Nurture Assumption*, which is listed in the bibliography.

48. James Côté, *Arrested Adulthood* (New York: New York Univ. Press, 2000).

49. Postman, *Building a Bridge*, p. 161.

50. Bryan Magee, *Confessions of a Philosopher* (New York: Random House, 1997), p. 87. The idea that we do not think in words didn't occur to me until I read Bryan Magee's realization that thoughts precede words.

51. Camus, *Myth of Sisyphus*, p. 94.

52. Mark Edmundson, *Teacher* (New York: Random House, 2002), p. 255.

53. Harold Bloom, *How to Read and Why* (New York: Scribner, 2000), p. 195.

54. Lawrence Kohlberg, *The Psychology of Moral Development* (San Francisco: Harper & Row, 1984). Kohlberg's work is increasingly the subject to criticism in light of the discoveries being made in neuroscience. Still, to develop morally through learning remains a noble aspiration.

55. Increasingly I find disparaging references in right-wing literature about being a citizen of the world. It is often described as something sinister and, perhaps, evil. This view seems to me an ignorant assumption that becomes an ethnocentric political tool for use against uneducated people.

56. In the case of difficult material, assistance from secondary books may be very helpful. I often buy *Cliffs Notes* after reading classics to see how my impression of the book compares with academia's.

57. Theodore Roszak, *America the Wise* (New York: Houghton Mifflin, 1998), p. 131.

58. Peter C. Whybrow, *American Mania* (New York: W. W. Norton, 2005), p. xix.

59. Thomas de Zengotita, *Mediated* (New York: Bloomsbury, 2005), p. 9.

60. Marshal McLuhan, *Understanding Media* (New York: McGraw-Hill, 1964).

61. Zengotita, *Mediated*, p. 11.
62. Neil Postman, *The End of Education* (New York: Alfred A. Knopf, 1995), p. 7.
63. Michael J. Sandel, *Democracy's Discontent* (Cambridge, MA: Harvard Univ. Press, 1996), p. 351
64. Postman, *Building a Bridge*, p.101.
65. Tyler Volk, *What Is Death* (New York: John Wiley & Sons, 2002), pp. 106-113.
66. Curtis White, *The Middle Mind: Why Americans Don't Think for Themselves* (New York: HarperSanFrancisco, 2003), p. 82.
67. William F. Allman, *The Stone Age Present* (New York: Simon & Schuster, 1994), pp. 209, 215. Randall White, "Production Complexity and Standardization in Early Aurignacian Bead and Pendant Manufacture: Evolutionary Implications," in *The Human Revolution: Behavioral and Biological Perspectives in the Origins of Modern Humans*, eds. Paul Mellars and Chris Stringer (Edinburg Univ. Press, 1989).
68. Ronald Gross, *Socrates' Way* (New York: Tarcher/Putnam, 2002), p. 29.
69. Robert N. Butler. *The Longevity Revolution* (New York: Public Affairs, 2008), pp. 38-39.
70. Mary Pipher, *Another Country* (New York: Riverhead Books, 1999), p. 27.
71. David Solie, *How to Say It to Seniors* (New York: Prentice Hall, 2004), p. 13.
72. Ibid., p. 15.
73. Ibid., p. 34.
74. Wendy Lustbader, *Counting on Kindness* (New York: Free Press, 1991), p. 2.
75. Ibid., p. 34.
76. This is my personal reaction to the play; it may not be a common interpretation.
77. Eugene O'Neil, *Long Day's Journey into Night* (New Haven, CT: Yale Univ. Press, 1955), p. 153.
78. I have not, however, wavered from the first time I bought into Kant's argument that people should be treated as ends in themselves. Still, it has taken me a long time to figure out at what point in our cultural history we missed the subtlety of the contempt that we come by as naturally as we breathe. The compassionate aspirations of our great religions fail when they come up against our Stone Age propensity for small group affiliation. To recognize and overcome that tendency takes an extraordinary amount of effort.

79. Neal Gabler, *Life: The Movie* (New York: Vintage Books, 1998).

80. Ibid., p. 4.

81. William A. Henry III, *In Defense of Elitism* (New York: Doubleday, 1994), p. 14.

82. Ibid., p. 20.

83. Ibid., p. 26.

84. There are critics who identify anything Kantian as being somehow dismissible simply because it is a part of Kantian philosophy. And while there are certainly flaws in some of Kant's arguments, no one in my experience has ever come up with a more plausible case for a viable morality than for treating others as ends in themselves and not as little more than a means to an end. As hard as this ethos may be to achieve, the aspiration realized would, in my view, lead to genuine civilization. So, before dismissing Kant's edict out of hand, let us first hear a superior argument for achieving peaceful coexistence.

85. Paul Woodruff, *First Democracy: The Challenge of an Ancient Idea* (New York: Oxford Univ. Press, 2005), pp. 3-6, 15.

86. Ibid., pp. 93–101.

87. Of course, this doesn't mean that people won't kill one another over differences at this level of relating. It just means they will do so because of ignorant assumptions.

88. The flip side is negative effects from this same capability. Just as tolerant people of common interest can come together, so can ideologues and terrorists.

89. It's important to point out that face-to-face communication involves emotions that cannot be discerned in any other way. But it's also important to note that in the distant future, technology is very likely to make face-to-face communication ubiquitous.

90. Gordon Allport, *The Nature of Prejudice* (New York: Addison-Wesley, 1954).

91. Ibid., pp. 261-281.

92. Ibid., p. 277.

93. Brian Mann, *Welcome to the Homeland* (Hanover, New Hampshire: Steerforth Press, 2006).

94. John Dean, *Conservatives without Conscience* (New York: Viking, 2006), pp. 31, 212. The study Dean cites is Jack Block and Jeanne H. Block, "Nursery School Personality and Political Orientation Two Decades Later," *Journal of Research in Personality* (2005).

95. Jack Block and Jeanne H. Block, "Nursery School Personality and Political Orientation Two Decades Later," *Journal of Research in Personality* (2005).

96. Sigmund Freud, *Civilization and Its Discontents* (New York: Dover Publications, 1994), p. 42. David Berreby, *Us and Them* (New York: Little, Brown), p. 169. Berreby takes Freud to task for having the arrogance to declare which differences are minor.

97. Laurence Rees, *Auschwitz: A New History* (New York: Public Affairs, 2005), p. xxi.

98. Martin Tolchin and Susan J. Tolchin, *A World Ignited* (Lanham, MD: Rowman & Littlefield, 2006), pp. 13-39.

99. Nicholas Wade, *Before the Dawn* (New York: Penguin Press, 2006), pp. 9-11. This remains a contentious argument in anthropology and is by no means settled.

100. Woodruff, *First Democracy*, pp. 23-24.

101. Martin Buber, *I and Thou*, trans. Walter Kaufmann (New York: Touchstone, 1970), p. 57.

102. Daniel Goleman, *Social Intelligence* (New York: Bantam Books, 2006), p. 107

103. Sam Keen, *Faces of the Enemy* (New York: HarperCollins, 1986), p. 12-13.

104. Buber, *I and Thou*, p. 103.

105. George Lakoff, *Don't Think of an Elephant* (White River Junction, VT: Chelsea Green Publishing, 2004), p. 19. Lakoff says it's a mistake to think that most people vote in favor of their self-interest. Instead, he points out, "They vote their identity." This book is an excellent guide for understanding politics and the language from which it derives its power.

106. The very idea of the existence of memes is a subject of continual debate. I'm not concerned, though, about whether they really exist or are simply metaphoric reflections that enable us to examine ideas from a useful perspective.

107. George P. Fletcher, *Loyalty* (New York: Oxford Univ. Press, 1993), p. 41.

108. A "gut reaction" is a common definition of truthiness, and indeed that may be the impetus. In any case, the effect is to put forth an assertion based upon identity, or what I characterize as truth by association.

109. Richard Hofstadter, "The Pseudo-Conservative Revolt," *The American Scholar*, 24, Winter 1954-55.

110. Dean, *Conservatives without Conscience*, p. 27.

111. Fletcher, *Loyalty*, p. 20. I changed five billion to six billion in the quote to make it current.

112. Ibid., p. 36.

113. Sagan and Druyan, *Shadows of Forgotten Ancestors*, p. 197.

114. Allport, *The Nature of Prejudice*, p. 405.

115. Ibid., p. 405.

116. Sagan and Druyan, *Shadows of Forgotten Ancestors*, p. 256.

117. Jonathan Haidt, *The Happiness Hypothesis* (New York: Basic Books, 2006), p. 181.

118. Frans de Waal, *Our Inner Ape* (New York: Riverhead Books, 2005). Chimpanzees and bonobos (a slightly smaller and more upright primate) are our closet kin; which one is closest is debatable. One of the most interesting aspects of our relationship with these two primates is that chimpanzees are socially aggressive while bonobos are more egalitarian.

119. Ibid., p. 59.

120. Richard Conniff, *The Ape in the Corner Office* (New York: Crown Business, 2005), p. 177. It's fascinating to discover that, even though we as primates are sharply attuned to discerning the subtleties of hierarchy, we do very poorly when tested to identify the facial expressions of others.

121. Waal, *Our Inner Ape*, p. 224.

122. Ibid., p. 247.

123. Goleman, *Social Intelligence*, p. 56.

124. Ironically this applies more to humans than to monkeys.

125. Marco Iacoboni, *Mirroring People* (New York: Farrar, Straus & Giroux, 2008), p. 4.

126. Liking those we emulate may not always be the case. Sometimes we align ourselves with the ones we feel are dominant, period.

127. Iacoboni, *Mirroring People*, p. 267.

128. Ibid., p. 7.

129. Lionel Tiger, *Optimism* (New York: Kodansha International, 1995), p. 70.

130. Tyler Volk, *What Is Death?* (New York: John Wiley & Sons, 2002). Volk devotes a chapter to this subject: "Managing Terror," pp. 101-125.

131. Nazi Germany provides a vivid example.

132. David Hume's assertion that an ought cannot be derived from an is, has been the subject of philosophical debate for more than two centuries. Stated more simply, Hume argues that we can't determine morality from facts. This may seem counterintuitive until you try to do it.

133. George Lakoff and Mark Johnson, *Metaphors We Live By* (Chicago, IL: Univ. of Chicago Press, 1980), pp. 5-7.

134. Ibid. No one, in my view, should get beyond high school without being fully aware of the power of metaphor, and I know of no better resource for doing so than this book and *Philosophy in the Flesh* by the same authors.

135. Charles D. Hayes, *The Rapture of Maturity* (Wasilla, AK: Autodidactic Press, 2004), pp. 62-67.
136. Tom Fenton, *Bad News* (New York: Regan Books, 2005), p. 81.
137. Ibid., p. 54.
138. It's worth noting that, even though many of the people who attended these lectures did not understand what was being said, they appreciated the respect of the speakers who treated them as if they did.
139. Cass R. Sunstein, *Infotopia* (New York: Oxford Univ. Press, 2006), p. 9. The term cocooning seems to have changed slightly over the past few years. It used to have more to do with spending one's time in the pursuit of private entertainment than seeking news and information.
140. Ibid., p. 8.
141. Ibid., pp. 7-19.
142. Ibid., pp. 215-224. Cascade effects are discussed throughout this book.
143. Fenton, *Bad News*, pp. 107-108.
144. This is not to suggest that critics do not have some discretion about their work, nor is it to suggest that they don't add some value to their respective trades. What matters is that the influential gravity of their business interest is pervasive, whether they choose to acknowledge it or not.
145. Eric Hoffer, *The True Believer* (New York: Harper & Row, 1951), p. 105.
146. Ibid., p. 91.
147. Juanita Brown, *The World Café* (San Francisco, CA: Berrett-Koehler Publishers, 2005), p. 40.
148. Daniel Yankelovich, *The Magic of Dialog* (New York: Touchstone, 1999), p. 29.
149. Ibid., p. 45.
150. Will Durant, *The Story of Philosophy* (New York: Pocket Books, 1926), p. xi.
151. Henry David Thoreau, *The Portable Thoreau,* ed. Carl Bode (New York: Penguin Books, 1962), p. 270.
152. William Barrett, *Irrational Man* (New York: Anchor Books, 1958), p. 7.
153. Colin McGinn, *The Making of a Philosopher* (New York: HarperCollins, 2002), p. 63. McGinn describes professional philosophy as an ego-driven blood sport. Near the end of the book he comes to the unsettling conclusion that professional philosophers are likely incapable of solving the problems they find most interesting. Better, in my view, to get it out of the academy and back onto the street.

154. Barrett, *Irrational Man*, p. 110.
155. Matthew Stewart, *The Truth About Everything* (Amherst, NY: Prometheus Books, 2005), pp. 24-26.
156. Postman, *Building a Bridge*, p. 95.
157. Ibid., p. 96.
158. Robert C. Solomon, *Spirituality for the Skeptic* (New York: Oxford University Press, 2002), p. 139.
159. Arthur Schopenhauer, *Wisdom of Life*, trans. T. Bailey Saunders (London: Swan Sonnenschein & Co., 1895), p. 11.
160. Mark Twain, *The American Claimant* (New York: Harper Brothers, 1899), p. 456.
161. Alan Watts, *The Wisdom of Insecurity* (New York: Vintage Books, 1951), p. 9.
162. Allport, *The Nature of Prejudice*, p. 166.
163. Watts, *The Wisdom of Insecurity*, p. 24.
164. Ralph Waldo Emerson, *Emerson Essays and Lectures* (New York: Library of America, 1983), 287.
165. Ibid., 294.
166. Ibid., 287.
167. Ibid., 296.
168. Ibid., 297.
169. John Taylor Gatto, *The Underground History of American Education* (New York: Oxford Village Press, 2003), p. 204.
170. John Keats, *John Keats: The Complete Poems*, (New York: Penguin Classics, 1973), p. 346.
171. Even if this is true, perception of truth is still a capacity that can be further developed through learning. Thus our capacity to perceive truth is more the point of appreciation than innate superiority.
172. Jonah Lehrer, *Proust Was a Neuroscientist* (New York: Houghton Mifflin, 2007), p. 70.
173. Robert A. Burton, *On Being Certain* (New York: St. Martin's Press, 2008), p. 139.
174. Ibid., p. 166.
175. Ibid., p. 218.
176. It is very disappointing to realize that psychologists can predict our behavior with a high degree of accuracy simply by changing the circumstantial set-up of the conditions we encounter. There are three books in the bibliography that I recommend for pursuing the context of human character: *Why We Believe What We Believe*, by Andrew Newberg, *Experiments in Ethics*, by Anthony Appiah, and *The Happiness Hypothesis,* by Jonathan Haidt.

177. Mihaly Csikszentmihalyi, *Flow* (New York: Harper & Row, 1990), p. 10.

178. I'm not suggesting that this is a conspiracy; rather, it's more of a product of industrial evolution, a dumbing down commensurate with the docility required for a substantial population to accept a life of mediocre compensation without stirring up too much of a fuss.

179. Barbara Oakley, *Evil Genes* (New York: Prometheus Books, 2008). People who cannot relate to others emotionally tend to be characterized as psychopaths. Moreover, as Oakley explains in this fascinating book, a genetic predisposition toward evil for many of us may tend to trump our knowledge and education, unless we have the capability and willingness to try to overcome our hardwiring.

180. Csikszentmihalyi, *Flow*, p. 10.

181. John Carey, *What Good Are the Arts?* (New York: Oxford Univ. Press, 2006), p. 54.

182. Ibid., p. 177.

183. Mihaly Csikszentmihalyi and Isabella Selega Csikszentmihalyi eds., *A Life Worth Living* (New York: Oxford Univ. Press, 2006), p. 4. Csikszentmihalyi writes, "A subtext of evolutionary psychology is often that the most authentic way to live is in accordance with the ancient genetic programs we have inherited and to discount the more recent developments of the human species as 'cultural' accretions of dubious standing and value."

184. A related example of how this plays out is found in how readily people identify with sports teams and become manic when their team is triumphant.

185. If, as a society, we really believed that education is the supreme good in life, not only would it not be an expensive enterprise to obtain a college education, but we would likely pay people to attend college.

186. Nancy C. Andreasen, *The Creative Brain* (New York: Dana Press, 2005), p. 101.

187. Simon Schama, *The Power of Art* (Great Britain: BBC, 2006).

188. I liken this kind of prediction to the late twentieth-century experience with desktop computers. For years, they were predicted to revolutionize the workplace, and yet nothing much seemed to happen. Then, about the time most of us had grown weary of the discussion, we realized we could not work without computers. Now the issue seems like ancient history.

189. Marc Freedman, *Prime Time* (New York: Public Affairs, 1999), p. 11.

190. Ernest Becker, *The Birth and Death of Meaning* (New York: Free Press, 1971), pp. 139-140.

191. Thoreau was a man of intense contradiction. His antics were cause for constant worry to his friend and mentor Ralph Waldo Emerson. But Thoreau could see through pretension regardless of its thickness, and he was not afraid to walk his talk.

192. Durant, *The Story of Philosophy*, p. 183.

193. Steven Pinker, *How the Mind Works* (New York: W. W. Norton, 1997), p. 370.

194. Talking on a cell phone while driving has been found in numerous studies to be almost as dangerous as driving while under the influence of alcohol.

195. David Berreby, *Us and Them* (New York: Little, Brown, 2005), p. 183.

196. One can make a counterargument that we should not let ourselves get in such a hurry as to be bothered by this kind of behavior, and it is a valid point. The willingness, though, to move along a little faster is nothing more than a respectful acknowledgment of another's presence.

197. James L. Payne, *A History of Force* (Sandpoint, ID: Lytton Publishing, 2004). Payne offers an intriguing view of history, showing how the use of force has been easing up for centuries in favor of voluntary alternatives leading, in turn, to more civilized behavior.

198. Viktor E. Frankl, *The Will to Meaning* (New York: Meridian, 1969), p. 70.

199. Nietzsche argued that Schopenhauer was wrong and that it is not the will, but the will to power that stands at the core of existence.

200. Nietzsche formulated the idea of the will to power as the driving force of life in direct opposition to Schopenhauer's notion of the will, which is but a blind and nonintellectual force and more like energy or nature than something that is actually willful. Schopenhauer's choice of words has caused so much misinterpretation that what was really intended is seldom brought to light.

201. David Denby, *Great Books* (New York: Simon & Schuster, 1996), p. 117. Denby also describes Plato's Theory of Forms as an elegant con game. p. 103.

202. Jared Diamond, *Guns, Germs, and Steel* (New York: W. W. Norton), 1997. Professor Diamond shows in great detail that it's not intelligence but rather geography and the availability of resources that determine success among the diverse peoples of the world.

203. Kwame Anthony Appiah, *Cosmopolitanism* (New York: W. W. Norton, 2006), p. 85.

204. It may not be a stretch, though, to suggest that they hate us for our ignorance and the arrogance that they perceive it represents.

205. Louise Richardson, *What Terrorists Want* (New York: Random House, 2006). This work shows in clear detail how people whom we would regard as ordinary citizens in most every way can become terrorists simply by being deluded by disaffection, assisted by an enabling community, and persuaded by a legitimizing ideology.

206. Karen Armstrong, C-Span2, interviewed on *Book TV*, Nov. 20, 2006. Armstrong was discussing her book *Muhammad: A Prophet for Our Time*.

207. This unlikely coalition, which includes many other diverse organizations, is united in common cause for net neutrality.

208. Merrill D. Peterson, *Adams and Jefferson* (New York: Oxford Univ. Press, 1976), pp. 111, 128. Both Adams and Jefferson died on the same day, July 4, 1826, fifty years to the day after American independence.

209. Peter C. Whybrow, *American Mania* (New York: W. W. Norton, 2005), p. 4.

210. See http://www.koko.org/ for information.

211. Bjørn Lomborg, *The Skeptical Environmentalist* (United Kingdom: Cambridge Univ. Press, 2001). The criticism of professor Lomborg is frequently so loud that it drowns his message that we should respond by doing the most cost effective things first.

212. Thom Hartmann, *Screwed* (San Francisco, CA: Berrett-Koehler, 2006), p. 42.

213. In every case where low wages prevail, a small percentage increase in the price of goods or services can double or triple the hourly wage. These days, for example, it is frequently cited in media that ten cents per head of lettuce could double the wages for farm workers. In every field of work where nonliving wages are customary, it's possible to find examples of people paid living wages for the same kind of work. Moreover, I believe that most people would pay a little extra for any and all goods and services in order to establish living wages. That this is impossible is a political assertion and not a reality.

214. Adam Smith, *The Theory of Moral Sentiments* (New York: Oxford Univ. Press, 1976). Smith's *An Inquiry into the Nature and Causes of the Wealth of Nations* is often cited as the grounds for unfettered capitalism, but this book on moral values shows clearly that Smith's work is often abused by those who claim he meant things that he clearly did not. His idea of justice is morally sympathetic to treating people as ends and not means.

215. Theodore Roszak, *The Making of a Counter Culture* (New York: Anchor Books, 1969), p. xi.

216. Ibid., p. 16.

217. Figuring out how much money has been wasted militarily is a formidable task. I have begun attempts on several occasions and have
given up because of the complexity of the subject. Even so, one only
has to realize how few nuclear weapons it would take to destroy life
as we know it, and then consider the untold thousands of decaying
weapons that now present disposal problems in Russia and the
United States, to get a sense of the magnitude of the waste.

218. Roszak, *Making of a Counter Culture*, p. 45.

219. Ibid., p. 11.

220. Barack Obama, *The Audacity of Hope* (New York: Crown Publishers,
2006), p. 42.

221. Durant and Durant, *Story of Civilization*, vol. 1, p. 1.

222. Wilson, *Consilience*, p. 52.

223. Of course, some people in academia would argue that to do this
would lower the level of discourse, but I would argue that there
must indeed be a discourse before we can worry about raising or
lowering it.

224. Herbert J. Gans, *Popular Culture and High Culture* (New York: Basic
Books, 1999), p. 91.

225. Anderson, *Reality Isn't What It Used To Be*, p. 156.

226. Terry Teachout, *The Skeptic* (New York: HarperCollins, 2002), p. 14.

227. David W. Stewart, *Adult Learning in America* (Malabar, FL: Robert
E. Krieger, 1987), p. 52.

228. Fenton, *Bad News*, p. 205.

229. Michael Kammen, *Visual Shock* (New York: Alfred A. Knopf 2006),
p. 384.

230. *Time,* "Person of the Year," December 25, 2006/January 1, 2007.

231. Neil Postman, *Amusing Ourselves to Death* (New York: Viking
Penguin, 1985), p. vii.

232. Steven Johnson, *Emergence* (New York: Simon & Schuster, 2001),
p. 13.

233. Judith Rich Harris, *The Nurture Assumption* (New York: Free Press,
1998).

234. Howard Gardner, *Five Minds for the Future* (Boston, MA: Harvard
Business School Press, 2006), p. 133. Gardner refutes Harris's
claim that peers outweigh the influence, but doing so without offering the research to back up the assertion in this case is inadequate.

235. Gordon Livingston, *Too Soon Old, Too Late Smart* (New York:
Marlowe & Company, 2004), p. 19.

236. Freud, *Civilization and Its Discontents*.

237. Chris Hedges, *American Fascists* (New York: Free Press, 2006), p. 35. Hedges provides a compelling argument that the divisiveness of the Christian Right and the threat posed by this movement is a recent phenomenon and has not always been the case. He describes the religious leaders who constitute the threat as dominionists. He writes, "Radical Christian dominionists have no religious legitimacy. They are manipulating Christianity, and millions of sincere believers, to build a frightening political mass movement with many similarities with other mass movements, from fascism to communism to the ethnic nationalist parties in former Yugoslavia. It shares with these movements an inability to cope with ambiguity, doubt and uncertainty. It creates its own 'truth.' It embraces a world of miracles and signs and removes followers from a rational, reality-based world. It condemns self-criticism and debate as apostasy. It places a premium on action and finds its final aesthetic in war and apocalyptic violence."

238. Karen Armstrong, *The Great Transformation* (New York: Alfred A. Knopf, 2006). Armstrong has written numerous books on this subject.

239. William Barrett, *The Illusion of Technique* (New York: Anchor Books, 1978), p. 86.

240. John F. Schumaker, *Wings of Illusion* (New York: Prometheus Books, 1990).

241. Barbara J. King, *Evolving God* (New York: Doubleday, 2007), p. 178.

242. Barrett, *Illusion of Technique*, p. 21.

243. King, *Evolving God*, p. 170.

244. Ibid., p. 52.

245. Of course, there are notable exceptions, such as Moses and the calf worshipers in the book of Exodus and the warnings to infidels in the Koran. But if the extreme edicts in the Bible and the Koran were taken literally with regard to what to do about outsiders, then religious practice would be untenable in any society that included nonbelievers. Moreover, stoning people to death for what are today considered minor indiscretions cannot be tolerated in civilized society.

246. Armstrong, *Great Transformation*, p. xii. Armstrong identifies the Axial Age as a pivotal time of spiritual development for humanity that occurred from about 900 to 200 BCE.

247. Ibid., p. xiii.

248. Ibid., p. 392.

249. King, *Evolving God*, p. 210.

250. Chris Hedges, *Losing Moses on the Freeway* (New York: Free Press), pp. 166, 173.

251. Gene D. Cohen, *The Mature Mind* (New York: Basic Books, 2005), p. 134.

252. Morris Berman, *Dark Ages America* (New York: W. W. Norton, 2006) and Jane Jacobs, *Dark Age Ahead* (New York: Random House, 2004). Berman's position represents but one example of those who think America has begun an era of rapid social and economic decline. Jacobs' case, in my view, is more credible. She calls our attention to five pillars of society in serious trouble: family and community, higher education, government, effective practice of science, and the self-regulation of those occupations deemed professional. Jacobs argues that decline in these areas of life are even more threatening than racism, environmental destruction and the growing divide between rich and poor. The reason, she says, lies in the fact that these fundamentals are crucial to society and that they are now in decay.

253. Daniel Kadlec, *Time,* July 31, 2006, p. 67.

254. Thoreau, *The Portable Thoreau,* p. 343.

255. David Graeber, "Army of Altruists," *Harpers*, January, 2007. This is a unique perspective and is deserving of much further study and consideration.

256. Abraham H. Maslow, *The Farther Reaches of Human Nature* (New York: Viking, 1971).

257. Of course, they still have a ranking system with a hierarchical order all its own, which can be very stressful, but it's barely noticeable as an issue among the general public. Servicemen and women are esteemed by nature of their enlistment; rank counts, but not as much as their simply being in the military.

258. Charles D. Hayes, *Beyond the American Dream* (Wasilla, AK: Autodidactic Press, 1998), pp. 202-204.

259. The late Milton Friedman was a tireless advocate for the freedom to choose in every aspect of life imaginable. He was vehemently opposed to collusion of government and big business against the interests of individuals. He objected to compulsory education because he thought that in its absence a self-interested ethos for literacy would enable us to rise above our current standards of mediocrity. He spoke often about his willingness to support a guaranteed income through a negative income tax. He is championed and often quoted by corporate interests with whom he had visceral ideological differences. The major disagreement I have with his philosophy is that he opposed a military draft and compared it to slavery. On this issue, I believe he was wrong. An obligatory draft is the only surefire way to keep political power in check. Being asked to

serve one's country by taking a turn in military service for a short period time is not in any measure comparable to slavery. But the misuse of a volunteer army is, indeed, comparable to tyranny.

260. Daniel Golden, *The Price of Admission* (New York: Crown, 2006). Golden elaborates on this idea and adds a whole host of additional obstacles that detract from the reality that our system of higher education is a meritocracy.

261. Many social critics have observed that not nearly as many people are marrying out of their respective social classes as they once did, which is making social class more rigid than it used to be.

262. Golden, *Price of Admission*, p. 289. Golden points out that admissions is a zero sum game and that colleges and universities increase their prestige by limiting access.

263. In some of my previous books I have written extensively about the fact that in many disciplines competence has become more important than paper credential. Computer technology is a good example. Computer technologists either know what they are doing or it is painfully obvious that they don't.

264. Lewis J. Perelman, *School's Out* (New York: Avon Books, 1992), p. 284.

265. Ibid., p. 297.

266. Ibid., p. 158.

267. Ibid., p. 131.

268. Walter Benn Michaels, *The Trouble with Diversity* (New York: Metropolitan Books, 2006), pp. 10-11.

269. Ibid., pp. 80-85.

270. Randall Collins, *The Credential Society* (San Diego, CA: Academic Press, 1979), p. 201.

271. Jeff Schmidt, *Disciplined Minds* (New York: Rowman & Littlefield, 2000), p. 41.

272. Ibid., p. 40.

273. Ibid., pp. 102-103.

274. It's kind of an open secret that this is already a frequent occurrence in many companies. It may be likened to a way of life by people who are self-employed, but the realty of real-time knowledge has yet to reach a tipping point where it radically changes our expectations about the acquisition of knowledge and the way we work.

275. Curtis White, *The Spirit of Disobedience* (Sausalito, CA: PoliPointPress, 2007), p. 119.

276. Frederick S. Lane, *The Decency Wars* (New York: Prometheus Books, 2006). Lane suggests that the public outcry, usually from social conservatives and referred to often in warring terms, is the

product of a cynical conservative movement that has more to do with profit than with decency. In other words, a lot of the hype about decency is misplaced and misconstrued emotion because most of the people who are most vociferous don't really understand the source of their anxiety.

277. Ibid., p. 281.

278. Ralph Waldo Emerson, *Emerson Essays and Lectures* (New York: Library of America, 1983), p. 952.

279. Bill Moyers, *Moyers On Democracy* (New York: Doubleday, 2008), p. 112.

280. Amy Goodman and David Goodman, *Standing Up to the Madness* (New York: Hyperion, 2008), p. 216.

281. David Sirota, *The Uprising* (New York: Crown, 2008), p. 5.

282. Thornton Wilder, *The Bridge of San Luis Rey* (New York: HarperCollins, 1955), p. 123.

283. Thoreau, *The Portable Thoreau*, p. 343.

284. Freedman, *Prime Time*, pp. 11-16.

285. Roszak, *America the Wise*, p. 193.

286. Pauline W. Chen, *Final Exam* (New York: Alfred A. Knopf, 2007), p. xv.

287. Pipher, *Another Country*, p. 192.

288. Edward O. Wilson, *The Creation* (New York: W. W. Norton, 2006), p. 10. I agree with those who say that Wilson is our present-day Thoreau. In this concise description of our species, Wilson captures the very essence of our existential dilemma and simultaneously aims at resolution.

BIBLIOGRAPHY

Adler, Mortimer J. *A Guidebook to Learning*. New York: Macmillan, 1986.

Allman, William F. *The Stone Age Present*. New York: Simon & Schuster, 1994.

Allport, Gordon W. *The Person in Psychology*. Boston: Beacon Press, 1968.

———. *Becoming*. New Haven, CT: Yale Univ. Press, 1955.

———. *The Nature of Prejudice*. Reading, MA: Addison-Wesley, 1954.

Anderson, Walter Truett. *The Truth About the Truth*. New York: Tarcher/Putnam, 1995.

———. *Reality Isn't What It Used to Be*. San Francisco: Harper & Row, 1990.

Andreasen, Nancy C. *The Creating Brain: The Neuroscience of Genius*. New York: Dana Press, 2005.

Appiah, Kwame Anthony. *Experiments in Ethics*. Cambridge, MA: Harvard University Press, 2008.

———. *Cosmopolitanism: Ethics in a World of Strangers*. New York: W. W. Norton, 2006.

———. *The Ethics of Identity*. Princeton, NJ: Princeton Univ. Press, 2005.

Arendt, Hannah. *The Life of the Mind*. New York: Harcourt, 1971.

Aristotle. "On Poetics." Translated by Ingram Bywater. In *Great Books of the Western World*. Vol. 42. Chicago: Encyclopedia Britannica, 1952.

Armstrong, Karen. *The Great Transformation: The Beginning of Our Religious Traditions*. New York: Alfred A. Knopf, 2006.

Aurelius, Marcus. "The Meditations of Marcus Aurelius." Translated by George Long. In *Great Books of the Western World*. Vol. 12. Chicago: Encyclopedia Britannica, 1952.

Barash, David P., and Nanelle Barash. *Madame Bovary's Ovaries: A Darwinian Look at Literature*. New York: Delacorte Press, 2005.

Barrett, William. *The Illusion of Technique*. New York: Anchor Books, 1978.

———. *Irrational Man: A Study in Existential Philosophy*. New York: Anchor Books, 1958.

Beah, Ishmael. *A Long Way Gone: Memoirs of a Boy Soldier*. New York: Sarah Crichton Books, 2007.

Becker, Ernest. *The Denial of Death*. New York: Free Press, 1973.

———. *The Birth and Death of Meaning: An Interdisciplinary Perspective on the Problem of Man*. New York: Free Press, 1971.

Berman, Morris. *Dark Ages America: The Final Phase of Empire*. New York: W. W. Norton, 2006.

Berreby, David. *Us and Them: Understanding Your Tribal Mind*. New York: Little, Brown, 2005.

Bloom, Harold. *How to Read and Why*. New York: Scribner, 2000.

Boorstin, Daniel J. *The Seekers: The Story of Man's Quest to Understand His World*. New York: Random House, 1998.

———. "The Amateur Spirit." In *Living Philosophies*. Edited by Clifton Fadiman. New York: Doubleday, 1990.

Botstein, Leon. *Jefferson's Children: Education and the Promise of American Culture*. New York: Doubleday, 1997.

Botton, Alain de. *Status Anxiety*. New York: Pantheon Books, 2004.

———. *The Consolations of Philosophy*. New York: Pantheon Books, 2000.

———. *How Proust Can Change Your Life: Not a Novel*. New York: Vintage Books, 1997.

Boym, Svetlana. *The Future of Nostalgia*. New York: Basic Books, 2001.

Bruner, Jerome. *Making Stories: Law, Literature, Life*. Cambridge, MA: Harvard Univ. Press, 2002.

Buber, Martin. *I and Thou*. Translated by Walter Kaufmann. New York: Touchstone, 1970.

Burton, Robert A. *On Being Certain: Believing You Are Right Even When You Are Wrong*. New York: St. Martin's Press, 2008.

Butler, Robert N. *The Longevity Revolution: The Benefits and Challenges of Living a Long Life*. New York: Public Affairs, 2008.

Campbell, Joseph. *Myths to Live By*. New York: Bantam Books, 1973.

Camus, Albert. *The Stranger*. Translated by Matthew Ward. New York: Vintage Books, 1989.

———. *The Myth of Sisyphus*. Translated by Justin O'Brien. New York: Vintage Books, 1955.

Carey, John. *What Good Are the Arts?* New York: Oxford Univ. Press, 2006.

Chen, Pauline W. *Final Exam: A Surgeon's Reflections on Mortality.* New York: Alfred A. Knopf, 2007.

Cicero. *On the Good Life.* Translated by Michael Grant. New York: Penguin Classics, 1971.

Claxton, Guy. *Wise Up: The Challenge of Lifelong Learning.* New York: Bloomsbury, 1999.

———. *Hare Brain, Tortoise Mind: How Intelligence Increases When You Think Less.* Hopewell, NJ: Ecco Press, 1997.

Cohen, Gene D. *The Mature Mind: The Positive Power of the Brain.* New York: Basic Books, 2005.

———. *The Creative Age: Awakening Human Potential in the Second Half of Life.* New Work: HarperCollins, 2000.

Collins, Randall. *The Sociology of Philosophies: A Global Theory of Intellectual Change.* Cambridge, MA: Belknap Press of Harvard Univ. Press, 1998.

———. *The Credential Society: An Historical Sociology of Education and Stratification.* New York: Academic Press, 1979.

Conniff, Richard. *The Ape in the Corner Office: Understanding the Workplace Beast in All of Us.* New York: Crown Business, 2005.

Corrigan, Maureen. *Leave Me Alone, I'm Reading.* New York: Random House, 2005.

Côté, James. *Arrested Adulthood: The Changing Nature of Maturity and Identity.* New York: New York Univ. Press, 2000.

Csikszentmihalyi, Mihaly. *Creativity: Flow and the Psychology of Discovery and Invention.* New York: HarperCollins, 1996.

———. *The Evolving Self: A Psychology for the Third Millennium.* New York: HarperCollins, 1993.

———. *Flow: The Psychology of Optimal Experience.* New York: Harper & Row, 1990.

Csikszentmihalyi, Mihaly, and Isabella Selega Csikszentmihalyi, eds. *A Life Worth Living: Contributions to Positive Psychology.* New York: Oxford Univ. Press, 2006.

Darwin, Charles. *The Descent of Man.* Amherst, NY: Prometheus Books, 1998.

Davidson, Richard J., and Anne Harrington. *Visions of Compassion: Western Scientists and Tibetan Buddhists Examine Human Nature.* New York: Oxford Univ. Press, 2002.

Dawkins, Richard. *The God Delusion.* New York: Houghton Mifflin, 2006.

———. *A Devil's Chaplain: Reflections on Hope, Lies, Science and Love.* New York: Houghton Mifflin, 2003.

———. *Unweaving the Rainbow: Science, Delusion and the Appetite for Wonder.* New York: Houghton Mifflin, 1998.

Dean, John W. *Conservatives without Conscience.* New York: Viking, 2006.

Deci, Edward L., and Richard Flaste. *Why We Do What We Do: Understanding Self-Motivation.* New York: Penguin Books, 1995.

Denby, David. *Great Books: My Adventures with Homer, Rousseau, Woolf, and Other Indestructible Writers of the Western World.* New York: Simon & Schuster, 1996.

Dennett, Daniel C. *Breaking the Spell: Religion as a Natural Phenomenon.* New York: Viking, 2006.

———. *Freedom Evolves.* New York: Viking, 2003.

———. *Darwin's Dangerous Idea.* New York: Simon & Schuster, 1995.

Diamond, Jared. *Collapse: How Societies Choose to Fail or Succeed.* New York: Viking, 2005.

———. *Guns, Germs, and Steel: The Fates of Human Societies.* New York: W. W. Norton, 1997.

Durant, Will. *The Story of Philosophy.* New York: Pocket Books, 1926.

Durant, Will, and Ariel Durant. *The Story of Civilization.* Vol.1, Our Oriental Heritage. New York: Simon & Schuster, 1935.

Dychtwald, Ken. *Age Power: How the 21st Century Will Be Ruled by the New Old.* Los Angeles, CA: Tarcher/Putnam, 1999.

———. *Age Wave: How the Most Important Trend of Our Time Will Change Our Future.* Los Angeles, CA: Jeremy P. Tarcher, 1989.

Edmundson, Mark. *Teacher: The One Who Made a Difference.* New York: Random House, 2002.

Emerson, Ralph Waldo. *Emerson Essays and Lectures.* New York: Library of America, 1983.

———. *The Collected Works of Ralph Waldo Emerson.* Cambridge, MA: Harvard Univ. Press, 1971.

———. *The Portable Emerson.* Edited by Carl Bode with Malcolm Cowley. New York: Penguin Books, 1946.

Enright, D.J., ed. *The Oxford Book of Death.* New York: Oxford Univ. Press, 1983.

Epictetus. *The Art of Living.* Interpreted by Sharon Lebell. New York: HarperCollins, 1994.

Erikson, Erik H. *Identity and the Life Cycle*. New York: W. W. Norton, 1980.

Erikson, Erik H., Joan M. Erikson, and Helen Q. Kivnick. *Vital Involvement in Old Age*. New York: W. W. Norton, 1986.

Evans, Dylan. *Emotion: The Science of Sentiment*. New York: Oxford Univ. Press, 2001.

Fenton, Tom. *Bad News: The Decline of Reporting, the Business of News, and the Danger to Us All*. New York: Regan Books, 2005.

Festinger, Leon. *A Theory of Cognitive Dissonance*. Stanford, CA: Stanford Univ. Press, 1962.

Feyerabend, Paul. *Conquest of Abundance: A Tale of Abstraction Versus the Richness of Being*. Chicago: Univ. of Chicago Press, 1999.

Flanagan, Owen. *The Problem of the Soul: Two Visions of the Mind and How to Reconcile Them*. New York: Basic Books, 2002.

Fletcher, George P. *Loyalty: An Essay on the Morality of Relationships*. New York: Oxford Univ. Press, 1993.

Frank, Robert H. *Luxury Fever*. New York: Free Press, 1999.

Frankl, Viktor. *Man's Search for Meaning*. New York: Pocket Books, 1984.

———. *The Will to Meaning: Foundations and Applications of Logotherapy*. New York: Meridian, 1969.

Freedman, Marc. *Prime Time: How Baby Boomers Will Revolutionize Retirement and Transform America*. New York: Public Affairs, 2000.

Freud, Sigmund. *Civilization and Its Discontents*. Translated by Joan Riviere. New York: Dover Publications, 1994.

Fromm, Erich. *The Sane Society*. New York: Rinehart & Winston, 1955.

Gabler, Neal. *Life: The Movie*. New York: Vintage Books, 1998.

Gans, Herbert J. *Popular Culture and High Culture: An Analysis and Evaluation of Taste*. New York: Basic Books, 1999.

Gardner, Howard. *Five Minds for the Future*. Boston, MA: Harvard University Press, 2006.

———. *The Disciplined Mind: What All Students Should Understand*. New York: Simon & Schuster, 1999.

———. *Frames of Mind: The Theory of Multiple Intelligences*. New York: Basic Books, 1993.

Gardner, Howard, Mihaly Csikszentmihalyi, and William Damon. *Good Work: When Excellence and Ethics Meet*. New York: Basic Books, 2001.

Gatto, John Taylor. "Against School." *Harpers*, September 2003, 33-38.

————. *The Underground History of American Education.* New York: The Oxford Village Press, 2003.

————. *Dumbing Us Down: The Hidden Curriculum of Compulsory Schooling.* Gabriola Island, BC: New Society Publishers, 1992.

Geldard, Richard. *The Spiritual Teachings of Ralph Waldo Emerson.* Great Barrington, MA: Lindisfarne Books, 2001.

Gergen, Kenneth J. *The Saturated Self: Dilemmas of Identity in Contemporary Life.* New York: Basic Books, 1991.

Gibbs, John C. *Moral Development and Reality: Beyond the Theories of Kohlberg and Hoffman.* Thousand Oaks, CA: Sage Publications, 2003.

Gilligan, Carol. *In a Different Voice: Psychological Theory and Women's Development.* Cambridge, MA: Harvard Univ. Press, 1993.

Glassner, Barry. *The Culture of Fear: Why Americans Are Afraid of the Wrong Things.* New York: Basic Books, 1999.

Gleiser, Marcelo. *The Prophet and the Astronomer: A Scientific Journey to the End of Time.* New York: W. W. Norton, 2001.

Golden, Daniel. *The Price of Admission: How America's Ruling Class Buys Its Way into Elite Colleges—and Who Gets Left Outside the Gates.* New York: Crown, 2006.

Goleman, Daniel. *Social Intelligence: The New Human Science of Relationships.* New York: Bantam Books, 2006.

Goodman, Amy, and David Goodman. *Standing Up to the Madness: Ordinary Heroes in Extraordinary Times.* New York: Hyperion, 2008.

Graber, Robert Bates. *Valuing Useless Knowledge.* Kirksville, MO: Thomas Jefferson Univ. Press, 1995.

Graeber, David. *Fragments of an Anarchist Anthropology.* Chicago, IL: Prickly Pear Press, 2004.

————. *Toward an Anthropological Theory of Value: The False Coin of Our Own Dreams.* New York: Palgrave, 2001.

Graff, Gerald. *Clueless in Academe: How Schooling Obscures the Life of the Mind.* New Haven, CT: Yale Univ. Press, 2003.

Grant, George. *Time as History.* Toronto, ON: Univ. of Toronto Press, 1995.

Greenspan, Stanley I., and Stuart G. Shanker. *The First Idea: How Symbols, Language, and Intelligence Evolved from Our Primate Ancestors to Modern Humans.* Cambridge, MA: Da Capo Press, 2004.

Griffin, Joe, and Ivan Tyrrell. *Human Givens: A New Approach to Emotional Health and Clear Thinking.* Chalvington, East Sussex, U.K.: Human Givens Publishing, 2003.

Gross, Ronald. *Socrates' Way: Seven Master Keys to Using Your Mind to the Utmost.* New York: Jeremy P. Tarcher/Putnam, 2002.

———. *The Independent Scholar's Handbook.* Berkeley, CA: Ten Speed Press, 1993.

———. *Peak Learning: How to Create Your Own Lifelong Education Program for Personal Enlightenment and Professional Success.* New York: Jeremy P. Tarcher/Putnam, 1991.

Haidt, Jonathan. *The Happiness Hypothesis: Finding Truth in Ancient Wisdom.* New York: Basic Books, 2006.

Harris, Judith Rich. *The Nurture Assumption: Why Children Turn Out the Way They Do.* New York: Free Press, 1998.

Harris, Sam. *The End of Faith: Religion, Terror, and the Future of Reason.* New York: W. W. Norton, 2004.

Hartmann, Thom. *Screwed: The Undeclared War Against the Middle Class.* San Francisco, CA: Berrett-Koehler, 2006.

Hayes, Charles D. *The Rapture of Maturity: A Legacy of Lifelong Learning.* Wasilla, AK: Autodidactic Press, 2004.

———. *Portals in a Northern Sky.* Wasilla, AK: Autodidactic Press, 2003.

———. *Training Yourself: The Twenty-First Century Credential.* Wasilla, AK: Autodidactic Press, 2000.

———. *Beyond the American Dream: Lifelong Learning and the Search for Meaning in a Postmodern World.* Wasilla, AK: Autodidactic Press, 1998.

———. *Proving You're Qualified: Strategies for Competent People without College Degrees.* Wasilla, AK: Autodidactic Press, 1995.

———. *Self-University: The Price of Tuition is the Desire to Learn. Your Degree is a Better Life.* Wasilla, AK: Autodidactic Press, 1989.

Hawken, Paul. *Blessed Unrest: How the Largest Social Movement in History Is Restoring Grace, Justice, and Beauty to the World.* New York: Penguin Books, 2007.

Hedges, Chris. *American Fascists: The Christian Right and the War on America.* New York: Free Press, 2006.

———. *Losing Moses on the Freeway: The Ten Commandments in America.* New York: Free Press, 2005.

———. *War Is a Force That Gives Us Meaning.* New York: Anchor Books, 2002.

Heilbrun, Carolyn G. *The Last Gift of Time: Life Beyond Sixty.* New York: Ballantine Books, 1997.

Henry, William A., III. *In Defense of Elitism.* New York: Doubleday, 1994.

Hillman, James. *The Force of Character: And the Lasting Life.* New York: Random House, 1999.

Hitchens, Christopher. *God Is Not Great: How Religion Poisons Everything.* New York: 12Twelve, 2007.

Hoffer, Eric. *The True Believer: Thoughts on the Nature of Mass Movements.* New York: Harper & Row, 1951.

Hofstadter, Richard. *Anti-Intellectualism in American Life.* New York: Vintage Books, 1962.

Holt, John. *Learning All the Time.* Reading, MA: Perseus Books, 1989.

Hudson, Frederic M. *The Adult Years: Mastering the Art of Self-Renewal.* San Francisco: Jossey-Bass, 1999.

Hume, David. *A Treatise of Human Nature.* Edited by L.A. Selby-Bigge. London: Oxford at the Clarendon Press, 1888.

Humes, Edward. *Monkey Girl: Evolution, Education, Religion, and the Battle for America's Soul.* New York: HarperCollins, 2007.

Iacoboni, Marco. *Mirroring People: The New Science of How We Connect with Others.* New York: Farrar, Straus & Giroux, 2008.

Jacobs, Jane. *Dark Age Ahead.* New York: Random House, 2004.

Jacobson, David. *Emerson's Pragmatic Vision: The Dance of the Eye.* University Park, PA: Pennsylvania State Univ. Press, 1993.

Janik, Daniel S. *Unlock the Genius Within: Neurobiological Trauma, Teaching, and Transformative Learning.* Lanham, MD: Rowman & Littlefield, 2005.

Johnson, Steven. *Everything Bad Is Good for You: How Today's Popular Culture Is Actually Making Us Smarter.* New York: Riverhead Books, 2005.

———. *Emergence: The Connected Lives of Ants, Brains, Cities, and Software.* New York: Simon & Schuster, 2001.

Kammen, Michael. *Visual Shock: A History of Art Controversies in American Culture.* New York: Alfred A. Knopf, 2006.

Kant, Immanuel. "An Answer to the Question: 'What Is Enlightenment?'" Translated by H. B. Nisbet. In *Kant's Political Writings.* Cambridge, U.K.: Cambridge Univ. Press, 1970.

———. "The Critique of Pure Reason," "The Critique of Practical Reason," and "The Metaphysic of Morals." Translated by J. M. D. Meiklejohn and W. Hastie. In *Great Books of the Western World.* Vol. 42. Chicago: Encyclopedia Britannica, 1952.

Kaufmann, Walter. *Existentialism from Dostoevsky to Sartre*. Cleveland, OH: Meridian Books, 1956.

Kaye, Harvey J. *Thomas Paine and the Promise of America*. New York: Hill & Wang, 2005.

Keats, John. *John Keats: The Complete Poems*. New York: Penguin Classics, 1973.

Keen, Sam. *Faces of the Enemy*. New York: HarperCollins, 1986.

Kegan, Robert. *In Over Our Heads: The Mental Demands of Modern Life*. Cambridge, MA: Harvard Univ. Press, 1994.

Kett, Joseph. F. *The Pursuit of Knowledge Under Difficulties*. Stanford, CA: Stanford Univ. Press, 1994.

Kierkegaard, Søren. *The Sickness Unto Death*. Edited and translated by Howard V. Hong and Edna H. Hong. Princeton, NJ: Princeton Univ. Press, 1980.

Kimble, Melvin A., ed. *Viktor Frankl's Contribution to Spirituality and Aging*. Binghamton, NY: The Haworth Press, 2000.

King, Barbara J. *Evolving God: A Provocative View on the Origins of Religion*. New York: Doubleday, 2007.

Knowles, Malcolm S. *The Adult Learner: A Neglected Species*. Houston: Gulf Publishing, 1990.

———. *The Modern Practice of Adult Education: From Pedagogy to Andragogy*. Chicago: Follett, 1980.

Kohlberg, Lawrence. *The Psychology of Moral Development*. San Francisco: Harper & Row, 1984.

Lakoff, George. *Don't Think of an Elephant*. White River Junction, VT: Chelsea Green Publishing, 2004.

Lakoff, George, and Mark Johnson. *Philosophy in the Flesh: The Embodied Mind and Its Challenge to Western Thought*. New York: Basic Books, 1999.

———. *Metaphors We Live By*. Chicago: Univ. of Chicago Press, 1980.

Landman, Janet. *Regret: The Persistence of the Possible*. New York: Oxford Univ. Press, 1993.

Lane, Frederick S. *The Decency Wars: The Campaign to Cleanse American Culture*. New York: Prometheus Books, 2006.

Langer, Ellen J. *Mindfulness*. New York: Addison-Wesley, 1989.

Lappé, Frances Moore. *Getting A Grip: Creativity and Courage in a World Gone Mad*. Cambridge, MA: Small Planet Media, 2007.

Lawrence-Lightfoot, Sara. *The Third Chapter: Passion, Risk, and Adventure in the 25 Years After 50*. New York: Farrar, Straus & Giroux, 2009.

Lehrer, Jonah. *Proust Was a Neuroscientist*. New York: Houghton Mifflin, 2007.

Lerner, Michael. *The Left Hand of God: Taking Back Our Country from the Religious Right*. New York: HarperCollins, 2006.

Livingston, Gordon. *Too Soon Old, Too Late Smart*. New York: Marlowe & Company, 2004.

Lomborg, Bjørn. *The Skeptical Environmentalist: Measuring the Real State of the World*. Cambridge, U.K.: Cambridge Univ. Press, 2001.

Lustbader, Wendy. *Counting on Kindness: The Dilemmas of Dependency*. New York: Free Press, 1991.

Magee, Bryan. *Confessions of a Philosopher: A Personal Journey Through Western Philosophy from Plato to Popper*. New York: Random House, 1997.

———. *The Philosophy of Schopenhauer*. New York: Oxford Univ. Press, 1983.

Mann, Brian. *Welcome to the Homeland: A Journey to the Rural Heart of America's Conservative Revolution*. Hanover, NH: Steerforth Press, 2006.

Markos, Louis. *From Plato to Postmodernism: Understanding the Essence of Literature and the Role of the Author*. Kearneysville, WV: The Teaching Company, 1999. Audiocassette.

Maslow, Abraham H. *The Farther Reaches of Human Nature*. New York: Viking Press, 1971.

May, Rollo. *Freedom and Destiny*. New York: W. W. Norton, 1981.

McGinn, Colin. *The Making of a Philosopher: A Journey Through Twentieth-Century Philosophy*. New York: HarperCollins, 2002.

McLuhan, Marshall. *Understanding Media*. New York: McGraw-Hill, 1964.

Michaels, Walter Benn. *The Trouble with Diversity: How We Learned to Love Identity and Ignore Inequality*. New York: Metropolitan Books, 2006.

Miller, Matthew. *The 2 Percent Solution: Fixing America's Problems in Ways Liberals and Conservatives Can Love*. New York: Public Affairs, 2003.

Morrow, Lance. *Evil: An Investigation*. New York: Basic Books, 2003.

Moyers, Bill. *Moyers On Democracy*. New York: Doubleday, 2008.

Murdoch, Iris. *Metaphysics as a Guide to Morals*. New York: Viking Penguin, 1992.

Nehamas, Alexander. *The Art of Living: Socratic Reflections from Plato to Foucault.* Berkeley, CA: Univ. of California Press, 1998.

Nietzsche, Friedrich. *The Portable Nietzsche.* Edited and translated by Walter Kaufmann. New York: Penguin Books, 1982.

———. *Beyond Good and Evil.* Edited and translated by R. J. Hollindale. New York: Penguin Books, 1973.

Novelli, Bill. *50+ Igniting a Revolution to Reinvent America.* New York: St. Martin's Press, 2006.

Nussbaum, Martha Craven. *Cultivating Humanity.* Cambridge, MA: Harvard Univ. Press, 1998.

Nuttall, A.D. *Why Does Tragedy Give Pleasure?* New York: Oxford Univ. Press, 1996.

Oakley, Barbara. *Evil Genes: Why Rome Fell, Hitler Rose, Enron Failed, and My Sister Stole My Mother's Boyfriend.* New York: Prometheus Books, 2008.

Obama, Barack. *The Audacity of Hope: Thoughts on Reclaiming the American Dream.* New York: Crown Publishing, 2006.

Olson, Kirsten. *Wounded by School: Recapturing the Joy in Learning and Standing Up to Old School Culture.* New York: Teachers College Press, 2009.

O'Toole, Patricia. *Money and Morals in America.* New York: Clarkson Potter, 1998.

Owen, David. *Maturity and Modernity: Nietzsche, Weber, Foucault and the Ambivalence of Reason.* London: Rutledge, 1994.

Parfit, Derek. *Reasons and Persons.* New York: Oxford Univ. Press, 1984.

Payne, James L. *A History of Force: Exploring the Worldwide Movement against Habits of Coercion, Bloodshed, and Mayhem.* Sandpoint, ID: Lytton Publishing, 2004.

Perelman, Lewis J. *School's Out: A Radical New Formula for the Revitalization of America's Educational System.* New York: Avon Books, 1992.

Peterson, Merrill D. *Adams and Jefferson: A Revolutionary Dialogue.* New York: Oxford Univ. Press, 1976.

Pinker, Steven. *The Blank Slate: The Modern Denial of Human Nature.* New York: Viking, 2002.

———. *How the Mind Works.* New York: W. W. Norton, 1997.

Pipher, Mary. *Writing to Change the World.* New York: Riverhead Books, 2006.

————. *Another Country: Navigating the Emotional Terrain of Our Elders.* New York: Riverhead Books, 1999.

Plato. "The Dialogues of Plato." Translated by Benjamin Jowett. In *Great Books of the Western World.* Vol. 7. Chicago: Encyclopedia Britannica, 1952.

Postman, Neil. *Building a Bridge to the Eighteenth Century.* New York: Alfred A. Knopf, 1999.

————. *The End of Education: Redefining the Value of School.* New York: Alfred A. Knopf, 1995.

————. *The Disappearance of Childhood.* New York: Vintage Books, 1994.

————. *Amusing Ourselves to Death.* New York: Viking Penguin, 1985.

Postrel, Virginia. *The Substance of Style: How the Rise of Aesthetic Value is Remaking Commerce, Culture, and Consciousness.* New York: HarperCollins, 2003.

Power, Samantha. *A Problem from Hell: America and the Age of Genocide.* New York: Basic Books, 2002.

Rawls, John. *A Theory of Justice.* Cambridge, MA: Belknap Press of Harvard Univ. Press, 1971.

Rees, Laurence. *Auschwitz: A New History.* New York: Public Affairs, 2005.

Richardson, Louise. *What Terrorists Want: Understanding the Enemy, Containing the Threat.* New York: Random House, 2006.

Richardson, Robert D., Jr. *Emerson: The Mind on Fire.* Berkeley, CA: Univ. of California Press, 1995.

Riesman, David. *The Lonely Crowd.* New Haven, CT: Yale Univ. Press, 2001.

Roderick, Rick. *The Self Under Siege.* Kearneysville, WV: The Teaching Company, 1993. Audiocassette.

————. *Philosophy and Human Values.* Kearneysville, WV: The Teaching Company, 1991. Audiocassette.

Rorty, Richard. *Philosophy and Social Hope.* New York: Penguin Books, 1999.

Roszak, Theodore. *America the Wise: The Longevity Revolution and the Real Wealth of Nations.* New York: Houghton Mifflin, 1998.

————. *The Making of a Counter Culture.* New York: Anchor Books, 1969.

Sagan, Carl. *The Varieties of Scientific Experience: A Personal View of the Search for God.* Ann Druyan ed. New York: Penguin Books, 2006.

————. *Billions and Billions: Thoughts of Life and Death at the Brink of the Millennium.* New York: Random House, 1997.

———. *Contact*. New York: Doubleday, 1997.

———. *The Demon-Haunted World: Science as a Candle in the Dark*. New York: Ballantine Books, 1997.

Sagan, Carl, and Ann Druyan. *Shadows of Forgotten Ancestors: A Search for Who We Are*. New York: Random House, 1992.

Sandel, Michael J. *Democracy's Discontent: America in Search of a Public Philosophy*. Cambridge, MA: Belknap Press of Harvard Univ. Press, 1996.

Santayana, George. *Skepticism and Animal Faith*. New York: Dover, 1923.

Sartre, Jean-Paul. *Being and Nothingness: A Phenomenological Essay on Ontology*. Translated by Hazel E. Barnes. New York: Washington Square Press, 1993.

Schacht, Richard. *Making Sense of Nietzsche*. Chicago: Univ. of Illinois Press, 1995.

Schama, Simon. *The Power of Art*. Great Britain: BBC, 2006.

Schmidt, Jeff. *Disciplined Minds: A Critical Look at Salaried Professionals and the Soul-Battering System that Shapes Their Lives*. Lanham, MD: Rowman & Littlefield, 2000.

Schopenhauer, Arthur. *Studies in Pessimism*. Translated by T. Bailey Saunders. London: George Allen & Company, 1913.

———. *Wisdom of Life*. Translated by T. Bailey Saunders. London: Swan Sonnenschein, 1895.

———. *Essays and Aphorisms*. Translated by R. J. Hollingdale. New York: Penguin Books, 1970.

———. *Essays of Arthur Schopenhauer*. Translated by T. Bailey Saunders. New York: A. L. Bert, 1949.

Schumaker, John F. *In Search of Happiness: Understanding an Endangered State of Mind*. Auckland, New Zealand: Penguin Books, 2006.

———. *The Age of Insanity: Modernity and Mental Health*. Westport, CT: Praeger, 2001.

———. *Wings of Illusion: The Origin, Nature and Future of Paranormal Belief*. New York: Prometheus Books, 1990.

Seneca. *Seneca: Letters from a Stoic*. Edited and translated by Robin Campbell. New York: Penguin Books, 1969.

Sennett, Richard. *Respect in a World of Inequality*. New York: W. W. Norton, 2003.

Shaw, George Bernard. *Man and Superman*. New York: Brentano's, 1903.

Shepard, Paul. *Coming Home to the Pleistocene*. Washington, DC: Island Press, 1998.

Shermer, Michael. *Why People Believe Weird Things: Pseudoscience, Superstition, and Other Confusions of Our Time.* New York: W. H. Freeman, 1998.

Singer, Peter. *The Life You Can Save: Acting Now to End World Poverty.* New York: Random House, 2009.

———. *How Are We to Live?* New York: Prometheus Books, 1995.

Sirota, David. *The Uprising: An Unauthorized Tour of the Populist Revolt Scaring Wall Street and Washington.* New York: Crown, 2008.

Slater, Philip E. *A Dream Deferred: America's Discontent and Search for a New Democratic Ideal.* Boston, MA: Beacon Press, 1991.

———. *The Pursuit of Loneliness.* 3rd ed. Boston, MA: Beacon Press, 1990.

Smith, Adam. *The Theory of Moral Sentiments.* New York: Oxford Univ. Press, 1976.

Smith, Harmon. *My Friend, My Friend: The Story of Thoreau's Relationship with Emerson.* Amherst, MA: Univ. of Massachusetts Press, 1999.

Smoot, George, and Keay Davidson. *Wrinkles in Time.* London: Little, Brown, 1993.

Solie, David. *How to Say It to Seniors: Closing the Communication Gap with Our Elders.* New York: Prentice Hall, 2004.

Solomon, Robert C. *Spirituality for the Skeptic.* New York: Oxford Univ. Press, 2002.

———. *A Passion for Justice.* New York: Addison-Wesley, 1990.

Spivey, Nigel. *How Art Made the World: A Journey to the Origins of Human Creativity.* New York: Basic Books, 2005.

Stack, George J. *Nietzsche and Emerson.* Athens, OH: Ohio Univ. Press, 1992.

Staub, Ervin. *The Psychology of Good and Evil: Why Children, Adults, and Groups Help and Harm Others.* New York: Cambridge Univ. Press, 2003.

Steinhorn, Leonard. *The Greater Generation: In Defense of the Baby Boom Legacy.* New York: Thomas Dunne Books, 2006.

Sternberg, Robert J., and Todd I. Lubart. *Defying the Crowd: Cultivating Creativity in a Culture of Conformity.* New York: Free Press, 1995.

Stewart, David W. *Adult Learning in America: Eduard Lindeman and His Agenda for Lifelong Education.* Malabar, FL: Robert E. Krieger, 1987.

Stewart, Matthew. *The Courtier and the Heretic: Leibniz, Spinoza, and the Fate of God in the Modern World.* New York: W. W. Norton, 2006.

————. *The Truth about Everything: An Irreverent History of Philosophy.* Amherst, NY: Prometheus Books, 2005.

Sunstein, Cass. *Infotopia: How Many Minds Produce Knowledge.* New York: Oxford Univ. Press, 2006.

Taylor, Shelley E. *Positive Illusions.* New York: Basic Books, 1989.

Teachout, Terry. *The Skeptic.* New York: HarperCollins, 2002.

Thomas, William H. *What Are Old People For? How Elders Will Save the World.* Acton, MA: VanderWyk & Burnham, 2004.

Thoreau, Henry David. *The Portable Thoreau.* Edited by Carl Bode. New York: Penguin Books, 1947.

Tiger, Lionel. *Optimism: The Biology of Hope.* New York: Kodansha International, 1995.

Tipler, Frank J. *The Physics of Immortality: Modern Cosmology, God and the Resurrection of the Dead.* New York: Anchor Books, 1997.

Tolchin, Martin and Susan J. Tolchin. *A World Ignited: How Apostles of Ethnic, Religious, and Racial Hatred Torch the Globe.* Lanham, MD: Rowman & Littlefield, 2006.

Turiel, Elliot. *The Culture of Morality: Social Development, Context, and Conflict.* New York: Cambridge Univ. Press, 2002.

Twain, Mark. *The American Claimant.* New York: Harper Brothers, 1899.

Twitchell, James B. *Living It Up: America's Love Affair with Luxury.* New York: Columbia Univ. Press, 2002.

Tyson, Neil deGrasse. *Death by Black Hole.* New York: W. W. Norton, 2007.

Vaillant, George E. *Aging Well: Surprising Guideposts to a Happier Life from the Landmark Harvard Study of Adult Development.* New York: Little, Brown, 2002.

Vidal, Gore. *Point to Point Navigation.* New York: Doubleday, 2006.

Volk, Tyler. *What is Death?: A Scientist Looks at the Cycle of Death.* New York: John Wiley & Sons, 2002.

Wade, Nicholas. *Before the Dawn: Recovering the Lost History of Our Ancestors.* New York: Penguin Press, 2006.

Waal, Frans de. *Our Inner Ape.* New York: Riverhead Books, 2005.

Watts, Alan. *The Wisdom of Insecurity.* New York: Vintage Books, 1951.

Weinberg, Steven. *Facing Up: Science and Its Cultural Adversaries.* Cambridge, MA: Harvard Univ. Press, 2001.

Weis, Robert S., and Scott A. Bass, eds. *Challenges of the Third Age: Meaning and Purpose in Later Life.* New York: Oxford Univ. Press, 2002.

White, Curtis. *The Spirit of Disobedience: Resisting the Charms of Fake Politics, Mindless Consumption, and the Culture of Total Work.* Sausalito, CA: PoliPointPress, 2007.

———.*The Middle Mind: Why Americans Don't Think for Themselves.* San Francisco, CA: HarperSanFranisco, 2003.

Whybrow, Peter C. *American Mania: When More Is Not Enough.* New York: W. W. Norton, 2005.

Wilson, Edward O. *The Creation: An Appeal to Save Life on Earth.* New York: W. W. Norton, 2006.

———. *The Future of Life.* New York: Alfred A. Knopf, 2002.

———. *Consilience: The Unity of Knowledge.* New York: Alfred A. Knopf, 1998.

———. *The Diversity of Life.* Cambridge, MA: Belknap Press of Harvard Univ. Press, 1992.

Wilson, David Sloan. *Darwin's Cathedral: Evolution, Religion, and the Nature of Society.* Chicago, IL: Univ. of Chicago Press, 2003.

Winston, Robert. *Human Instinct: How Our Primeval Impulses Shape Our Modern Lives.* New York: Bantam Press, 2002.

Wood, John. *Leaving Microsoft to Change the World: An Entrepreneur's Odyssey to Educate the World's Children.* New York: HarperCollins, 2006.

Woodruff, Paul. *First Democracy: The Challenge of an Ancient Idea.* New York: Oxford Univ. Press, 2005.

———. *Reverence: Renewing a Forgotten Virtue.* New York: Oxford Univ. Press, 2001.

Wright, Robert. *Nonzero: The Logic of Human Destiny.* New York: Vintage Books, 2001.

———. *The Moral Animal: Why We Are the Way We Are: The New Science of Evolutionary Psychology.* New York: Pantheon Books, 1994.

Yankelovich, Daniel. *The Magic of Dialogue: Transforming Conflict into Cooperation.* New York: Touchstone, 1999.

Zengotita, Thomas de. *Mediated: How the Media Shapes Your World and the Way You Live in It.* New York: Bloomsbury, 2005.

INDEX

277

ABOUT THE AUTHOR

C harles D. Hayes is a self-taught philosopher and one of America's strongest advocates for lifelong learning. He spent his youth in Texas and served as a U.S. Marine and as a police officer before embarking on a career in the oil industry. Alaska has been his home for more than 30 years.

Hayes' book *Beyond the American Dream: Lifelong Learning and the Search for Meaning in a Postmodern World* received recognition by the American Library Association's *CHOICE* Magazine as one of the most outstanding academic books of the year. His other titles include *Existential Aspirations: Reflections of a Self-Taught Philosopher*; *The Rapture of Maturity: A Legacy of Lifelong Learning*; *Training Yourself: The 21st Century Credential*; *Proving You're Qualified: Strategies for Competent People without College Degrees*; and *Self-University: The Price of Tuition is Desire. Your Degree is a Better Life.* His first work of fiction is *Portals in a Northern Sky*.

Promoting the idea that education should be thought of not as something you get but as something you take, Hayes' work has been featured in *USA Today*, in the *UTNE Reader*, on National Public Radio's *Talk of the Nation* and on Alaska Public Radio's *Talk of Alaska*. His web site, **www.autodidactic.com**, provides resources for self-directed learners—from advice about credentials to philosophy about the value lifelong learning brings to everyday living. In 2006, Hayes established **www.septemberuniversity.org**, a site devoted to ongoing dialogue among September University participants in search of the better argument.

WHAT OTHERS SAY ABOUT
THE WORK OF CHARLES D. HAYES

"In a world of flabby, fragmentary, and postmodernist thinking, Hayes offers a glowing tribute to old-fashioned curiosity and reason. Clear thinking is as human and healthy as breathing. Charles Hayes encourages us to give it a try."

BARBARA EHRENREICH,
author, *Fear of Falling* and *Blood Rites*

"In the midst of all the frantic hype and fluff that deluge Americans every day and produce so much ovine behavior, it is an inspiration to hear from someone who both cherishes and exemplifies independent thinking."

PHILIP SLATER, author,
The Pursuit of Loneliness and *A Dream Deferred*

"Reading *Portals* is like looking through a kaleidoscope in which break-neck adventure and science fiction occasionally reconfigure themselves into patterns of ancient wisdom—don't start unless you have enough time to finish it, because you won't be able to put it down."

MIHALY CSIKSZENTMIHALYI,
author, *Flow* and *The Evolving Self*

"Charles Hayes' voice is one of experienced wisdom, grappling artfully with the 'existential' questions we all grapple with, well or poorly. His answers, his appreciation of the role of Emersonian ecstasy in education, and his reflections on things that matter, are well worth your consideration."

ROBERT C. SOLOMON, author,
Spirituality for the Skeptic: The Thoughtful Love of Life
and coauthor, *A Passion for Wisdom*